LOVE
Psychoanalytic Perspectives

LOVE

Psychoanalytic Perspectives

JUDITH F. LASKY and
HELEN W. SILVERMAN
Editors

NEW YORK UNIVERSITY PRESS
NEW YORK AND LONDON

© 1988 by New York University
All rights reserved
Manufactured in the United States of America

Library of Congress Cataloging-in-Publication Data
Love : psychoanalytic perspectives.
   Papers presented at a conference held February 15,
1986; sponsored by the Psychoanalytic Society of the
Postdoctoral Program of New York University.
      1. Love—Congresses.   2. Love—Psychological aspects—
Congresses.   3. Interpersonal relations—Congresses.
I. Lasky, Judith F., 1945–   .   II. Silverman, Helen W.,
1937–   .   III. Psychoanalytic Society (New York
University. Postdoctoral Program in Psychotherapy and
Psychoanalysis)
HQ801.L656   1988   306.7   87-25030
ISBN 0-8147-5036-2

Clothbound editions of New York University Press books
are Smyth-sewn and printed on permanent and durable acid-
free paper.

Book design by Ken Venezio

To Richard
         [J.L.]

To Johanna
         [H.S.]

Contents

Preface	ix
About the Contributors	xi
Introduction	1
1. Eros, Agape, Amor, Libido: Concepts in the History of Love *Waltraud Ireland*	14
2. Love: Transcultural Considerations *Robert Endleman*	31
3. What Is This Thing Called Love? The Popular Ballad as a Framework for Changing Conceptions of Love *Barbara Cohn Schlachet and Barbara Waxenberg*	52
4. Love in a Hall of Mirrors: Reciprocal Transference Relationships in Marriage *Walter Gadlin*	63
5. Sibling Relationships and Mature Love *Judith F. Lasky and Susan F. Mulliken*	81
6. Perversion: The Terror of Tenderness *Leanne Domash*	93
7. Differential Roles of Narcissism in Healthy and Pathological Love Relationships *Michael P. Varga*	104
8. Fantasies of Love and Rescue in Fatherless Adolescent Boys *Patrick R. Lane*	111
9. Falling in Love and Being in Love: A Developmental and Object-Relations Approach *Eileen J. Setzman*	122
10. Trust and Testing in Love Relations *Peter Lawner*	133

11. The Struggle to Love: Reflections and Permutations
    Joan O. Zuckerberg — 147

12. The Self and Loving
    Harold B. Davis — 159

13. Aspects of the Erotic Transference
    Helen W. Silverman — 173

14. Should Analysts Love Their Patients? The Resolution of Transference Resistance Through Countertransferential Explorations
    Robert S. Weinstein — 192

15. Mature Love in the Countertransference
    Irwin Hirsch — 200

16. The Classical Psychoanalytic Stance: What's Love Got to Do With It?
    Andrew B. Druck — 213

    Index — 229

Preface

Love is the province of many human studies, such as literature, history, and the arts. No one discipline claims exclusivity; each offers its particular perspective. Psychoanalysis has a unique contribution to make toward understanding the human capacity to love. The investigation of how and why we connect with others, why we want and need to, and the distortions that can occur in these processes are central concerns of psychoanalysis. In this light, the current emphasis on narcissism can be seen as a reflection of concerns about the inability to love.

This book grew out of a conference on "Love: Psychoanalytic Perspectives." The idea behind the conference was to make explicit the tenets and assumptions about love that are implicit in psychoanalysis. "Love: Psychoanalytic Perspectives" was held on February 15, 1986, the day after Valentine's Day, a fitting occasion to speak of love.

The conference was sponsored and organized by the Psychoanalytic Society of the Postdoctoral Program. The Psychoanalytic Society is a professional, scientific, and educational organization composed of graduates, faculty, and supervisors of the New York University Postdoctoral Program in Psychotherapy and Psychoanalysis. The Postdoctoral Program offers advanced training to doctoral-level psychologists in the theory and practice of psychoanalysis, and it is one of the few psychoanalytic institutes to provide training in several different theoretical orientations. All of the authors are members of the Psychoanalytic Society.

The papers presented at the conference reflected the diversity and range of these theoretical positions. The capacity crowd and the audience enthusiasm suggested a high degree of professional interest in the topic and led us to think about publishing the papers as a book. While this book is based in large part on papers presented at the conference, it is not a proceedings of the conference. Chapters were added to make the book more comprehensive, and papers were expanded and revised for publication.

We would like to thank the Conference Committee—Bernice Barber,

Harold B. Davis, Leanne Domash, Andrew Druck, and Susan Mulliken—for their creative ideas and hard work in producing this conference. Without the group effort the conference would have remained only a good idea.

We extend our thanks to the paper and panel presenters and workshop leaders for their lively contributions, which enabled us to draw a large crowd and to offer the audience of the conference itself what was an interesting and thought-provoking day.

We would also like to express our appreciation to our editor, Kitty Moore, for her unflagging interest in and enthusiasm for this project, and for her helpful guidance in transforming the papers from the spoken word into a book.

About the Contributors

Harold B. Davis is Associate Professor in the Clinical School Psychology Program at the City College, CUNY, and a supervisor and a faculty member at the Institute for Contemporary Psychotherapy. He is past president of the Psychoanalytic Society of the Postdoctoral Program. He maintains a private practice in New York City.

Leanne Domash is Consulting Psychologist, Beth Israel Hospital, and Adjunct Assistant Professor of Psychiatry, Mt. Sinai School of Medicine. She is the author of articles on creativity, object relations theory, and narcissism. She is in private practice in New York City.

Andrew B. Druck is Assistant Clinical Professor of Medical Psychology, Columbia University College of Physicians and Surgeons, and is on the faculty of the Institute for Psychoanalytic Training and Research (IPTAR). He is in private practice in New York City.

Robert Endleman is Professor Emeritus of Sociology, Adelphi University, and Advisory Editor of the *Journal of Psychoanalytic Anthropology*. He is the author of *Psyche and Society* and many other books and articles in psychoanalytic social science. He is a practicing psychoanalyst.

Walter Gadlin is Assistant Clinical Professor of Medical Psychology at the Columbia University College of Physicians and Surgeons. He is currently in private practice of psychoanalysis and family therapy in New York City.

Irwin Hirsch is Codirector, Manhattan Institute for Psychoanalysis, and Associate Professor of Psychology and Supervisor, Postdoctoral Program in Psychotherapy, Adelphi University. In addition, he is on the faculty of the Psychoanalytic Institute, Postgraduate Center for Mental Health, and he has published numerous articles. He is in private practice in New York City.

About the Contributors

Waltraud Ireland was originally trained as a historian at the Johns Hopkins University. She is a faculty member of the Center for the Study of Anorexia and Bulimia and in private psychoanalytic practice in New York City.

Patrick R. Lane is the former Assistant Director and Coordinator of Adolescent Outpatient Services, Maimonides Community Mental Health Center. He is currently Clinical Adjunct Professor at New York University and Yeshiva University and maintains a private practice in New York City.

Judith F. Lasky is a supervisor at the doctoral programs of City, Yeshiva, Adelphi, and Pace Universities and a faculty member and supervisor at the Institute for Contemporary Psychotherapy. She is Vice-President of the Psychoanalytic Society of the Postdoctoral Program and maintains a private practice in New York City.

Peter Lawner is Instructor in Psychology/Psychiatry, Harvard Medical School, and is a clinical supervisor at Massachusetts General Hospital, Beth Israel Hospital, and the Massachusetts Mental Health Center, and formerly supervisor in the New York University Clinical Psychology Doctoral Program. He also maintains a private practice in Cambridge, Massachusetts.

Susan F. Mulliken is on the faculty of the Manhattan Institute for Psychoanalysis and is in private practice in New York City.

Barbara Cohn Schlachet is on the faculty of the New York University Postdoctoral Program in Psychotherapy and Psychoanalysis and the Institute for Contemporary Psychotherapy. She is in private practice in New York City. She and her coauthor, Barbara Waxenberg, also perform in New York City cabarets.

Eileen J. Setzman is on the faculty of the National Institute for the Psychotherapies and is a supervisor at the Metropolitan Institute for Training in Psychoanalytic Psychotherapy. Dr. Setzman has a private practice in New York City.

Helen W. Silverman is on the supervisory faculty of the doctoral programs of Adelphi University and Long Island University. She is President of the Psychoanalytic Society of the Postdoctoral Program and maintains a private practice in New York City.

Michael P. Varga is an instructor at the New School for Social Research and a supervisor and faculty member at Washington Square Institute for Psychotherapy, Advanced Institute for Psychotherapy, and Institute for Contemporary Psychotherapy. He is in private practice in New York City.

Barbara Waxenberg in on the faculty of the New York University Postdoctoral Program in Psychotherapy and Psychoanalysis and the Manhattan Institute for Psychoanalysis. She is in private practice and teams with coauthor Barbara Cohn Schlachet in New York cabaret performances.

Robert S. Weinstein has held staff and supervisory positions at the Neurological Institute, Columbia Presbyterian Medical Center, and New York Medical College. Currently, he is on the faculty of the Brooklyn Institute for Psychotherapy and in private practice in New York City.

Joan O. Zuckerberg is on the supervisory faculty of Yeshiva University and the National Institute for the Psychotherapies, and she is a founding faculty and board member of the Brooklyn Institute of Psychotherapy. She has written extensively in the area of psychoanalytic psychology and is in private practice in Brooklyn and New York City.

LOVE
Psychoanalytic Perspectives

Introduction

Love, a word with ancient Aryan roots, is extremely difficult to define. The dictionary gives as its first definition, "A feeling of strong personal attachment induced by that which delights or commands admiration, by sympathetic understanding, or by ties of kinship; ardent affection; as, the love of brothers and sisters" (*Webster's* 1959). The search for new words and definitions to describe loving attachments and delight in the beloved returns for each generation of lovers and poets.

The need for attachment and connection with others is universal and inborn; it is necessary in order for us to survive as a species. Love is at the heart of human experience. The love of the parent for the child is the necessary background out of which all human emotional and intellectual capacities develop. Later in life, it is actively sought as a way of refinding that earlier attachment and overcoming human separateness. The loss, or lack, of love is among the most painful of human experiences.

And yet, though the need to love may be a universal quality of man, one has to learn to love. It is a developmental task. If not used and developed within a certain time period, love—like speech, another inborn capacity unique to man—does not grow to its full flowering in complexity, subtlety, and communication. The culture in which one lives will define the various love relationships that are possible. One of the most common misconceptions about love is that it is absolute, that one has it or one does not, and that it arises "naturally," as if love were an instinct that does not require nurture. As we move up the phylogenetic scale, love, like other complex behaviors, is ruled not by the biological alone but by an interaction between psyche and biology, within a cultural context.

While the importance of love has certainly been recognized in the development of psychoanalysis, a unified theory has not yet emerged. Bergmann (1982), a current thinker on love, points out, "Love . . . has through the centuries evoked a wealth of images, metaphors, and poetry but [it has] . . . seldom fostered the epistemological wish to discover its nature" (p. 88). Freud is one who did wish to discover the nature of love, and Bergmann's writings (1971, 1980, 1982) have contributed to the delineation and elucidation of Freud's unfinished project of developing a theory of love.

Love has a central place in the theory and practice of psychoanalysis. It was Freud's remarkable discovery of transference love that led to the development of the psychoanalytic method. Critical to this discovery was the observation that the love toward the analyst that emerged in treatment was a repetition and transformation of personal history, a kind of ghostly love, rather than a real love for the analyst. At first this love was considered a resistance to the treatment because it turned the patient's attention toward the person of the analyst and away from themselves and their reasons for seeking treatment. But Freud's courageous pursuit of this material led him to discover that it was precisely this repetition that would enable him to see the infantile love relationships in vivo and thus learn where they had gone wrong. The unmasking of this mysterious and archaic intruder into the present allowed the patient to understand his past and to reshape his future. Freud believed transference love to indeed be love, but with "perhaps a degree less freedom than the love which appears in ordinary life and is called normal" (1915, p. 168). Present day psychoanalytic practice continues to be centered on the medium of the transference relationship as the means of exploring the individual's experience of love.

Freud's focus was on the contributions and resistances to love stemming from the oedipal phase. Bergmann (1971) has pointed to the ways in which Mahler's (1967) studies of the early infant experiences of bonding, symbiosis, separation, and individuation have deepened our understanding of the earliest roots of love. Bak (1973) has focused on love as an emotional state aimed at undoing the early mother-infant separation and other later separations. Balint (1948) and Altman (1977), from different perspectives, have looked at love and sexuality, and concluded that how they are distinct is as important as how they are interwoven. Thus psychoanalytic theory continues to add new dimensions to its understanding of the nature of normal and pathological love relations.

Our three opening chapters consider in some detail the importance of historical and cultural aspects in the experience of love. Although drawing from different disciplines these essays share the observation that the cultural context casts its stamp on the public form of love relationships and on our private vision of love.

In seeking the historical sources of our conceptions of love, Waltraud Ireland reviews the ideas of love in ancient Greece, early Christianity, the later medieval period, and psychoanalysis. She informs us that Plato developed a hierarchy of love, in which the highest form, agape, a philosophical or spiritual love commonly referred to as Platonic love, was reached through a form of male to male attachment. For the ancient Greeks the strongest bond of love was between men. Freud (1910) distinguished between the erotic life of antiquity which glorified the instinct (even when directed toward an inferior object) and the erotic life of his day which despised the instinctual activity and extolled only the merits of the object. Ireland points out that idealization of the love object was not central in ancient Greece. It was not until the advent of courtly love that idealization and the woman as the ideal revered object, became important. Ironically, Christianity, because of its repressive and ascetic currents, gave impetus to the idealization of woman as love object. The cult of the Virgin Mary was the precursor of courtly love (amor), which led directly to our notions of romantic love. In placing the current trends of psychoanalysis regarding love in a historical framework, she observes that psychoanalysis has focused on the psychopathology of sexuality rather than on various states of love.

Writing as a sociologist and psychoanalyst, Robert Endleman illustrates some differing ways in which love and the love object are defined in several tribal cultures and then compares their views of love with that of Western culture. These cultures seem to lack a concept of romantic love as known in the West, that is, they do not exhibit an idealization of the love object or of the process of loving. Endleman states that he is looking at these groups not as a cultural relativist but as a transculturist who believes that there are universal standards and meanings of certain behavior.

Other scholars have taken a different position and argued that cultural practices should be looked at from within the culture in which they arise in order to determine their meaning. For example, it may be only from a Western ethnocentric position that parents who send their children to live with aunts and uncles are seen as uncaring; the parents themselves may endow this with a different meaning. Similarly, adult love might exist in some of these cultures, but in a form that is not readily identifiable to an outside observer, because of the difficulty in disentangling the elements of sex and love. (The question of the nature of the relationship between sex and love is complicated, from a theoretical and developmental point of view as well as from a cultural one.) Our implication is that it is important to maintain a relativistic position, especially when treating people of different ethnic backgrounds and family styles. That a culture seems more restrictive or permissive may not be an indication of how well its members can love, but rather may reflect how they are expected to love.

Barbara Cohn Schlachet and Barbara Waxenberg look at our own culture from a sociological perspective in their study of the effects of popular music as one of the most potent disseminators of cultural expectations regarding the learning of love. Much as the telling of myths and chanting serve as vehicles of cultural goals in tribal societies, so popular music serves in ours. "Love is linked more than any other behavior . . . to language in general, but in those forms most richly endowed with popular and suggestive terms, clichés, metaphors, and accepted symbols. Love is both the best conductor and the best stimulant of expression" (De Rougemont 1963, p. 19). It is not merely that poets and musicians speak best of love but that how they speak of love is part of how we experience love. The authors emphasize ways in which love is differentially defined for men and women, the conflicts these differences may cause, and the way in which changing sex roles affect the clarity of what is communicated. They describe changes in attitudes toward love as reflected in the lyrics of song, from the twenties and thirties to the present: from the celebration of romance as salvation to the hardhearted nonenduring view of relationships. The authors make note that it is during adolescence that this music plays such a formative role. This is the time that we begin to branch out and discover love objects outside the family and popular songs meet a need to find a new vocabulary of love.

In the same way that the ideals of romantic love differ from society to society, and change within a society, ideals of other kinds of love change as well. An example is love between parent and child. Major changes in child-rearing practices have taken place in our own society in this century. For instance, infants of the upper classes were sent out to wet nurses, and very early in their lives, children of the poor were sent to work. The rigid feeding schedules advocated by the child-rearing manuals of the 1920s and 1930s are now looked upon with horror. Then, picking up the baby when it cried was thought to spoil the child, and mothers only admitted doing so in whispers to each other. Now the cry of a baby is thought to be a communication, and whether it is physical discomfort or emotional need it is heeded. Changes in the style and patterns of child-rearing lead to new ways of demonstrating and expressing parental love. It would not be unexpected to find this leads to changes in the forms of adult love and the adult object choice.

Failure to achieve what the culture defines as a satisfactory love relationship is one of the most usual reasons for which people seek psychoanalytic treatment. It is not surprising that much of the psychoanalytic thinking on love deals with problems, failures, and difficulties in the capacity to love. Choosing a love object and dealing with the feelings engendered by an intimate relationship are two major categories of problems.

The undesired interweaving of past and present in the choice of a love object was originally noted by Freud in 1905 and emphasized again in 1915. Some ways in which past love attachments may prevent current love relationships from being fully satisfactory are elaborated by Walter Gadlin, Judith F. Lasky and Susan F. Mulliken, and Leanne Domash in their chapters.

Gadlin uses material from individual analysis and marital treatment to present a vivid example of a marital relationship whose difficulties in large measure can be traced back to each partner's wish to repeat some parts (and to avoid others) of their relationship with their parents in childhood. He describes how over the course of a marriage a once satisfactory adjustment may turn unsatisfactory as one or both partners develops and moves on. The function of the marital therapy described by Gadlin is to deal with the changed expectations of each partner and to discover the changed aspects of identifications expressed in their loving each other.

Not only parents but also siblings can serve as models for later love relationships, as Lasky and Mulliken suggest. Several patterns are described in a strongly clinical presentation. The sibling may be the direct model, or a rejected model, for later love choices. In addition, people may identify with their siblings so completely that they choose a partner who is appropriate for the sibling, not for themselves. The authors note that even an absent or dead sibling may serve as a model for adult relationships.

Domash sees the repetition of an unsatisfactory mother-child relationship as one explanation for the adult choice of an unsatisfying love partner in a perverse love relationship. In such a relationship one may choose an abusive object, who is similar in that aspect to the earlier object, and thus repeat the absence of affection and tenderness that was part of the earlier relationships.

These three chapters illustrate a variety of ways in which earlier relationships may cast a shadow that limits the possibility of a satisfying and successful relationship, without the individual's being aware of this process. Thus, one aspect of the therapeutic task is to help the person distinguish between aspects of past relationships that cannot be changed and possibilities within the present one.

The attempt to make up in current life for unsatisfying love relationships in the past may also cause problems in current love relationships, and Michael P. Varga, Patrick R. Lane, and Eileen J. Setzman each consider this area.

Varga looks at situations where individuals try to compensate for feelings of being unloved and ill-treated in childhood by loving someone as they would have wanted to be loved as a child. The problem with such a solution is that those who deny their underlying anger about the past must defensively idealize the partner and denigrate themselves, thus making for a relationship that is limited in the free expression of all feelings.

Lane presents a circumstance where the loss of a love object (the father) in adolescence leads some children to attempt to find a new father in circumstances (the therapeutic situation) where that is not a real possibility. What makes this particularly problematic for these adolescent boys is that they need both a good inner representation of a father, and a real father, and they have neither. Also they are not free as an adult would be to find a relationship that might in some ways compensate for this lack. This contribution reminds us of the importance of taking into account the individual's developmental level when we are trying to understand the difficulties in love that they are facing.

Setzman's main point is that falling in love is a normal developmental phase but that some people get stuck repetitiously at that stage where their concern is only for the self. They are unable to move to the stage of being in love, a more evolved and developed state, which includes caring for the other. She attributes this problem to a frustrating mother-child relationship. The individual may attempt to make up for this deficit in later adult relationships, however when undoing past deficits is all that is sought, the individual may find him or herself endlessly seeking a new relationship in order to continually experience the joys of falling in love without the demands of a real relationship.

In these examples the individual is looking to love objects for what they cannot provide. The treatment task would be to help clarify what a particular relationship may or may not offer. It is a common misconception that analysis will encourage partners either to leave a marriage or to maintain a status quo. Rather, psychoanalysis leads the person to an assessment that is based on current reality rather than on infantile wishes and conflicts.

Many patients have difficulties in tolerating either the positive or the negative feelings involved in the experience of love. In this instance the ability to learn to trust another person plays an important part. Peter Lawner and Joan O. Zuckerberg here suggest that the analyst can succeed in helping the patient by providing a different type of experience for the patient.

Lawner discusses some hostile and provocative behavior that a patient may engage in, not to express hostility but to test the concern and love of others. When the patient does that in a therapeutic setting it becomes important for the therapist to respond differently than people do in the rest of the patient's life. He sees variations in the levels and expression of testing as occurring most frequently when some new aspect of the relationship is about to appear. If the analyst is able to tune in to this type of communication, he can respond with understanding and interpretation to this behavior so as to break the self-destructive cycle and allow the trusting feelings to emerge.

Zuckerberg raises the question of adjusting the treatment to suit the needs of the patient who has problems in the area of love. She notes how difficult it is for patients with a real deficit in their love history to love another person. In these instances there is resistance to or an inability to form the therapeutic attachment that will be necessary for the treatment process to proceed. The therapist must use himself as an instrument to encourage an attachment. It is that attachment, once formed, that will help move the individual in the direction of a genuine love relationship.

Idealization, discussed by Freud (1914) in relation to love, remains a controversial area of theoretical and clinical interest. Harold B. Davis reviews the role of idealization in love from a variety of theoretical positions. Idealization, which includes an overestimation of the object, is considered a part of normal love for both the Freudian and self-psychology schools, as long as it does not include denigration of the self. We would suggest, however, that Freudians and self psychologists differ in the weight given to idealization, and that self psychology sees it as playing a more important part in love. Interpersonal, Jungian, and Existential perspectives share the view that mature love requires an accurate perception of the other, with which idealization would interfere. This is surely one instance where one's theoretical perspective will lead one to treat the particular phenomena in differing ways.

As Endleman and Ireland suggest, idealization of the love object is not a part of every culture or historical period's view of love. This raises the question of what it is in a particular culture that gives rise to the propensity for forming idealizations: Do groups that don't idealize the beloved idealize some other aspect of their society or family? What part does the intense mother-child relationship play in its development? Is idealization of the love object diminished in societies where extended families and other kin are involved in child care?

Most analysts would agree that in our culture, romantic love involves idealization as well as idealization of love itself. Many patients come to treatment unhappy because they are not feeling the depth and intensity of feeling they wish or expect to feel. Setzman describes patients who are, in effect, addicted to the phase of falling in love, where idealization is at its peak, but who are not able to make the transition to a more steady state of being in love. Varga suggests that idealization is a part of a healthy love relationship when it is connected with caring but not when it is serving as a defense against underlying hostility.

Hostility although controversial is seen by many analysts to be inherent in love relationships. In popular conceptions of love, love itself is idealized, and its essential ambivalence ignored. Forgotten in recollections of love are the bursts of hate and anger, the fears of abandonment, the frustration, the lack of total satisfaction. In loving and in remembering love hostile feelings may be denied. Mother love is considered the purest form of selfless love in its ideal, yet even in the best of relationships between mother and child there must be the painful awareness of separateness, loss, hate, and anger. Varga describes a defensive idealization that is employed to deny any underlying hostility. Domash discusses the hostility that may overwhelm love relationships when the individual himself has been the victim of abuse during childhood. Drawing upon the work of Stoller, she goes on to suggest that since it is inevitable that we all experience some frustration or dissatisfaction in growing up, hostility is an aspect of all relationships. According to Domash, hostility can be integrated into a loving and caring relationship and, in a sense, can enrich the experience. Silverman discusses aspects of the erotic transference itself, which, although ostensibly loving, may either be a disguise for, or a defense against, expressions of hostility. Lawner describes instances where seemingly hostile and provocative behavior is actually intended to pave the way to greater closeness.

Idealization, trust, and hostility are complicated concepts as well as complex feelings. Love is composed of many experiences and emotional states, and is not a singular entity. Love is so complex intrapsychically that perhaps we should not ever expect a final integration of all its components. The aim of psychoanalysis is to enable a person to become more aware of and more tolerant of the intricate nature of love relationships and to become more aware of the particular ways one approaches such relationships.

It is noteworthy that the problems of loving dealt with by our authors are almost entirely those occurring in the domain of passionate love. Passionate love seems to be what comes to mind when one thinks of love, and it is problems in this area that bring people into treatment. It is possible to come up with some examples of problems in other aspects of love (i.e., failures in maternal or paternal love) for which someone might seek treatment, but not many. Passionate love seems to be most central to one's adult experience, and thus most explicitly missed if lacking. This may also reflect our culture's high valuation of the experience of romantic love, and one could hypothesize that in cultures that place more emphasis on love of one's extended family or love of one's country, difficulties in those areas could motivate an individual toward treatment. It may be the task of psychotherapy and psychoanalysis to help illuminate other aspects of love in addition to the passionate, including the less dramatic everyday shadings of love.

Introduction

The last section covers the treatment situation and how love effects it. Helen W. Silverman writes about love on the part of the patient, transference love, while Robert S. Weinstein and Irwin Hirsch discuss it from the analyst's point of view. Andrew B. Druck suggests that love may be an inherent part of the analytic stance itself.

Silverman explores the nature of the love that the patient feels for the analyst and how it enters the treatment. She indicates some factors above and beyond the patient's unique psychodynamics that will affect the form and function of the erotic transference. These factors include the gender of the patient and analyst, the role of reciprocal transferences of each to the other, and the impact of the cultural milieu. She notes the taboo against discussing the analyst's sexual reactions in response to the erotic transference of the patient. She regards erotic transference and the analyst's response to it as inevitable, interactive, and ubiquitous in treatment. She also raises the question of the fate of this love after the patient leaves treatment and suggests that the erotic feelings may be transformed into an aim-inhibited love that includes appreciation and continued interest.

Weinstein suggests that there is a time and a place in a successful treatment when loving feelings on the analyst's part may occur. These, he indicates, can be presented to the patient in such a way that they confirm the patient's experience, without either offering the patient the possibility of gratification, which would cause their continued attachment to the therapist, or acting them out, which would be destructive to the patient.

Hirsch suggests that the intimacy and intensity of the analytic situation create circumstances where feelings of love do emerge in the patient and may also emerge in the analyst. He sees this as a natural part of the treatment process and as a particularly useful clue to what is going on in the patient at a particular time, and suggests that these feelings then can be used as a basis for interpretations. He views the therapeutic situation as one in which patient and therapist interact and in which each may influence the feelings and reactions of the other.

Druck focuses his attention on aim-inhibited love and places the erotic feelings of the analyst in the realm of countertransference. He suggests that concern for patients, appreciation of their experience, attention to their productions, and respect for their autonomy and potential are all formal aspects of the analytic process that may be regarded as expressing an aim-inhibited love. This love bears some resemblance to the love of a friend for another, or a parent for a child. This kind of love perhaps relates more to the Greek notion of agape than to eros, or passionate love, in that it focuses on the growth and development of the patient and contains a sense of their future—a perspective that a patient or a child usually are not able to have.

We noted earlier the complexity of love as an emotional state, and the treatment situation is not immune from the consequences of that. Many of our authors comment on the variety of ways in which love can enter the treatment situation and effect it. Hirsch makes the interesting comment that it is the patient who has most benefited from loving experiences who will most readily evoke love in others, including his or her analyst. Zuckerberg notes that it is particularly those who have been deprived of love who need the love of the therapist in order to have their own potential for growth stimulated. An example of this might be seen in Lane's fatherless adolescent boys, who seek the analyst's love in part as a compensation for their deprivation and, in part because there are other paternal functions that they need to have filled. Domash refers to another group which might be considered to have been deprived of love, the narcissistic personality, but here the patient "fights" the analyst's empathy and love in order to maintain an attachment to an unloving, but familiar object. Among the patients described by Silverman are those who seek to arouse the analyst's love in order to prevent further analytic work from taking place.

It should be apparant from this brief comparison that the role of love in the treatment will vary with theoretical orientation, patient dynamics, analyst characteristics, and timing in the treatment process. Any assessment of its growth-enhancing or inhibiting qualities cannot be made without all of these factors being considered.

Psychoanalysis today encompasses a variety of viewpoints that differ in the importance given to biological, environmental, and intrapsychic factors in human development and functioning, and in the language used to discuss psychological experience. It is interesting to see that although coming from varying orientations, our contributors concern themselves with similar issues: the relationship between childhood experience and adult love, the psychological requirements for loving, the feelings encompassed by the experience of love, the appearance of love in psychoanalysis, and the treatment of love problems. As psychoanalysts, we are most familiar with the pathology of love, with the difficulties people have in finding and maintaining a love relationship. Psychoanalysts are the historians of the individual's passage through love from infancy to adulthood and the unravelers of behaviors that are barriers to love. Poets and lovers may find the best words to describe the experience of love. Psychoanalysts can help explain where the power of this experience comes from and why it is so eagerly sought.

It is difficult to write of love and to conceptualize it in the absence of a unified theory. Psychoanalysis is probably the field of knowledge most likely to develop a theory of love, but it is clear that questions remain to be answered. Why is the differentiation between carnal love and romantic love so pervasive that in the dictionary definition of love the notion of erotic love is not a part of the first definition? Does involvement in one kind of love, that is, erotic, preclude involvement in love of other kinds, or is the loving person one who may have many simultaneous kinds and levels of love relationships? Why does a culture emphasize and idealize one kind of love above another? Answers to such questions will help to clarify both the similarities and differences between love and other human experiences.

In adolescence, one begins to leave one's primary family and develop new attachments. In adulthood, the formation of a new family brings with it new identifications and self-perceptions. In maturity, the forms of attachment may change so as to encompass a larger realm of involvement. Through love, ego ideals may be achieved and replaced by others, identifications with early objects may recede into the background and new ones come forth, idealizations may be surrendered as realistic satisfactions are appreciated. Love is a way of transcending the self and of participating in another's transformation as well. The force of love oscillates between the loss of the self in fusion with another, and the consolidation and emergence of new aspects of self. Out of love, with its roots in the past, grow the possibilities for the future.

REFERENCES

Altman, L. 1977. Some vicissitudes of love. *Journal of the American Psychoanalytic Association* 25:35–52.
Bak, R. 1973. Being in love and object loss. *International Journal of Psychoanalysis* 54:1–8.

Balint, M. 1948. On genital love. *International Journal of Psychoanalysis* 29:34–40.

Bergmann, M. 1971. Psychoanalytic observations on the capacity to love. In J. McDevitt and C. Settlage, eds., *Separation-individuation: Essays in honor of Margaret S. Mahler*, pp. 15–40. New York: IUP.

———. 1980. On the intrapsychic function of falling in love. *Psychoanalytic Quarterly* 49:56–77.

———. 1982. Platonic love, transference love, and love in real life. *Journal of the American Psychoanalytic Association* 30:87–111.

De Rougemont, D. 1963. *Love declared: Essays on the myths of love.* New York: Random House.

Freud, S. 1905. Three essays on the theory of sexuality. *Standard edition* 7:135–243.

———. 1910. A special type of object choice made by men. *Standard edition* 11:165–75.

———. 1912. The dynamics of transference. *Standard edition* 12:99–108.

———. 1914. On narcissism. *Standard edition* 14:69–102.

———. 1915. Observations on transference-love. *Standard edition* 12:157–71.

Mahler, M. 1967. On human symbiosis and the vicissitudes of individuation. *Journal of the American Psychoanalytic Association* 15:740–63.

Webster's international unabridged dictionary. 1959. 2nd ed. Springfield: Merriam.

1. Eros, Agape, Amor, Libido: Concepts in the History of Love

Waltraud Ireland

The suffering and ecstasy of love have been central and enduring themes of imaginative literature throughout the ages. Still, the configuration of this sought-after emotion continues to be enigmatic and to elude scientific specificity. There is no agreed upon definition of love. The concept itself is loosely applied to a variety of human relationships with both animate and inanimate objects, and little clarity has emerged as to the common thread uniting these diverse expressions of love or distinguishing one type of love experience from another.

The literature on love is characterized by a high degree of ambivalence, a weaving back and forth between the two opposite poles of love and hate. It touches upon the other fundamental polarities governing human existence that influence our ideas on love, such as male and female, good and evil, life and death, nature and nurture, fantasy and reality, active and passive. It is as if two seemingly opposite views about love, as either something terrifying or as something comforting, are constantly struggling for expression.

On the idealizing side, love is salvation, "a central condition of human existence" necessary for survival (Gaylin 1986, p. 1). It is portrayed as an experience beyond mere necessity, one by which man is enabled to transform the animal side of his nature (Singer 1984). Love is thus seen as being beyond mere sexuality and the procreative imperatives of the species, processes for which love is not necessary. Seen from this perspective, love is a uniquely human event and, like art and religion, both an artifact of civilization and an intrinsically civilizing force. It is viewed as a universal tendency, altruistic in its nature, enriching the lives of those touched by it. It is offered as a panacea that conquers and cures all, symbolized recently by the slogan "make love, not war." In the idealizing tradition, love is made for marriage "like a horse and carriage." Perhaps not surprisingly, this benevolent vision of love is associated with a female prototype, the most sublime expression of which is embodied in the Virgin Mary (Adams 1961; Hunt 1959; de Riencourt 1974; De Rougemont 1983; Singer 1984).

Pitted against this cult of love are sentiments that bespeak a kind of wariness—even fear—of love, as if it were a danger or a disease against which one needed to be inoculated. Far from being a pleasure and benefit, it is viewed as a kind of madness that ultimately impoverishes the lovers and pulls them into a widening circle of pain and suffering, with the ever-present threat of loss of love and even death in suicide (Bak 1973). It is held to be egotistic and exclusionary, at odds with the conventions of society and a threat to the institution of marriage, which love is said to enter only to destroy. Far from being immortal, love is seen as transient, like a fever that comes and goes beyond the lovers' control. André Maurois (cited in Bessel 1984) called romantic love one of the worst inventions bequeathed to humanity by the Middle Ages. The female prototype of this vision of love is the biblical Eve, the seductress of man (D'Arcy 1956; de Riencourt 1974; Hunt 1959; Lerner 1979).

In view of the ambivalence surrounding the subject of love, it is not surprising that the literature on love is permeated by value judgments and efforts to construct hierarchies of love, ranging from spiritual to carnal love, heterosexual to homosexual love, conjugal to romantic love, true to inauthentic love, and mature to immature love. Writing about love seems to encourage the penchant to moralize about it and to channel the expression of love in particular directions. As a result, we know more about what writers have thought love ought to be than about the true nature of different love experiences. We know more about interpersonal love than about the love of art, of music, or of God. Early psychoanalytic theory tended to view these more abstract forms of love reductionistically as sublimated expressions of the sexual drive; other views have also been suggested.

In the Western tradition, the literature on love has evolved around the discussion of three major concepts: eros, agape, and amor, with libido, as the latest concept, introduced by psychoanalysis, being seen as a variant of eros. Eros has to do with desire and passion, with man's sexual appetitive nature, which at its most elemental level, has been described as the "zeal of the organs, male and female, for each other" (Campbell 1973, p. 161); in contrast, agape is seen as a higher, transfiguring, spiritual order of love. While placed at opposite poles, eros and agape share certain characteristics, in that both are general and impersonal in their operation, with minimal regard for the individuality and personality of the love object. With the rise of the idea of amor in the eleventh century, love took on an altogether new dimension, one in which personal preference, individual experience, and the personality of the beloved were given a unique status (Campbell 1973). With Freud's development of the libido theory at the turn of this century, love received a psychological dimension, which opened up new ways of understanding the vicissitudes, conflicts, and ambivalences of love.

The conventions of love in the Western world have their origins in classical Greece, as conveyed to us by Plato in *The Symposium* (1974). Plato recounts a myth about the origin of love in which themes of loss, longing, and refinding, which are echoed in contemporary psychoanalytic views on love, predominate. According to this myth, mankind existed originally as three distinct sexes, male, female, and a third sex, hermaphrodite, now extinct, combining the characteristics of the first two. Physically, the human being was a rounded whole, with a duplicate of everything: four arms, legs, eyes, and ears; two sexual organs and two faces turned in opposite directions. So adaptive was this race of man that the gods felt challenged and determined to weaken it by cutting each human being in half and by creating in each half the overwhelming longing to be reunited with the half from which it had been severed. Instead of sparring with the gods, mankind became preoccupied with itself and with issues of completion. As Plato (1974) said:

> It is from this distant epoch, then, that we may date the innate love which human beings feel for one another, the love which restores us to our ancient state by attempting to weld two beings into one and to heal the wound which humanity suffered. (p. 59)

By cutting the race of man in two, Zeus is said to have created the sexual categories of homosexuals (male halves pursuing male halves), lesbians (female halves pursuing female halves) and heterosexuals (male and female halves of the bisected hermaphrodite)—the latter being considered an inferior category.

In this view, as Bergmann (1982) has pointed out, love is the consequence of man's hubris in challenging the gods and is meted out as a kind of punishment. The idea of love is thus already in its origin inextricably intertwined with notions of loss, deficiencies of the self, and a longing for a symbiotic union once enjoyed.

Plato also has been credited by such authors as Bergmann (1982) and de Riencourt (1974), with the achievement of moving the discussion about love from the mythological to the philosophical plane. According to Plato, eros is a universal principle active in every striving for good and for happiness. The striving itself is prompted by the consciousness of a need for a good or happiness not as yet attained, and it thus implies an awareness of a deficiency in the self and a belief in the existence of an object who has what one believes oneself to lack.

But this striving could take many forms, dependent on whether the lover was in pursuit of earthly or heavenly Aphrodite. With his famous ladder of love Plato established the convention of a hierarchy of love that those capable of "growing wings" might ascend. At its lowest rung, eros had to do with the pursuit of physical pleasures, its natural object being physical procreation. In an ascending order, the other stages moved from the love of particular examples of physical beauty to love of beauty itself, and finally reached the highest stage, agape, the love of wisdom, which, akin to a religious experience, was held to offer the possibility of attaining knowledge of universal truths.

Platonic love, at its highest level, is thus an affair of the soul, of two noble minds coming together for the purpose of spiritual procreation, an activity of which only men were capable according to Plato. All other expressions of eros were merely imperfect approaches to the ideal. As a philosopher, Plato gave the highest honor in the pantheon of love to the activity he knew best, philosophizing. He has little to say about interpersonal forms of love but a great deal to say about what from a psychoanalytic perspective would be viewed as sublimated forms of eros. In love as in politics, Plato was very much concerned with what made a life worth living.

What is striking about *The Symposium* is the conspicuous absence of women as either objects or subjects of eros, and of any reference to conjugal love. While the portrayal of women in the *Iliad* and in the Greek tragedies bespeaks a time when women enjoyed considerable power and influence and participated in public life, in Plato's time the status of women had significantly declined. The marriages of upper-class women were arranged by their families, for the purpose of producing children and keeping house. Women had little education and did not participate in public life. They simply were not considered worthy objects of romance. Their uses were summed up by Demosthenes (cited in O'Faolain and Martines 1973), a public figure of the time, in this statement: "Mistresses we keep for pleasure, concubines for daily attendance upon our person, wives to bear us legitimate children and be our faithful housekeepers" (p. 9). Omitted in this statement is the extent to which male homosexuality was practiced and tolerated in the upper-class culture of classical Greece and the romantic function of that homosexuality. The ideal romantic couple of that time was an older male (though not too old) and a youth on whom would be showered the affection and solicitous attention that in other times and places came to be associated with heterosexual love. The romance was expected to end when the boy reached maturity (Dover 1978; Hunt 1959). In fact, love between men figures prominently in Plato's ladder of love, which he felt could be ascended only on the basis of sublimated homosexuality. While he did not, at least in *The Symposium,* condemn the physical expression of this love, he left no doubt that he preferred its sublimated variant.

Finally, the omission of women in a treatise on love may also be attributable to the intellectual revolution with which the name of classical Greece is associated and of which Plato's philosophy is but one manifestation. This revolution is embodied in the systematic effort to supplant earlier mythopoeic modes of apprehending and interpreting the world with the methodology of the analytical, logically reasoning mind—a faculty believed to be uniquely male. That was the point in history when mind was set up against feeling and culture against nature. The value of spiritual over physical procreation lay thus in its independence from nature—and women (de Riencourt 1974; Plato 1974).

The next major change in how love was viewed found its source in Christianity, which was in its expansionary bloom in the first centuries of this era. By then classical Greece had become absorbed, along with a diversity of other cultures, into the Roman Empire, which in turn had come under increasing pressure from tribes outside the Roman pale and from centrifugal social and cultural forces within. The feminine emotionalism derided by the masculine and rationalist orientation of classical Greek culture had collected around a host of mystery cults from the

Near East. Christianity represented a creative synthesis that drew on Greek thought, Judaic messianic faith and ethical will, and the symbolism and emotionalism of rival mystery cults. The new creed had an immeasurably larger impact on the daily lives of men and women than the concept of Platonic love ever had.

Christianity placed the concept of love in the heart of its teachings. Love was the essence of God and thus the ultimate reality, and the love of God was equivalent to the love of man—of all mankind, indiscriminating and regardless of personal merit. As Matthew 5:43–46 states: "And [God] makes his sun to rise on the evil and on the good, and sends rain on the just and on the unjust" (May and Metzger 1965). In the act of loving God, both the love of the self and the love of the other were constituted, as exemplified in the typically Christian saying from Galatians 5:14, "Love thy neighbor as thyself" (May and Metzger 1965), however imperfect both of you may be. Again and again Christian teachings reiterated the need to love especially those we do not care for—after all, loving those we find congenial requires little effort—as exemplified in the command from Matthew 5:43–46, "love your enemies and pray for those who persecute you" (May and Metzger 1965). The new creed saw as the mark of the Christian the capacity to return good for evil, and required that an end be put to the cycle of revenge, as a way of putting into practice the joining of love with compassion and mercy. This mysterious idea, embodied in Christ's crucifixion, was portrayed as a sign of God's love of mankind. It has engaged Christian writers grappling with its meaning and implications throughout the ages. Kierkegaard (cited in Kaplan 1971) again underscored it when he wrote: "Perfect love means to love the one through whom we are made unhappy" (p. 575). The American writer Hawthorne (cited in Campbell 1973) expressed his understanding thus: "Man must not disclaim his brotherhood even with the guiltiest" (p. 173).

The new creed, based on principles of love, charity, humility, and chastity, was expected to permeate and shape the manner in which a Christian conducted his everyday life, both within the family and the community. Every aspect of human life was transformed by Christian principles. While Christianity inspired an ardent, passionate love, it was a love divorced from sex. With its repressive attitudes toward sex, Christianity greatly accentuated conflict and guilt regarding activities the pursuit and varied gratification of which had been by and large uncomplicated in the classical world. It forbade the separate enjoyment of sex, love, and marriage that had been customary in the ancient world, by condemning prostitution and adultery as well as homosexuality. At the same time it made difficult the simultaneous enjoyment of love and marriage, for as St. Paul admonished in Galatians 5:16–17, "The desires of the flesh are against the 'Spirit' and the desires of the Spirit against the flesh" (May and Metzger 1965). Celibacy and virginity were celebrated as the highest ideals, and men and women were encouraged to live together in spiritual marriages. Ironically, Christianity's repressive attitude toward sex accomplished its precise opposite—it succeeded in giving love and sex a value they had not held before. As Freud (1912) noted:

It can easily be shown that the psychical value of erotic needs is reduced as soon as their satisfaction becomes easy. An obstacle is required to heighten libido. . . . In this context it may be claimed that the ascetic current in Christianity created psychic values for love which pagan antiquity was never able to confer on it. (pp. 187–88)

Equally ironic, as Christianity became heir to the collapsing Roman Empire, the advocacy of celibacy turned out to be poor population policy. It became preferable to "marry rather than to burn." In time, marriage was made a holy sacrament, created as a bulwark against promiscuity and adultery and for the purpose of procreation. Contrary to the practice in classical times, it was indissoluble for either partner. Whatever was licit or illicit within marriage was so for both sexes. As noted in 1 Corinthians 7:4–6, sex for pleasure was considered anathema, "He who too ardently loves his own wife is an adulterer" (May and Metzger 1965). Many people found the dilemmas posed by the new creed insoluble and fled to a celibate life in the monasteries and convents (Brown 1971; de Riencourt 1974; Hunt 1959).

Yet married life attained a quality and a value under the aegis of Christian love that it had not attained in the classical world. Companionship, mutual affection, and respect were at least ideals the couple could expectantly strive toward, as is reflected in Ephesians 5:22–28, 33: "Husbands, love your wives as Christ also loved the Church" (May and Metzger 1965)—the Church, incidentally, viewing itself in its corporate identity as female.

The emergence of the female principle in Christianity can be seen most graphically in the gradual evolution of the cult of the Virgin Mary, mother of God, as the great mediator between heaven and earth, very much like the role expected of mothers in the human family. Mary had been left out of the Holy Trinity as being a mere mortal, and yet by the time of the Crusades in the eleventh century, she overshadowed the Trinity in importance. De Riencourt (1974) reports that it was rumored at this time that God had changed sex. Adams (1961) conveys that countless miracles were attributed to Mary; she inspired the Gothic style of architecture and had vast numbers of cathedrals and churches constructed and dedicated in her honor, with an unprecedented expenditure of manpower and scarce resources.

But in the wake of the cult of the Virgin Mary, there followed an unprecedented shift in the object of love. Not heaven and the heavenly queen, but earth and mortal woman came to be seen as the true domain of love. Between the eleventh and fourteenth centuries an understanding of love developed in Western Europe that has been described as different from anything preceding it and that has been characterized by Campbell (1973) as "one of the most important mutations not only of human feeling but also of the spiritual consciousness of our human race" (p. 162). This new understanding was courtly love, or amor.

Its efflorescence is connected with the Crusades of the eleventh century, organized by the papacy against Islam in Spain and in the Middle East. In the wake of the establishment of this contact with Islamic civilization, there arose, first in southern France and later throughout Western Europe, a love poetry in which the passionate love of woman is celebrated. This poetry was spread throughout the land by poets, troubadors, and minnesingers traveling from court to court. This poetic legacy of courtly love is enshrined in the romances of Tristan and Isolde, Lancelot and Guinevere, Troilus and Cressida, and Parsifal, as well as in the real-life romance of Heloïse and Abelard.

The love experience celebrated in these romances of amor, or courtly love (the other name by which we know it), was the agony of earthly love, in Campbell's (1972) words, "bitter sweetness and sweet bitterness" (p. 211). What came to be valued above all else was the pursuit of love as unfulfilled desire. The idea of being in love became a kind of religion, as if the Christian saying "God is love" had been reversed, except that at the heart of this religion stood a woman of decided personality. What distinguished amor from eros and agape was that love became specific, personal, and discriminating. The eyes and the heart of the lover were intensely engaged in selecting the beloved, who could not be easily exchanged for another object. For a woman to be a worthy object of the kind of service amor demanded of the lover, she had to be preferably a lady of exalted station—distant, and married, and thus unattainable.

Courtly love has often been decried for celebrating adultery or not respecting marriage bonds. The reasons for this seem to lie more in the nature of medieval marriage than in courtly love's promoting adulterous love as an end in itself. At the heart of courtly love was a love freely chosen and bestowed, and this was an act in which partners in a medieval marriage were thought unable to engage, being themselves pawns in the service of consolidating family, property, and political interests (de Riencourt 1974; Huizinga 1954; Hunt 1959).

The conventions of amor revolve around a knight secretly entering the service of his beloved as an ennobling and civilizing experience, in the course of which he has to prove his valor. In the words of Andreas Capellanus (cited in Hunt 1959), "Oh, what a wonderful thing is love, which makes a man shine with so many virtues and teaches everyone, no matter who he is, so many good traits of character" (p. 171). The relationship of the knight to his lady was modeled on that of the vassal to his feudal lord and governed by mutual rights and obligations. The knight had to submit to whatever tests of valor his lady might devise. In fact, so-called courts of love were set up at various European courts to discuss and arbitrate disputes that might arise among lovers. Generally, the knight proved his valor at popular sports events, such as tournaments and jousts. According to Campbell (1970a), "The disciplines the knight subjected himself to in order to gain favor [in the eyes of his lady] sometimes approached the lunacy of the penitential grove" (p. 175). Each successful completion of such a test was supposed to lead to an increase in the degree of intimacy permissible to the lovers.

The character and conventions of courtly love owe a great deal to the needs of a military, hereditary aristocracy, which was beginning to take shape at this time, to differentiate itself as a class from the peasantry on the one hand and the clergy on the other. With the code of chivalry, this aristocracy had devised highly ritualized rites of passage for becoming, militarily, the perfect knight. In absorbing the arts of courtly love, the knight subjugated himself to tests, the successful completion of which, he believed, would make him a more civilized and noble human being.

Jaeger (1985) tells us that "Courtliness and courtly humanity were next to Christian ideals the most powerful civilizing forces in the West since ancient Rome" (p. 261). Or in the words of Huizinga (1954), "In no other epoch did the ideal of civilization amalgamate to such a degree with that of love" (p. 108).

Adhering to the ideas of courtly love, however, was something inherently subversive or, considering the religious character of medieval society, heretical. These ideas had taken hold in areas that had been on or outside the perimeter of the influence of the Roman Empire and had been only recently converted to Christianity, mostly by means of force. From this perspective, courtly love is seen as a reaction to the claims of absolute authority of the Christian church, headquartered in Rome. That amor is an anagram of Roma became especially significant in this context as embodying opposition to Rome (Campbell 1970b; De Rougement 1983). In upholding the tenets of courtly love, the knightly class was setting up its own value system and its own moral authority and thus contributing to the individuating process that came to a head with the Reformation. What is certain is that the Church felt threatened and that it organized in the thirteenth century in the south of France the so-called Albigensian crusade in which the adherents of courtly love were included among the sects slated for extermination (Campbell 1970b; de Riencourt 1974; De Rougemont 1983).

There existed a wide chasm between the professed ideals of courtly love and the lived reality. "Civilization," in the words of Huizinga (1954), "always needs to wrap up the idea of love in veils of fancy, to exalt and to define it, and thereby to forget cruel reality" (p. 127). In the end the exalted treatment of women in courtly love had much to do with the male need to practice heroism in love as it was practiced on the battlefield. Christine de Pisan (cited in Huizinga 1954), who lived in the fourteenth century and has been accorded by the current feminist movement the status of one of the earliest feminist writers, argued:

All the conventions of love are the work of men; even when it dons an idealistic guise, erotic culture is altogether saturated by male egotism; and what else is the cause of the endlessly repeated insults to matrimony, to woman and her feebleness, but the need of masking this egotism? One word suffices to answer all these infamies: it is not the women who have written the books. (p. 127)

Alongside the literature celebrating courtly love in its sublimated forms, there had also grown up a literature glorifying the arts of seduction, thus enhancing female vulnerabilities and the dangers of love. For, as Huizinga (1954) so eloquently portrayed, despite the conventions of courtly love, the "sexual life of the higher classes remained surprisingly rude" (p. 109).

And yet, however artificial in its conventions, courtly love planted a seed that continues to germinate and that has had a powerful influence on the relations between the sexes in the West. It implanted the idea that love must be a genuinely reciprocal relationship based on mutual admiration and respect, including fidelity, even though, paradoxically, courtly love existed within an adulterous framework.

We know from psychoanalysis, of course, that wherever woman is placed on a pedestal and elevated above the full range of her humanity, the other image of woman as one who engulfs, hurts, destroys, and magically seduces is pushed into the unconscious, there to assume demonic proportions. The massive "return of the repressed" with respect to women occurred in the witch hunts of the sixteenth and seventeenth centuries, when the feared image of woman as being in league with the devil gained the upper hand. (For an excellent discussion of this subject see Thomas [1975]).

It was Freud who set the foundations for a psychology of love that could cast light on the vicissitudes of love itself and on the causes of human conflicts with love. According to Freud, all forms of love are expressions of libido (the Latin form of the Greek *eros*) based on desire or need. Infantile and unconscious prototypes help determine the nature of adult forms of love, as expressed in Freud's (1905) statement: "The finding of an object is in fact a refinding of it" (p. 222). The capacity to love is achieved only through reaching the genital stage by the fusion of two libidinal currents, the affectionate or tenderness current, which goes back to infancy, and the sensual current, which emerges at puberty. Even manifestly nonsexual forms of love are in this view related to the operation of libido, albeit in its aim-inhibited sublimated form (Freud 1905).

Freud (1905) distinguished two types of love, the narcissistic and the anaclitic, both a considerable source of difficulty in man's love life. In its extreme form, narcissistic love refers to a person immersed in self-love who uses objects primarily to enhance the self, while the extreme of anaclitic love involves intense object dependence. In these extreme forms, either type of love leads to psychic impoverishment by virtue of bondage either to the object or to the narcissistic self. The findings of psychoanalysis leave no doubt that the act of love requires an interweaving of both self-love and object love. According to Loewald (1978),

> Our love life develops in such a way that one main current desires and longs for other persons as objects of desire, while the other, more ancient, current remains "narcissistic." . . . Love then is a force or power that not only brings people together . . . but equally brings oneself together into that one individuality which we become through identification. (pp. 39–40)

In a report on recent psychoanalytic views of love, Kernberg (1977) also states that the state of being in love enhances both normal narcissism and the capacity for object love.

For Freud, the capacity for love as well as the difficulties with loving are rooted in the incestuous fantasies making up the Oedipus complex. Basing their views on further refinements of psychoanalytic theory, such authors as Bergmann (1971) and Bach (1985) now suggest that the capacity has its origin in the preoedipal period, most specifically in what Margaret Mahler calls the symbiotic phase, and later subphases. The state of bliss thought to be experienced in the mother-infant symbiosis, in which the two are as one, is seen as coming to an end in the separation-individuation phase with the attainment of individuation. Loewald (1978) states that "individuation of the individual comes about by the losses of separation" (p. 46). Depending on the solidity of this achievement, the search for love more or less seeks to undo this state of separateness. It also seeks to restore to the self the sense of perfection believed to have been enjoyed in the original mother-infant unit. The idealization of the object, much commented on by Freud and other writers on love, thus functions as a compensation for a perceived deficiency in the self, as does love's possessiveness; one seeks to lay claim in others to what one fears the self does not possess. To Freud (1921) it was obvious that:

> the object serves as a substitute for some unattained ego ideal of our own. We love it on account of the perfections which we have striven to reach for our own ego, and which we should now like to procure in this roundabout way as a means of satisfying our narcissism. . . . (pp. 112–13)

Some of this, as Bergmann (1971, 1982) reminds us, echoes themes developed by Plato.

According to Freud (1915a), the driving force behind love is the pursuit of pleasure and the avoidance of unpleasure. Freud defined loving "as the relation of the ego to its sources of pleasure . . ." (p. 135). Whether love is the love of pleasure is a question writers on love pondered long before Freud. Spinoza (cited in Hazo 1967) said that "love points toward something more than pleasure, toward perfection, happiness and blessedness" (p. 76). Reik, who strongly disagreed with Freud's formulations, wrote that the "peak of love is beatitude" (cited in Hazo 1967, p. 411). The difficulty of Freud's equation of love with pleasure has to do with the variety of pleasures available to the human mind in both fantasy and reality, including the pleasures of pain, and how to distinguish among them. Indeed, the close proximity of pain to pleasure and the frequent transformations of pleasure into suffering and hate are at the heart of the difficulty. To be sure, Freud (1915b) was mindful of the close connection between love and hate in the unconscious mind, stating, "It might be said that we owe the fairest flowerings of our love to the reaction against the hostile impulses which we sense within us" (p. 299). But with the growing emphasis in our culture on love as an ethical force, this connection has receded into the background. As Altman (1977) recently put it:

This other side of love should be a cautionary tale. The need to disown hate might even be the root cause of our need to place so much emphasis on love, to ask so much of it. . . . Perhaps man would love more if he could also hate cheerfully. (p. 42)

Despite considering love, together with work, as a cornerstone of communal life, Freud was suspicious of the binding capacity of genital love, placing greater stock in the capacity of sublimated forms of love to create both lasting ties and the cultural achievements that define a civilization (Freud 1905, 1930). Passionate love not only threatened ego boundaries but made the lover dependent for his happiness on the external world and exposed him to the risks of extreme suffering. Thus, Freud (1930) cautioned, "For that reason the wise men of every age have warned us most emphatically against this way of life" (p. 101).

Among the early psychoanalysts, there were some who objected to the close association between love and sexuality as postulated in the libido theory. Reik (1944) insisted that sex and love are not the same and that the ego functions play a larger role in the psychogenesis of love than do the sexual drives. In fact, Reik considered the transfer of the ego ideal to another person the most characteristic attribute of love. But in view of the close connection between love and hate in the unconscious mind, Reik also saw love as a kind of a reaction formation against hate, envy, jealousy, and greed, and he thought that an incapacity to hate made for an incapacity to love. For Fromm (1963), the primary function of love is as a protection against isolation: "The basis for our need to love lies in the experience of separateness and the resulting need to overcome the anxiety of separateness by the experience of union" (p. 6). Love is, according to Fromm, an art that has to be learned, inasmuch as the instinctual connections have been lost in man.

For many years, little that was truly new was added to Freud's store of observations and conjectures about love. The subject does not even appear as a separate listing in glossaries of psychoanalytic terms or indexes of publications (Altman 1977). The evidence suggests a real resistance among psychoanalysts to exploring the complexities of love. Altman observes that an attitude of inquiry was precluded by the apparent belief that the nature of love was understood by virtue of "its known provenance in the sexual drives" (p. 36).

Balint (1948) was among the first to bring the issue into focus again and to initiate the process of reevaluating the assumptions underlying the psychoanalytic theory of love. Balint questioned whether the attainment of genital primacy was indeed the sine qua non of genital love, seeing it instead as a necessary but not a sufficient condition: "Genital love . . . uses the genital sexuality only as a stock on which to graft something essentially different . . ." (p. 36). These essential differences included "idealization, tenderness, and a special form of identification" (p. 36). More recently, Altman (1977) also concluded that "there are many who have reached what is called genital primacy whose aim-inhibited sublimatory derivatives are nonexistent" (p. 49). In a sense, Balint (1948) wondered whether genital love is all there is to love. He called genital love doubly artificial, stating:

firstly, constant interferences with free sexual gratification build up external and internal resistance against pleasure . . . , secondly, the demand for prolonged, perpetual regard and gratitude forces us to regress to the archaic and infantile forms of tender love. (p. 37)

Balint (1968) later opposed primary love to Freud's concept of primary narcissism as a basic constitutional predisposition whose aim it is to "establish—or, probably, re-establish—an all-embracing harmony with one's environment, to be able to love in peace" (p. 65).

Over the last two decades, principally as a result of work by Bergmann (1971, 1980, 1982), Altman (1977), Kernberg (1974a, 1974b, 1977), and others, the awareness has grown that psychoanalysis lacks a consistent theory of love. Echoing Balint's (1968) objections, Kernberg (1977) came to the conclusion that the "concept of 'genital primacy' as simply the capacity to achieve orgasm in sexual intercourse badly needs revision" (p. 83); Altman (1977) added that "libido is not the full measure of love. Love is more than the expression of the energy of the sexual instinct" (p. 38). It was hard not to infer that much of the past psychoanalytic literature on love had more to do with the psychology and psychopathology of sexuality—with the conditions that interfere with the development of the capacity for love—than with the various states of loving.

It thus appears that psychoanalysis is rediscovering love on the basis of a more differentiated investigation of it. Love is now seen as having its seasons, with associated meaning and experiences that change in the different stages of the life cycle. Men and women are said to relate differently to the experience of love based on the complex biological, social, and cultural configurations that make up gender. Kernberg (1974a, 1974b, 1977) has begun to investigate the developmental tasks required for the capacity of falling and remaining in love, concluding that "sexual love is a complex, emotional disposition which integrates sexual excitement, tenderness, genital identification, a mature form of idealization, and a deep commitment to an object relation" (Kernberg 1977, p. 94). Kernberg considers sexual passion an integral component of this commitment, a view shared by Altman (1977) and Bergmann (1971).

As indicated above, however, love between people does not exhaust the possibilities of love. Where in the psychoanalytic theory of love do we fit the experience of love that comes from art, music, scientific and intellectual creativity; the satisfaction that comes with the completion of an intensely experienced piece of work, whatever its nature; the bliss, possibly "oceanic feeling," or what Balint (1968) referred to as the "harmonious, interpenetrating mix-up" (p. 66) that may be present in watching a sunset, or when one is at peace with oneself and one's surroundings? And who is to say which form of love makes the larger contribution to man's happiness?

REFERENCES

Adams, H. 1961. *Mont-Saint-Michel and Chartres*. New York: New American Library of World Literature.
Altman, L. 1977. Some vicissitudes of love. *Journal of the American Psychoanalytic Association* 1:35–52.
Bach, S. 1985. *Narcissistic states and the therapeutic process*. New York: Aronson.
Bak, R. C. 1973. Being in love and object loss. *International Journal of Psychoanalysis* 54:1–8.
Balint, M. 1948. On genital love. *International Journal of Psycho-analysis* 29:34–40.
———. 1968. *The basic fault: Therapeutic aspects of regression*. London: Tavistock.
Bergmann, M. S. 1971. Psychoanalytic observations on the capacity to love. In J. B. McDevitt and C. F. Settlage, eds., *Separation-individuation: Essays in honor of Margaret S. Mahler*, pp. 15–40. New York: IUP.
———. 1980. On the intrapsychic function of falling in love. *Psychoanalytic Quarterly* 49:56–77.
———. 1982. Platonic love, transference love, and love in real life. *Journal of the American Psychoanalytic Association* 1:87–112.
Bessel, H. 1984. *The love test*. New York: Morrow.
Brown, P. 1971. *The world of late antiquity, AD 150–750*. London: Thames and Hudson.
Campbell, J. 1970a. *The masks of God: Creative mythology*. New York: Viking.
———. 1970b. *The masks of God: Occidental mythology*. New York: Viking.
———. 1972. *The flight of the gander*. Chicago: Gateway Edition.
———. 1973. *Myths to live by*. New York: Bantam.
D'Arcy, M. D. 1956. *The mind and heart of love*. London: Faber and Faber.
de Riencourt, A. 1974. *Sex and power in history*. New York: McKay.
De Rougemont, D. 1983. *Love in the Western world*. Trans. M. Belgion. Princeton: Princeton University Press.
Dover, A. J. 1978. *Greek homosexuality*. Cambridge: Harvard University Press.
Freud, S. 1905. Three essays on the theory of sexuality. *Standard edition* 7:135–243.
———. 1912. On the universal tendency to debasement in the sphere of love (Contributions to the psychology of love, II). *Standard edition* 11:177–90.
———. 1915a. Instincts and their vicissitudes. *Standard edition* 14:109–40.
———. 1915b. Thoughts for the times on war and death. *Standard edition* 14:273–300.
———. 1921. Group psychology and the analysis of the ego. *Standard edition* 18:65–143.
———. 1930. Civilization and its discontents. *Standard edition* 21:57–146.

Fromm, E. 1963. *The art of loving.* New York: Bantam.
Gaylin, W. 1986. *Rediscovering love.* New York: Viking Penguin.
Hazo, R. 1967. *The idea of love.* New York: Praeger.
Huizinga, J. 1954. *The waning of the Middle Ages.* New York: Doubleday–Anchor.
Hunt, M. M. 1959. *The natural history of love.* New York: Grove.
Jaeger, C. S. 1985. *The origins of courtliness.* Philadelphia: University of Pennsylvania Press.
Kaplan, D. M. 1971. On transference love and generativity. *Psychoanalytic Review* 58:573–79.
Kernberg, O. F. 1974a. Barriers to falling and remaining in love. *Journal of the American Psychoanalytic Association* 22:486–511.
———. 1974b. Mature love: Prerequisites and characteristics. *Journal of the American Psychoanalytic Association* 22:743–68.
———. 1977. Boundaries and structure in love relations. *Journal of the American Psychoanalytic Association* 25:81–114.
Lerner, L. 1979. *Love and marriage: Literature and its social context.* London: Arnold.
Loewald, H. 1978. *Psychoanalysis and the history of the individual.* New Haven: Yale University Press.
May, H. G., and B. M. Metzger, eds. 1965. *The Oxford annotated Bible with the Apocrypha.* New York: Oxford University Press.
O'Faolain, J., and L. Martines, eds. 1973. *Not in God's image: Women in history from the Greeks to the Victorians.* New York: Harper and Row.
Plato. 1974. *The symposium.* Trans. W. H. Harmondsworth. New York: Penguin.
Reik, T. 1944. *A psychologist looks at love.* New York: Farrar and Rinehart.
Singer, I. 1984. *The nature of love,* vols. 1–2. Chicago: University of Chicago Press.
Thomas, K. 1975. *Religion and the decline of magic.* New York: Macmillan.

2. Love: Transcultural Considerations

Robert Endleman

Few psychoanalysts or cultural anthropologists have focused on love in their writings. The psychoanalytic literature contains many indirect references to love in terms such as "object cathexes" and "libidinal ties" but little about love itself. At the same time, anthropological literature, while containing a great deal about sex, is also strangely silent on the topic of love.

GENERAL TRANSCULTURAL CONSIDERATIONS

Love and the relation of love and sex are handled differently in different societies.

First, I want to make clear what I mean by a transcultural view. *Transcultural* is used here, in preference to the more common term *cross-cultural,* to emphasize that I posit basic psychological universalities, applicable to all human beings, *trans*culturally, underlying the *cross*-cultural variations among different cultures. Psychoanalysis asserts, and anthropological studies confirm, that basic human problems are universal to all. This universality rests on the human species's having a common and singular phylogenetic history. Phylogenetic history gave us not only upright posture and bipedal locomotion but an extraordinarily vulnerable neonate absolutely dependent on physical and psychological care for survival. It also gave us the particular human sexuality, which is lifelong; nonseasonal; extremely peremptory; prodigious; precocious; prolific; potentially labile in aim, modality, and object; variably connected to the anatomical distinctions of the two sexes; and complexly connected to that other primary instinctual drive, namely, aggression. (See Endleman 1981, pt. 2, for fuller development.) The transcultural view emphasizes the universality of the basic instinctual drives of sex and aggression and the necessity of each society to come to terms with these drives. It also refers to the universality of the basic maturational and developmental stages and of basic mechanisms of defense and adaptation such as repression, reaction formation, identification, and so on, which are the repertoire of human beings in all societies.

Variable across cultures are the details of how all of these are worked out and expressed. The culture can emphasize the erotic drive itself, the object being less important (such as the societies of ancient Greece and the Mohave Indians). Or it can consider the sexual drive itself problematic and emphasize the question of the object: Who is the object? Which objects are taboo? Is the object highly individualized, as it is in modern Western culture? The culture may have concepts of many different kinds of love—for example, mother-child love, nonerotic love between siblings and other relatives, love in friendship. There may or may not be a highly developed concept of romantic love.

It should be clarified that romantic love is a special development of late medieval to modern Western societies (De Rougemont 1940). Since the tribal societies to be discussed will be considered in relationship to love, it is appropriate briefly to describe what is meant by romantic love. In this kind of love the choice of object is highly individualized and idealized, and there is an enormously heightened sexual attraction, which may in turn be highly sublimated and may even preclude physical sexual contact. It is believed that the partners were "fated" for each other by mysterious, perhaps supernatural powers and that any resistance to that fate is futile. The partner is seen as the "one and only in the whole universe." The lover is prepared to carry out any sacrifice for the beloved. The state of "being in love" in this romantic way is seen as a kind of madness, suspending all normal capacities for rational judgment. (See Freud [1921] comparing such a state of "being in love" with a kind of hypnosis.)

In this essay, I shall concentrate on anthropological and other accounts of various societies, some tribal, some transitional from tribal to modern, others superficially but not yet entirely modern. I shall focus on adult relationships, mostly between men and women, omitting other kinds of love, and referring to parent-child ties as precursors to the later adult relations.

In anthropological writings we find very full accounts of the "sexual life of the savages" and very little reference to love. Love is rarely a prerequisite to marriage or to nonmarital sexual contact (even in the social ideal, let alone in reality). All societies have marriage in some form, defined as a long-term publicly recognized mating between two persons, usually one male and one female, involving clear mutual rights and obligations. Partner choice is always regulated, limited to certain categories of persons (the mate is chosen from within a category—endogamy rules—and outside a category, such as close kin—exogamy rules). Rarely must the prospective mates love each other; indeed, in many cases it is considered undesirable. Bride and groom may not have even met before the marriage ceremony. Close affection, even love, might develop after the marriage. In plural marriage, with polygyny (plural wives) or polyandry (plural husbands), love between spouses is even less expected.

THE MOHAVE INDIANS

The Mohave Indians of Arizona, an agricultural people with exogamous patrilineal clans, were intensively studied in the 1930s by the anthropologist and psychoanalyst George Devereux (1937, 1939, 1950, 1961). The Mohave have a very active heterosexual life, with a great many partners, and serially monogamous marriage, usually with affection between partners, though without deep and abiding love, and rarely with any romantic love.

In Devereux's voluminous accounts of the sexual practices (see particularly 1950) the word or the concept of "love" rarely appears at all. An exception is the following brief notation: "Persons 'in love' are usually monogamous" (1950, p. 89). The state of "being in love" is evidently rare and exceptional, and it is certainly not considered a prerequisite for sexual contact, but where it does occur, the usual promiscuity of nearly all Mohave is momentarily suspended.

Devereux sees the Mohave attitudes and practices as fitting exactly the pattern of ancient Greece as contrasted with our own. The contrast is characterized by Freud as follows:

The most pronounced difference between the love life of antiquity and ours lies in the fact that the ancients placed the emphasis on the impulse itself, while we put it on its object. The ancients extolled the impulse and were ready to ennoble through it even an inferior object, while we disparage the activity of the impulse as such and only countenance it on account of the merits of the object. (Freud 1905, p. 149)

Devereux sees the Mohave practices, even as they include promiscuity and do not include a concentration on one particular object, as not incompatible with regarding them as having achieved psychosexual maturity, or genitality. Their sexuality is not infused with neurotic or guilt-laden motivations, nor is it used to act out neurotic fantasies. They can "form numerous socially meaningful object relationships" (1950, pp. 86, 125). Other psychoanalytic observers might question Devereux's assignment of "maturity" on the grounds that the Mohave rarely maintain a prolonged and constant attachment to any one other person as "object."

The Mohave rarely have a prolonged "aim-inhibited courtship," since sexual gratification with momentarily desired partners is allowed and encouraged. It is impossible under these cultural conditions to "overvalue any particular sexual object, or love itself" (Devereux 1950, p. 93). That is, there is simply no "romantic love," and little or no idealization of partners or potential partners. The state of "being in love," referred to above, appears to be a partial exception. It is not clear how closely that state, as Devereux sees it, resembles what Freud (1921) refers to by that name as a state akin to being in a hypnotic trance. It also seems rare that people put themselves in a state of debasement as a price of "love" (cf. Freud 1912).

When we look at the infant- and child-rearing forerunners of the adult Mohave's sexuality, we find that early infancy is a kind of paradise for the Mohave child: he is breast-fed on demand for a long period, and weaned late, gradually, and very gently (Devereux 1961, p. 222). There is very little emphasis on the anal stage, which is extremely casual and overlaps with the late oral stage, and later with the early phallic. The baby and young child are not protected from adult sexuality, which goes on semipublicly in the small (usually one-room) crowded houses. The Mohave place little value on privacy. Awareness of sexuality is early and casual, and has no aura of mystery or guilt. Little boys' erections are recognized and positively remarked upon. Except for incest taboos, there is very little restriction on sexual expression or curiosity.

APACHES

Another American Indian people, the Mescalero Apaches, were studied by the psychoanalyst L. Bryce Boyer and his anthropologist wife Ruth Boyer (Boyer 1964, 1979; Boyer and Boyer 1967, 1972). In many formerly tribal societies undergoing intensive acculturation, different elements of the aboriginal culture are transformed at different rates and to different degrees. One of the most resistant patterns is the complex of socialization and care of infants and young children, since these are (more than other elements of culture) under the influence of unconscious factors derived in turn from the infancy and childhood of the older generation. For the Apaches, this means that child-rearing practices may be largely unchanged from aboriginal times.

Their infant and child care involves gross inconsistencies. The neonate is a kind of monarch of the household. The mother, when present, breast-feeds him on demand. However, she frequently abandons him to the care of anyone available, including siblings under five years old. At the birth of a new baby two or three years later, the older toddler is abruptly displaced and subjected to such harsh, even brutal treatment that the mortality rates at this age are very high. In aboriginal times, such treatment was seen as justifiable to harden children—if they survived—to the omnipresent dangers of a hostile human and animal environment. It probably also functioned, not necessarily by conscious intent, to protect parents from the incapacitating grief that could otherwise occur with the death of the child (Boyer 1964, p. 224).

What does the displaced toddler do with the resulting rage? It is taboo to vent it on the newborn intruder and brings harsh punishment. He is allowed to vent it somewhat on the mother, on older siblings, and, it appears, on small animals, as it is permitted for children to torture and torment them. It has also been noted that children will tense the muscles that would have been used in a temper tantrum, then suddenly become limp, with a masked and withdrawn facial expression. Such stoicism, a vehicle of passive aggression, befitted aboriginal Apache warriors.

The aboriginal gender division of labor was very clear-cut. Men of this nomadic tribe hunted and made war. In aboriginal times they were also allowed plural wives; frequently these wives were sisters. Women gathered wild plants, maintained households, and raised children. Since 1873, reservation confinement transformed former gender relations. Men's old roles are gone, but women's household and childrearing are mainly intact. Children grow up in an environment where males are nominal leaders but where women are obviously dominant in family relations. Also, with the survival of matrilocality and some matrilineal descent, women have strong bonds of solidarity with each other; men do not. The closest emotional bonds are between women, not between a woman and a man, nor between men. Relations between the sexes are strained. Many men are demoralized and take a passive-dependent or passive-aggressive position toward women. Hostility between men and women abounds.

There is much sexual activity by children throughout childhood, which is pointedly ignored by the adults. In aboriginal times, girls were married soon after their puberty ceremony and were expected (unrealistically) to be virgins at marriage. Nowadays there is much sexual activity among adolescents, and much premarital pregnancy. While boys are warned about the dangers of the reputedly dentate female genitals, adolescents are pressured toward promiscuous sexuality to prove their masculinity, challenged sexually to service middle-aged women, and ridiculed if they do not. Children also witness both aggressive and sexual encounters of one parent with the other, or another partner. Fathers are frequently absent for long periods. With polygyny, they could leave one wife for a period with another elsewhere. There is no indication that marriage is based on love. Women commonly leave behind their young children, for varying periods of time, while they go to "party" or to "fool around." A man catching his wife in an infidelity might be physically brutal to her and could even, with impunity, thus cause her death. In tribal times, he might slash her nose, even cut off the end of it. Both men and women drink alcohol heavily, lose self-control, have violent encounters and sexual bouts. Intense sexual attraction is commonly attributed to love magic practiced by a shaman. Transgressions, sexual or violent, are excused as caused by drunkenness, or by such love magic.

External object consistency [1] is not prominent in their sexual relationships. These are vitiated, in any case, by the pervasive hostility between the sexes. Although overt homosexuality is virtually absent, there is evidence of pervasive latent homosexuality in males (Boyer 1964).

In summary, adult relations are marked by a great deal of sexual activity with many partners, low external object consistency, and high intersexual hostility and suspicion. The plurality of partners is like the situation of the Mohave, as is the lack of idealization of partners or of anything approximating romantic love. The adult picture is unlike the cheerful promiscuity of the Mohave, and comes as a sequela to a much more troubled infancy and childhood.

THE ANYI OF THE IVORY COAST, AFRICA

In the second of their two unusual psychoanalytic-anthropological researches on formerly tribal West African societies, three Swiss psychoanalysts, Paul Parin, Fritz Morgenthaler, and Goldy Parin-Matthèy, worked among the Anyi (or Agni) of the former French colony, now independent state, the Ivory Coast (1971: *Fürchte deinen Nächsten wie dich Selbst;* 1980: misleadingly translated as *Fear Thy Neighbor as Thyself*).[2]

Many members of this ethnic group came to a series of sessions structured much like psychoanalytic therapeutic sessions, with one or another of the three psychoanalysts. The sessions went on over a period of several months. Along with these probes of their subjects' inner lives, the authors got basic ethnographic data on the group.[3] They had daily contact with the people of the community, medically treated patients at their clinic, saw Anyi psychiatric patients at a hospital, and collected 130 Rorschach protocols. In addition, the authors read previously published literature on the group. They developed an account of the Anyi people that is both intensive and extensive.

Though partially modern, like the Mohave and the Apache, at the time of the study, the Anyi retain, largely unchanged, elements of earlier tribal life—in particular, much of their traditional child-rearing and socialization.

Among the Anyi, the neonate enjoys the situation of nursing at the mother's breast, which appears to be a blissfully satisfying fusion-symbiosis charged by the nursing mother's sensual gratification. The mother does not talk or smile to the infant, or otherwise emphasize the distance between the two. This lasts for about a year, or until the new baby arrives. Then comes abrupt weaning, in which the mother rejects, neglects, and abandons the child and places him with another family. Maternal attention is then shifted to the new baby. Given a very high infant mortality rate, the authors hypothesize that mothers become unconsciously reluctant to invest long-term cathexis in the child. (Compare the Boyers' account of similar practice among the Apaches, and accounts of many other tribes.)

In place of anal sphincter training, the baby is given twice-daily enemas. The child is expected to endure, passively, this phallic-anal attack. Absent are Western-type anal reaction formations. Because of the passive mode of this kind of anal treatment and the easier displaceability from anal to genital experience for the girl than for the boy, the girls would appear to have a smoother psychosexual development from there on than do the boys, who have strong anxieties and fears in later development, including wariness toward women. Both sexes come to fear anyone at all close to oneself, especially sexual partners and spouses.

There are no phallic-phase taboos placed on autoerotic stimulation (used abundantly for self-comfort) or on viewing adult sexual intercourse. In children's primal-scene fantasies coitus is an aggressive assault, with oral, anal, or genital violation or mutilation, or the woman tearing off the man's clothing and castrating and devouring him. For girls, the oedipal situation is clearer, simpler, less troubled. Western-style penis envy is rare. The male has more trouble with the phallic-oedipal stage. He must give up identification with the mother and does not (usually) have a present, loving, caring father with whom to identify, or to experience as a distinct oedipal rival for the mother. Males tend to ignore or deny the existence of rivalry.

Abundant male castration anxiety focuses more on fear of the mother than of the father. This appears in adults' pervasive fear of witches (female), who may poison, mutilate, or abandon an individual or attack him orally or anally. Males also want nurturance from a powerful, dominating, male chief/king, who combines idealized paternal and maternal qualities. Males thus become anxious, troubled adults, less self-confident than the women, and less competent in males' economic and political tasks than the females are at the feminine tasks of household maintenance, food preparation, and caretaking.

Matrilineal kinship negates fathers' authority over children (relevant for boys' oedipal conflicts), and the married couple rarely live together. This results in the father's being experienced by the child as an alien interloper. His authority is not introjected. Hence there are grave problems of superego formation. In late adolescence boys have a great deal of sexual activity without strong object ties: the partner is less a love object than a means of narcissistic gratification. Emotional relations between the sex partners, as between husband and wife later, are laden with conflict and tension. Both have grave difficulties moving toward a good, enduring object tie.

Intense attachments do exist in this culture, but they are not expected to endure. A woman's adage is, "One is not always in love with the same man." Both sexes say, "Fear the person who is close to you." Men see women as too demanding and think they need to withdraw. This is the advantage of polygyny. With plural wives, the men seem to feel less pressured by these demands. Divorce is common, and external object consistency is rare in affairs or marriage.

Although there are sporadic references to people "loving," or, rarely, "being in love with," certain others, and although there are certainly nonmarital sexual affairs and marriage, the prevailing picture is that "The Anyi cannot afford to let themselves become involved in long-lasting love relationships" (Parin et al. 1980, p. 388).

The authors see some strength in this, in that the adult Anyi are remarkably resilient and flexible, able to shift rapidly from conscious to unconscious and back, among different defenses, and among different kinds of object relations, all equally unstable and nonpermanent. As in many other previously tribal societies, modernization has more gravely affected the role of men than of women.

THE PEOPLE OF LUSAKA, ZAMBIA

Ilsa Schuster's *New Women of Lusaka* (1979) describes women from many tribal ancestries, most from matrilineal kinship systems, who are now working in modern offices of state and business organizations. The study deals with the work, social lives, and personal lives of these women. They are educated and literate, and ostensibly fully part of the modern technological society of a newly independent nation-state. Schuster reconstructs the infant- and child-rearing they experienced at the hands of their traditionally minded mothers and kin and learned how they raised their own children. The methods show substantial continuity. Also, the different ancestral tribes seem largely similar on these matters. Schuster is not a psychoanalytically oriented anthropologist, but the empirical data she provides enable psychological reconstruction.[4]

In earliest infancy the baby is with the mother at all times, held next to her body or carried on her back, and breast-fed on demand. This infantile paradise is abruptly ended with the arrival of the next baby or with weaning at eighteen to twenty-four months. Then the toddler is left very much on its own, shunted from one relative to another. The child is exposed to a large extended family and might develop a close object tie with any of these kin. Yet there is likely to be poor external object consistency in the life of the baby, the child, and later the adult.[5] Children rarely live with both parents, or, unless very young, with a divorced mother. Older children may live with a divorced father and his new wife. On vacation from boarding schools, adolescents may stay with relatives, not necessarily nuclear family kin. Rarely do kin have enthusiasm in their care for the child, by Western standards, and may seem, by those standards, to be exploiting the youngster for babysitting and household chores. Such unstable, temporary arrangements were common in tribal-traditional times as well as today. From a Western view, such child care seems haphazard and negligent, resulting, at least indirectly, in high infant and early childhood mortality rates, from malnutrition, accidents, complications from simple childhood illnesses, and misuse of modern infant formulas. The situation is similar to that of many other recently tribal societies. The high infant mortality rates may cause parents to feel, unconsciously, or even close to consciously, reluctant to invest emotional attachment in the child for fear of devastating grief at its loss. Clearly, a major theme is lack of external object consistency.

The adult scene in the capital city Lusaka is a mixture of tribal-survival and modern conditions. The arriving high-school-educated young women have an unprecedented level of personal freedom and income. The men they encounter expect easy sexual liaisons without long-term commitment. The woman can resist and find herself lonely and isolated, or she may comply, learn to play the game, become devious and deceitful, juggle several lovers at once. This is a life of much partying and sex, much mutual exploitation, little love, and no commitment. After a while the young woman may experience emptiness and a sense of meaninglessness. By then she cannot resume a more traditional tribal life, in part because she has had at least one out-of-wedlock baby, cared for by some kin.

Marriage is a possible option, which many do pursue. It is not an unqualified improvement in the young woman's position, since any desirable husband, who would be traditionally patriarchal, does not want a "modern" wife. He greatly restricts the wife's life, her freedom of movement and socializing, which results in a shocking change from her single-state freedom. If he allows her to continue her work, he takes control of her income. They both want to have babies right away. While he may have been attentive to her in the courtship period, even professing "love," once married this all ceases, and he takes the traditional male freedoms, including extramarital sex. If she has an extramarital affair, she risks being beaten or even killed by her husband. If a woman is beaten, people assume she deserved it. Her husband's suspiciousness may be so extreme she can feel virtually a prisoner in their residence. Close emotional ties, let alone deep love, are very unlikely. Though modern statutory marriage is monogamous, some men insist on customary traditional law, by which they can have more than one wife. This further reduces the woman's rights or satisfactions in marriage. Divorce is common, with settlements disadvantageous to the wife. Divorce had also been common in tribal conditions, but there the women were central to the production process, and so had more power. In this culture, then, modernization has hurt women relatively more than men, which is in contrast with the cases discussed above.

By the age of thirty, most women are veterans of many relationships and also of one or more marriages that have ended in divorce. They have had a great deal of sexual experience and very little, if any, love. Romantic love may be a fantasy of some adolescent girls, but it is one rapidly dissolved by experience. Relations between men and women are permeated with mutual suspicion and hostility combined with a great amount of sexual activity desired by both sexes. Sexual jealousy is rampant, deep love and devotion rare. Lack of external object consistency is the overriding theme. This carries over from childhood and from tribal-traditional to modern conditions.

THE "SAMBIA" OF NEW GUINEA

Yet another variation are the "Sambia" (pseudonym) of New Guinea, reported by the anthropologist Gilbert Herdt in *Guardians of the Flutes* (1981).[6]

With the Sambia, relations between husband and wife are tense, anxious, and distant. The man and the woman live in categorically separated worlds. The whole culture institutionalizes a polarization of matters masculine and feminine. There is practically no companionship or sharing between husband and wife, and Herdt's detailed monograph scarcely ever mentions love. Fathers do no coparenting. By contrast, there is an intense and long-lasting bond between mother and baby.

For the boy, this means an intense and close tie to the mother in infancy and early childhood, from which she evidently also obtains important sensual gratification (missing in the rather perfunctory marriage). This close mother-son tie continues until he is about seven years old. He is then roughly torn away from the mother and forced to embark on the male initiation ceremonies, which are intended to make a man of him, to masculinize him. He is to become the fierce brave warrior, a character trait demanded of all adult males. Part of this process involves homosexual fellatio, which is practiced daily, by which the young boy, as fellator, is supposed to acquire, literally, the strength and power of semen from an older boy or young man. Later he will take the other role in this daily ritual. This is accompanied by other practices of male initiation, supposedly secret from the women. The sacred lore includes a basic myth about what it means to be male including tales of male superiority and dominance over women. (Many features are those of male initiation ceremonies anywhere in the tribal world. See Endleman 1967; Bettelheim 1954; Róheim 1950.)

In late adolescence the young Sambian is married off to a girl who is probably prepubertal and a stranger to him. Until she reaches menarche, she also performs fellatio on him, and he may at the same time continue fellatio with young boy initiates. When she reaches menarche, he starts genital coitus with her, and at the birth of the first baby, he is supposed to give up the homosexual activities entirely, and most men do. From there on, most of the men are exclusively heterosexual in practice. But contact with the wife is not frequent and is shadowed by his fears of being sexually depleted by her. Herdt reports that there is no exclusive homosexuality in adult males, yet it seems clear there is no surfeit of loving tenderness between husband and wife. Whether there is any tender love or caring in any of the homosexual contacts is not evident from the anthropologist's account.[7]

Similar patterns (intense and prolonged male initiations, strong male-female antagonisms, homosexual rituals imposed on all growing males to create a powerful male warrior) appear in a number of other New Guinea societies, at least one in the New Hebrides, and some in Australia.[8] In most of these, heterosexual contact (even between husband and wife) is hedged with many restrictions and taboos and is commonly believed to be dangerous and depleting. Still, it is the dominant mode of sexual contact in adulthood, attesting to the strength of the drive, even where not facilitated of accompanied by love or tenderness, much less by "romance" or idealization, and even where homosexual expression is pervasive and/or institutionalized.

It also demonstrates how precarious is the attainment of what Freud saw as the ideal of "love," that is, the fusion of sexual excitement and desire with tenderness, affection, and caring concern.

SEX WITHOUT LOVE?

At this point the reader may be wondering whether societies exist in which there is usually love or even strong affection between the male and the female in a mating or sexual relationship, or where the relationship is an enduring one, with high external object consistency. The answer is a carefully qualified yes.

Certain of the American Plains Indians, according to *some* accounts, developed the husband-wife ties more personally than did any other reported primitive groups. Courtship could last for years, and a bride might be wooed for weeks after marriage before consummation (Mead 1949; p. 211). But Mead and other anthropologists see such tenderness and affection as rare in the tribal world.

In Mangaia, as elsewhere in Polynesia, people have a very active heterosexual life, essentially promiscuous, with strong feelings of sexual jealousy, but no concept of love in the Western sense. Only in old age are there relations marked by affection, even willingness to sacrifice for each other (Marshall 1971). Harold Schneider (1971) reports that in the Turu of Tanzania, along with sexually restrained and loveless arranged marriages, there are intense, passionate extramarital affairs. Schneider calls this—with questionable basis—"romantic love." It does involve highly individualized choice with strong sexual attraction, but there is no idealization of the partner or feeling of being fated for, or willing to sacrifice for, each other. The passion here seems to depend on the affair's being illicit.

CONCLUSIONS

In the tribal or tribal-transitional societies considered here, it is rare to find "love" in a manner familiar in the West, and rarer still "romantic love" in the Western sense. There is a great variety of patterns of sexual behavior. Much sexual activity with a plurality of partners is common, but rarely with strong affection or tenderness, or concern for the welfare of, or willingness to sacrifice for, the partner.

In many societies there is very little external object consistency in adult sexual activities. These are also likely to be societies showing very little external object consistency in infant and child care. Many tribes show a familiar pattern: neonatal paradise of total attention from the nursing mother, followed by neglect, extrusion, and abandonment, turning over the child to a variety of more or less negligent surrogates (Apaches, Anyi, Lusaka).

We can hazard, on psychoanalytic grounds, some interpretation of the prevalent promiscuity of such societies, by analogy with psychoanalytic experience with promiscuous persons in our society. A male may react to the childhood trauma of expulsion, abandonment, and neglect by repeating in adulthood, now with the roles reversed: he has an exciting sexual affair with a woman, full of sensual passion, then abruptly abandons her and moves on the the next. The repetition-compulsion causes him to do this over and over again, with an endless succession of partners. The inner pain is never assuaged, and each time, it is inflicted on the other. For the female, the sequence may begin with intense rage against the mother, turning to the father for consolation, not getting it, and feeling disappointment again. This is repeated in reverse in adulthood by subjecting the male partner to such abandonment (or subjecting herself to this rejection—or doing both), again reliving but never really assuaging the pain. Intense unconscious sadistic and masochistic motivations are to be inferred, on both sides. These may be overtly expressed by a prevalent war of the sexes, each harboring suspicions and hostilities toward the other, with evident "reality" justification.

Many societies do have positive feelings between the sexes, with accompanying sexual promiscuity and no deep attachment or commitment (Mohave, Mangaia, other Polynesians). But rarely do we find in those societies anything like what Freud posited as the ideal of mature love, namely, the fusion of sexual passion with tender caring and long-term concern for the object. It should go without saying that "love" in that ideal sense is probably rare in our society as well. But in the societies discussed here, it is not even experienced as an *ideal*, whereas in Western culture it is.

In these societies, the prevalent promiscuity probably has different dynamics, rooted in the fact that they, like the ancient Greeks, emphasize and positively value erotic feelings for their own sake and almost without regard to particular objects. Infancy and childhood are a kind of pansexual paradise with almost no restrictions (other than the incest taboos) and almost no consideration of individualization of objects. Many other societies have in effect institutionalized the very prevalent hostility and suspicion between the sexes, frequently accompanied by poor external object consistency. Some of those have, for males, an intense prolonged mother-child tie until latency, followed by initiation ceremonies lasting many years, with universal institutionalized male homosexuality, followed by heterosexual loveless marriage (Sambia, Etoro, many other tribes).

COMPARISON WITH OUR SOCIETY

How would we describe our contemporary society in terms of these issues? Considering the tremendous cultural variation within the United States and Western culture in general, the task is almost impossible. Individual and family variations, too, are probably much greater in complex modern societies than in any of the homogeneous tribal societies considered here. However, some observations can be made.

Almost any aspect of problems discussed in reference to a tribal group can be found in some individuals in modern society. Many people find it impossible to fuse sensuality with tender concern for the partner. It is likely, however, that the individuals concerned will consider that something is wrong in such a situation, either normatively—since we do consider it desirable to combine sex and tenderness—or in terms of psychic health, or simply in terms of suffering. Many individuals need an endless succession of partners. Many are involved in an endless war of the sexes. Romantic love is touted as an ideal in this society, even as a necessary prerequisite for marriage. But many regard it as a joke, or at least a myth, something not really connected with their own experience. Many reject the prevailing mythologies and regard marriage choice as essentially a practical matter. Many enjoy extramarital affairs without guilt. Others do so, but with guilt. Many take a casual approach to sex. Some idealize the partner, many never do. External object consistency may be absent as often as present. Though it is normative to provide highly individualized, lasting, loving care to infants and young children, many parents act more like Apaches or Anyi or Lusakans and subject their children to neglect or even brutality, and at the very least feel much unconscious—sometimes even conscious—ambivalence toward their children, based on their own unresolved inner turmoil.

We can describe the norms of our society more easily than the empirical behavioral reality. We are supposed to develop the capacity to experience intense, lasting, individualized love attachment to a very few particular persons; to make in a few of these cases a relationship that fuses sensuality with tender devotion; to maintain in other cases such a "love" as an aim-inhibited erotic connection. We should have the capacity to be willing to sacrifice for the beloved partner, without hostility or ambivalence. We are supposed to provide protection and tender loving care to our children, and constancy, consistency, a good balance of loving warmth and consistent discipline. We are supposed to be able to "tame" our sensual passions, find modes to satisfy them consistent with the needs of an orderly society. In our close personal love and sexual relations, we are not supposed to "use" our partners.

Needless to say, the reality is commonly far different from these norms—how commonly it is difficult to assess. Where the discrepancy is accompanied by feelings of psychic distress, such as guilt, anxiety, self-contempt, psychoanalysts often see these people in their practice. But there is no way of knowing how prevalent these difficulties are in the population that does not seek treatment. Sociological studies can provide some evidence of variations from these norms. Divorce rates are charted assiduously, providing currently (1980) an estimate that one out of two newly contracted marriages in the United States today will end in divorce. This may be regarded as one rough measure of external object consistency. Child abuse is dealt with by the criminal law, as is brutality toward spouses, and the statistics seem to some observers disturbing. Extramarital philandering is sometimes tabulated, particularly where it has led to crimes of passion. Sexual deviance in the form of homosexuality, while uncertain in prevalence gets attention in a number of evaluative ways. And various "liberation" groups are working to change the norms and their administration (e.g., in the justice system) in reference to many forms of conduct traditionally considered deviant, in the areas of sexuality, love, and marriage. Many aspects of family, such as custody of children, are being subjected to controversial challenges. Controversy rages about pornography and sexual education in the schools.

We can also look at our society in terms of Devereux's distinction, after Freud, between cultures that emphasize the sexual instinct itself, regardless of object, and those that focus attention on the object. Western culture, in general, emphasizes the object, its choice, its particularity, the dilemmas experienced by contrasting desire toward a very particular object (e.g., one that is taboo in some way) and powerful cultural norms, with the drive being seen as problematic. In such a culture, the object is highly individualized, and in extreme cases, like that of romantic love, also highly *idealized*—a phenomenon rare or nonexistent in all of the tribal-transitional cases we have considered in this paper, and probably in most tribal societies.

Where does such idealization come from? It must derive from some characteristics of child development common in the West and not found in the societies considered here. For example, it would seem necessary to have some degree of security about survival, thus reducing the probability that caretaking mothers would harbor intense unconscious ambivalence, even hatred, toward the infant. This is only the first step. The path to idealization still needs to be spelled out.

Erich Fromm postulates in *The Art of Loving* (1956) that love, defined as "the overcoming of human separateness, . . . the fulfillment of the longing for union" (p. 27), is a universal need of all human beings. The data on the various societies considered here should lead us to question whether this need is universal, unless we include in it attachment to *any* other human being, or any succession of a number of different other human beings. Fromm's own formulation, however, implies a highly individualized attachment, which is likely to be rooted in a highly individualized and basically unambivalent relation to the particular caretaker over a prolonged period from the neonatal state onward; his formulation is thus ethnocentrically Western.

From a transcultural psychoanalytic-anthropological perspective, we cannot accept a Western conception of love as universal. We can, however, see in all societies human beings struggling with the problems and vicissitudes of sex and the dilemmas of how that might, or might not, be combined with "love."

NOTES

1. This phrase is introduced here, in the negative, to refer to the person's having a plurality of objects in rapid succession—e.g., many sexual partners, or, in infancy, many caretakers—none of them strongly attached to the child. It is to be distinguished from the term *object constancy* or *libidinal object constancy* (Mahler et al. 1975, pp. 109ff.), which in psychoanalytic writings refer to an *intra*psychic state, i.e., constancy of the *inner* object. Though probably most cases of, e.g., shallow promiscuity derive from the infant's not having reached "object constancy" internally, we are unsure, without full clinical evidence, that that is the case. Therefore, unless the authors of the ethnopsychoanalytic study clearly refer to object constancy defect (e.g., Parin et al. 1971), I use here the term *external object consistency*.
2. The title used in the English translation has a serious error: it *should* be "Fear Thy Next-of-Kin . . ." or "Fear the One Closest to You . . . ," not "Fear Thy Neighbor. . . ." This is important because the basic theme is suspicion and hostility toward people *in close relationship to oneself*.
3. Various ethnographic elements in the Parin team's account, including aspects of economic organization, have been challenged by some critics. See, for example, Lumsden 1982; see also replies by Boyer and Boyer (1982), Freeman (1982), and Parin et al. (1982); all are reprinted in Stein 1982.
4. Ethnographic and descriptive information about Lusaka are from Schuster's account. Psychoanalytically phrased interpretations, e.g., about inferred unconscious motivations and discussion of external object consistency, are mine.
5. Schuster questions whether we can properly refer to poor object consistency for traditional generations (recent personal communication). My response is that this is my psychoanalytic interpretation, based on the evidence available. Schuster also notes that from the Zambians' viewpoint, the shunting around of children is seen not as "neglect" but rather as a good deed for a barren sister or an aging grandparent needing help at home, etc. (personal communication). These strike me as rationalizations, and also as examples of the probably insoluble problem of competing conceptions of reality among

participants and various kinds of social scientific and psychological observers.
6. See also discussion of this book in Endleman 1986, pp. 193–95, and a psychoanalytically sophisticated review of it by Hippler (1985).
7. For a coherent psychoanalytic developmental account, we need data about topics not covered in Herdt's monograph, e.g., the *girls'* development, the nature of the object tie in fellatio, and the existence of deviants (boys unenthusiastic about fellatio, men unwilling to give it up).
8. See Endleman 1986, pp. 195–97, for detailed references and brief summary discussion of the well-documented cases: the Etoro, Kaluli, Baruya, Marind-Anim, Jaqai, Anyu, Boadzi, Keraki, and Kiwai of New Guinea; the Malekula of New Hebrides; the Aranda and the Nambutji of Australia.

REFERENCES

Bettelheim, B. 1954. *Symbolic wounds.* New York: Free Press.
Boyer, L. 1964. Psychological problems of a group of Apaches: Alcoholic hallucinosis and latent homosexuality among typical men. In W. Muensterberger and S. Axelread, eds., *The psychoanalytic study of society* 3:203–77. New York: IUP.
———. 1979. *Childhood and folklore: A psychoanalytic study of Apache personality.* New York: Psychohistory Press.
———, and R. M. Boyer. 1967. Some influences of acculturation on the personality traits of the old people of the Mescalero and Chiricahua Apaches. In W. Muensterberger and S. Axelread, eds., *The psychoanalytic study of society* 4:170–84. New York: IUP.
———, and ———. 1972. Effects of acculturation on the vicissitudes of the aggressive drive among the Apaches of the Mescalero Indian Reservation. In W. Muensterberger and A. Esman, eds., *The psychoanalytic study of society* 5:40-82. New York: IUP.
———, and ———. 1982. Comment on Lumsden review (of Parin et al. 1980). *Journal of Psychoanalytic Anthropology* 5:419–23.
De Rougemont, D. 1940. *Love in the Western world.* Trans. M. Belgion. New York: Harcourt, Brace, World.
Devereux, G. 1937. Institutionalized homosexuality of the Mohave Indians. *Human Biology* 9:498–527. (Reprinted in Ruitenbeek 1963.)
———. 1939. Mohave culture and personality. *Character and Personality* 8:91–109.
———. 1950. Heterosexual behavior of the Mohave Indians. In G. Róheim, ed., *Psychoanalysis and the social sciences* 2:85–128. New York: International Universities Press.
———. 1961. *Mohave ethnopsychiatry and suicide: The psychic disturbances of an Indian tribe.* Washington, D. C.: Smithsonian Institution Press.

———. 1980. *Basic problems of ethnopsychiatry*. Chicago: University of Chicago Press.
Endleman, R. 1967. *Personality and social life*. New York: Random House.
———. 1981. *Psyche and society: Explorations in psychoanalytic sociology*. New York: Columbia University Press.
———. 1986. Overview essay: Homosexuality in tribal societies. *Transcultural Psychiatric Research Review* 23:187–218.
Freeman, D. M. A. 1982. Commentary on Lumden review essay (on Parin et al. 1980). *Journal of Psychoanalytic Anthropology* 5:424–28.
Freud, S. 1905. Three essays on the theory of sexuality. *Standard edition* 7:135–243.
———. 1912. On the universal tendency to debasement in the sphere of love. *Standard edition* 11:177–90.
———. 1921. Group psychology and the analysis of the ego. *Standard edition* 18:65–144.
Fromm, E. 1956. *The art of loving*. New York: Harper and Row.
Herdt, G. 1981. *Guardians of the flutes: Idioms of masculinity*. New York: McGraw Hill.
Hippler, A. 1985. Review of Herdt, *Guardians of the flutes*. *Journal of Psychoanalytic Anthropology* 8:212–13.
LaBarre, W. 1954. *The human animal*. Chicago: University of Chicago Press.
Lumsden, D. P. 1982. Enemas and ethnopsychoanalysis in West Africa (review essay on Parin et al. 1980). *Journal of Psychoanalytic Anthropology* 5:386–403. Response to commentaries on same, pp. 434–64.
Mahler, M. S., F. Pine, and A. Bergman. 1975. *The psychological birth of the human infant*. New York: Basic Books.
Marshall, D. S. 1971. Sexual behavior on Mangaia. In D. S. Marshall and R. C. Suggs, eds., *Human sexual behavior: Variations in the ethnographic spectrum*, pp. 103–62. New York: Basic Books.
Mead, M. 1949. *Male and female*. New York: Morrow.
Parin, P., F. Morgenthaler, and G. Parin-Matthèy. 1971. *Fürchte deinen Nächsten wie dich selbst: Psychoanalyse und Gesellschaft am Modell der Agni in Westafrika*. Frankfurt am Main: Suhrkamp.
———, ———, and ———. 1980. *Fear thy neighbor as thyself: Psychoanalysis and society among the Anyi of West Africa*. Trans. Patricia Klamerth. (Abridged English translation of Parin et al. 1971.) Chicago: University of Chicago Press.
———, ———, and ———. 1982. Reply to D. P. Lumsden review. *Journal of Psychoanalytic Anthropology* 5:404–18.
Róheim, G. 1950. *Psychoanalysis and anthropology*. New York: IUP.
Ruitenbeek, H., ed. 1963. *The problem of homosexuality in modern society*. New York: Dutton.
Schneider, H. K. 1971. Romantic love among the Turu. In D. S. Marshall and R. C. Suggs, eds., *Human sexual behavior: Variations in the ethnographic spectrum*, pp. 59–70. New York: Basic Books.

Schuster, I. G. 1979. *New women of Lusaka*. Palo Alto: Mayfield.
Stein, H. F., ed. 1982. Symposium: Psychoanalytic ethnography, the nature of data, and the problem of interpretation. (reviews and replies on Parin et al. 1980). *Journal of Psychoanalytic Anthropology* 5:385–463.

3. What Is This Thing Called Love?

The Popular Ballad as a Framework for Changing Conceptions of Love

Barbara Cohn Schlachet and
Barbara Waxenberg

In this culture, two important requisites of adulthood are knowing how to communicate about love, and understanding the rituals of courtship and relationships. Through reading a common literature, viewing the same films, and singing the same songs, we learn how love is patterned and expressed in culture. These are obviously not the sole channels, yet they do offer a powerful source for our knowledge. John Money, in his text *Love and Love Sickness,* writes: "The prime source of sex-shared love education is music—the lyrics of popular songs. They are a virtual barometer of where adolescents are at, in love and sex" (1980 p. 64). And as Richard Rodgers has pointed out (in words, not music), "Setting words to music gives them weight, makes them somehow easier to say and helps them to be remembered. . . . It may be that we can sing what we often cannot say, whether it be from shyness, fear, lack of the right words or the passion or dramatic gift to express them" (1973, p. xiii).

The lyrics of popular songs of the forties and fifties set the tone for expectations of love of that period. For women, especially, love was to be immediate, nonambivalent, urgent, idealizing, everlasting, painful, completely satisfying (even if in a masochistic framework), and, above all, passionate. This was an ideal of love and loving far more in tune with Jung—"the woman is increasingly aware that love alone can give her her full stature" (1928, p. 185)—than with Sullivan—"When the satisfaction or the security of another person becomes as significant to one as is one's own satisfaction or security, then the state of love exists" (1945, p. 20).

In the bittersweet ballads of the Depression, war, and postwar years, love was strangers magnetically drawn to one another across a crowded room, the rescue fantasy of "Someday My Prince Will Come," the fidelity of " 'Til Then," the merging of two personalities usually at the expense of the submerging of one. There was to be no room for doubt ("He's your fella and you love him, that's all there is to that") or for the inevitable erosions of familiarity, the monotonously repetitious crises of daily living, or the ineluctable vicissitudes as romance evolves to include marriage, children, and aging. In an earlier time, in a different setting, even Freud had speculated as to whether all love was like that—a kind of sickness and craziness, an illusion, a blindness to what the loved person is really like (Malcolm, 1981).

Music has always reflected, defined, and informed conceptions of love, whether the singer was a troubadour gently strumming medieval notions of romantic love or the rock musician insisting on its erotic components. Lomax tells us that "the first function of music . . . is to produce a feeling of security for the listener by voicing the particular quality of a land and the life of its people." He goes on to remind us that a line from a song may bring back all the familiar emotions of home in an almost magical summing up of patterns of family, love, conflict, and work, which give a community its special feel and which shape the personalities of its members, preparing them to dance, worship, fight, or make love in ways normal to their place (1960, p. xv). In Shakespeare's words, music is the "food of love." Love of God is expressed in hymns, love of country in anthems, love of school in alma maters, love of children in lullabies, and our love for one another in the romantic ballad. Music evokes memories of the past, speaks in tones of the present, and inspires the future. In sound and lyrics, music tells us much about what we construe to be love, what we can expect from love, and what we should offer the loved person. It tells us whom to love, how to love, and how to avenge or mourn when love is lost. Particularly at this time—when the media have such a powerful impact on all aspects of our lives; when music seeps out of unseen speakers in an elevator, blares out of a box on the street, and accompanies us as we drive; and when people wearing earphones are a common street sight—it has become a primary mediating and disseminating force, describing and prescribing differences in gender roles, generations, social class, and culture. There is no defense against its impact for anyone who has intact hearing and understands the language. A culture's beliefs are embodied in song: I'm happy to be free; what the world needs now is love; doesn't anybody stay in one place anymore; these boots are made for walking; come on and cry me a river; my lover will save me. In *Sirens of Song*, Pauletich states that a life could be ruled by the jukebox, by going from song to song for the cheapest advice to be found (1980). As psychoanalysts we speak to few, but music is a universal language and speaks to everyone.

As theorists, we have always been indebted to myth as a reflection of those aspects of human life and development within a given culture that are shared by the greatest number of people. If a theoretical perspective departs too far from current mythology, then its relevance must be questioned, or, at the very least, the differences between theory and mythology must be addressed. It may be that our theories are pointing the direction for a radical break with tradition, but this cannot be assessed or approached in a meaningful way without first articulating the tradition. We propose that popular music to a large extent embodies the mythology of the twentieth century, particularly since the advent of radio, movies, records, tapes, television, and videotapes. Music is no longer the province of the itinerant troubadour but has exploded insistently into the public domain, so that most of the country is apt to be hearing the same songs at the same time.

What struck both of us as we began our research for this essay was the paucity of material on this subject in the psychological or social-science literature. It seemed incredible that something that had loomed so large in our own lives and in the life of our society had escaped serious and extensive consideration by social scientists.

Since the overwhelming majority of songs are concerned with love and male-female relationships, what does popular music tell us about love? In what ways have our conceptions of love changed over the past sixty years? Are these changes reflected in psychoanalytic theory? These are weighty questions, and we can only begin to touch upon them. What we intend to address are the changes in views of love as they have been reflected in popular music, with particular attention paid to gender issues. Other chapters in this volume will be presenting psychoanalytic conceptions of love. We hope to consider how these conceptions converge and diverge from the perceptions of love that all of us in the dominant culture share.

In an article describing the shifts in taste in popular music, Mooney (1969) characterizes the music of the 1920s as shaped primarily by a white middle class, self-consciously hedonistic, relatively prosperous at a time when, particularly during the Depression of the 1930s, income was so narrowly distributed that people had difficulty acquiring necessities. Even the infusion of jazz and the acceptance of black musicians onto the musical scene were carefully homogenized into the big band, carefully orchestrated, "symphonic" format of mainstream music.

Love was sweeping the country, and Pessen, an historian, writes that 85% of the "good" songs were love songs, "joyous or sad, reciprocated or unrequited," and, in response to the winds blowing from Vienna, sprinkled with masochism, cynicism, and addiction—to love, not drugs, although Cole Porter did lament getting no kicks from cocaine (1985 p. 193). It was Ginger and Fred meeting, misunderstanding, separating, and finally glamorously reuniting in top hat, tails, and sequined gowns to the lush strains of "The Way You Look Tonight," or Jeannette pleading with Nelson, "Lover Come Back to Me," or a dimpled Shirley describing Heaven as "the day I found, and put my arms around, the right somebody to love." For ten cents, one could have not only a dance but two movies, a serial, a newsreel, and endless coming attractions. But for couples struggling with the survival issues and harsh realities of the Depression, these escapist fantasies were hard and unrealistic romantic acts to follow, and set up expectations for love and loving far beyond reach.

Richard Rodgers notes,

The music of the 20's and 30's represents . . . the voices of *two* times separated by a single day late in 1929—the day of the Great Wall Street Crash. . . . The Twenties sang of carefree nights and the frenetic days that rushed headlong into the nightmare and fantasy of the Thirties. Both had their reality; both voiced it. This was a score of years in which love grew from an idle and pleasant pastime into a vital avocation—romance. Breadlines seemed less burdensome if one could sing. (1973, p. xiv)

So while money was scarce, romance was available to all.

As Mooney points out, these intense lovelorn ballads appealed to a consumer who was older than the buyers of today and more openly identified with middle-class values. Lyrics tended to be subtle and understated, aimed at an audience of some maturity and education but still lacking in the bite and sardonicism that makes Sondheim so appealing today. But the Gershwins did refer to Russian plays, Robins and Ranger to the Parthenon and to castles on the Rhine, and, perhaps most sophisticated of all, Cole Porter to the Colosseum, Louvre Museum, Bendel bonnets, and Shakespeare sonnets—all a far cry from June-moon rhyming schemes.

The generations that grew up between the 1920s and the early 1950s were as much influenced by Victorian gentility as by the infiltration of the psychosexual theories of Freud into popular culture. Sexuality had begun to show itself in a more obvious way in popular lyrics than it had in the early part of the century, although by and large, sexuality was still permeated with the ideals of monogomous love. To quote Mooney,

> Sex could be truly good and beautiful, truly redeemed, only if part of a romantic love affair. If not chastity, if not marriage, there must be Love. And this love must be, as in a marriage, monogomous, exclusive, rather than promiscuous. Love was not to be treated casually. One might defy the Victorian double standard but must uphold courtly fidelity. (1969, p. 15)

Woman and adolescent girls formed the main audience for this music, for they were as Pauletich has described, easy marks for the appeal of popular songs, the hope for easy fulfillment through love. For women, to aspire to love was to aspire to power, the only kind of power that women could get. A woman's power over one man was her means to power in a world in which power was wielded by men (1980).

In her quest for that love, no humiliation was too great to be embraced, and, in fact, self-abasement and denial were the hallmarks of a loving woman. "Can't Help Loving That Man of Mine," "Stormy Weather," "Something Wonderful," "The Man That Got Away," "I'll Be Around," "Happiness Is Just a Thing Called Joe," "My Man," "'Tain't Nobody's Business If I Do," "I Got It Bad and That Ain't Good"—these songs all communicate this. For all their apparent acquiescence to the values of partriarchy, however, underlying many of these lyrics, is more than a *soupçon* of contempt, for, after all, a man is just a man. The woman grants him forgiveness from aloft; she, a woman, having learned right and wrong at her mother's knee, is above such behavior and is, therefore, his superior. Men are little boys who never grew up and must be taken in hand, chided for their transgressions, and set on the proper path. It is interesting that women sing of the treachery and beastliness of men, their flaws, their faithlessness and passion for roving, and women's own hopeless enslavement in songs that until recently were written predominantly by men.

All of this was to change radically with the advent of rock, which exploded upon the American scene in the late 1950s as an attitude and as a musical form. Rock was James Dean, Marlon Brando, and Elvis Presley; it was rebellion and sexuality, raw and unchained. A rock band was a male team, struttingly tough, challenging, antiestablishment, lonely, indifferent to the future, building its own legends. Women were viewed instrumentally and functionally, to be taken or left. Romantic involvement was no longer a necessary ingredient in any relationship and might even be an obstacle to open, free enjoyment.

Thus the music of the sixties began to portray changes in the patternings of male-female relationships. In a content analysis of the lyrics of the most popular songs of the 1950s and 1960s, Carey (1969) notes marked differences in portrayal of courtship patterns in the two decades. Where many of the hit tunes of 1955 describe a man powerlessly and helplessly in love, at the mercy of a woman who determines the course of the relationship, the rock lyrics of 1966 give initiative and power to the man. It is he who pursues or terminates the involvement. Women no longer inhabit pedestals but are often reduced to the status of sexual objects. Songs in the sixties became increasingly raunchy, with explicit references to erotic sensation and sexual arousal. But although the underlying rationale for sexual pursuit was frequently the irresistible tidal force of love, love was no longer defined in terms of deep romantic involvement, but was a more ephemeral linking. To love someone could mean simply that you were "turned on." The earlier requirement of romantic love as a prerequisite for sexual involvement was abandoned, and sexual relationships were considered to be legitimate in their own right. George S. Kaufman once quipped that Irving Berlin's "I'll be loving you always" should be rewritten, "I'll be loving you Thursday," and rock seems to have adopted some of this cynicism. Affairs were not expected to be permanent or necessarily exclusive. Those diagnosed as unhealthy, that is, those in which one of the partner's demands could not be met, were expected to be terminated. This deemphasis on romantic love allowed for more personal freedom; relationships could be temporary or long-lasting. Forever was no longer a given. All of this was in keeping with the human-potential movement of the late sixties and early seventies, with its emphasis on personal control of destiny, self-actualization, and individual choice, and with the sexual revolution and the more widespread rejection of middle-class morality. The song lyrics of this period celebrate autonomy, both in personal relationships and in relation to the larger community.

In this respect, it might be illuminating to compare Woods, Campbell, and Connelly's 1932 handling of the theme of a woman's neediness in their recipe "Try a Little Tenderness" with Bob Dylan's 1964 version. While both songs describe the woman as dependent and clinging, seeking security in the sheltering arms of a strong protector, Woods, Campbell, and Connelly cater to her desires in a patronizing, self-serving fashion. A little consideration, they suggest, goes a long way with women who regard "love as their whole happiness." Dylan, on the other hand, unmoved by her protestations and apparent desperation, turns his back and, while acknowledging her search for an unswerving defender, informs her that "It ain't me Babe" (it is interesting to note the frequency with which women are referred to as "Babe" or "Baby" in the lyrics of popular songs.)

Earlier in this essay, we referred to Sullivan's view of love as a balancing of concern for the satisfaction and security of the other with consideration for one's own well-being. But Sullivan did not specifically address what happens when these needs collide. At what point does compromise shade into sacrifice and self-abnegation become self-renouncing? To what extent does one give up or submerge one's own needs and take pleasure from participating in the fulfillment of the other person's? The idea of sacrifice for love is a recurrent theme in lyrics as well as literature, but it has received bad reviews particularly since the 1960s. Love that requires sacrifice has been judged to be love that is suspect. Furthermore, sacrifice is too often an ignoble act—an effort to bind the receiver in ties of guilt and gratitude.

The concept of love cannot be addressed without exploring this dialectic of separateness and connectedness. Each of us throughout life struggles with forming intimate and loving relationships while maintaining a fundamental integrity of the self. What then are the prototypes for adult love, for the kind of loving that enriches the self?

Whereas Freud saw love as developing out of the ability to sublimate instinctual drives, relational theorists view it as inherent in the early parent-child bond. Klein speaks of the child's love for parents and siblings as not simply stemming from the youngster's need for his or her objects as sources of gratification but as involving what she describes as "a profound need to make sacrifices," a desire to make others happy because of genuine sympathy and concern (1964, p. 65).

This "no man is an island" theme is central to the work of Fairbairn and Guntrip, both of whom recognize that the capacity to stand alone must be viewed within the framework of a coexisting and continuous-through-life need for relationships with other persons. Fairbairn (1952) describes emotional health as a state of mature interdependence, which he contrasts with the largely skewed dependence of infancy, where parental love is, under the best of circumstances, unconditional.

Kernberg (1977) stresses that there can be no meaningful love relations without a persistent sense of self, that is, without the firm boundaries that generate both a sense of identity and continuity—and an accompanying anxious awareness of the indissoluble separateness of persons from one another. Passion, particularly sexual passion, involves crossing these boundaries to a state of transcendence in which the individual experiences him- or herself as being at one with the loved person. Thus the processes of separateness and connectedness are intimately interwoven in loving; separateness carries with it expectations of loneliness and longing and fear for the frailty of all relations; the transcendence of union provides a sense of permanence, of new creation, and of oneness with the world.

Gilligan's (1982) work on morality is relevant here. Gilligan posits that men and women possess different standards of morality because of the ways in which relatedness and autonomy are selectively reinforced for each sex. Thus each sex perceives a danger that the other fails to see—men in connectedness, women in separation. It is interesting, in this context, to note how frequently men's songs focus on autonomy—"Don't Fence Me In," "By the Time I Get to Phoenix," "I'll Go My Way by Myself." "I Did It My Way," "It Ain't Me Babe," "Babe I'm Gonna Leave You," and the scores of other vagabond songs in popular and folk music. Fairbairn has emphasized that the desire for contact and nurturance is often experienced as sexual desire, for this is more acceptable than the acknowledgment of one's longing to be cared for. Although this is obviously a reality for both sexes, it seems particularly relevant to men because of the pressure to be achieving and self-reliant.

A woman's life, in contrast, is characterized by embeddedness in social interaction and personal relations. Traditionally, she has been defined in relationship to others—as someone's daughter, someone's wife, someone's mother. In inescapable ways, she finds herself feeling responsible for the well-being and success of others, and her self-worth reverberates with her success in relating. This is reflected in her music, which deals almost uniformly with relatedness. "As long as he needs me," she sings, "I'll cling on steadfastly," no matter what adversities and infidelities, throughout life. Even such songs as "Strong Woman Number," for the 1979 off-Broadway show "I'm Getting My Act Together and Taking It on the Road," have tongue firmly planted in cheek, for the songstress is well aware that her protestation of assertiveness and autonomy may not get her anywhere.

Our study of the twentieth-century ballad shows a pole-to-pole progression, a movement from passivity to activity, and from embeddedness to autonomy, that is particularly apparent in the songs of male rock groups. The songs of the twenties and thirties focus on romance and lament love's demise ("When you're alone the magic moonlight dies"), while the rock music of the eighties celebrates quick sexual attachment, individuality, and material gain. In today's rock music, particularly heavy-metal rock, the medium has truly become the message: packaging is everything, extravagance of dress and presentation prevail. Lyrics are drowned in a cacophony of sound in which the erotic beat overrides all. The pendulum has swung, but it has swung too far in the direction of what seems but a struttingly aggressive caricature of true individuality and independence, where narcissism and autonomy are confused and undifferentiated.

Today's music continues to stress love as a dominant theme, but, as reported by Robert Palmer in a *New York Times* article, it is no longer the transcendent and irresistible force that could accomplish any deed or overcome any obstacle that was extolled by some of the rock lyricists of the sixties. Today's versions of love and romance regard relationships in a stark light, stripped of roseate hues, hard of head and heart. Where the Beatles strummed, "All you need is love," the songwriters of the eighties argue that romance is no longer primary and actually places third, somewhere after materialistic acquisitiveness and sex. Despite the fact that male dominance continues to be celebrated, the protest against rock lyrics that demean women seems to have had a broad and salutary effect. Holly Near, singing feminist and gay love songs, can sell out a concert hall, but heavy-metal rock, which appeals largely to white male teenagers, continues to treat women as either temptresses or chattel and is more popular than ever.

Perhaps what is most interesting about the popular music of the eighties is its sheer volume—not only accoustically but numerically. Where music was once enduring and lyrics were expressive of thought as well as feeling, it is now being mass-produced and mass-consumed at an ever-increasing rate. The Hit Parade of the forties and fifties and the Top Ten have been replaced by a weekly Top Forty, and, for the most part, the components change every week.

The consumers of popular music are presented with a dazzling array of styles, titles, groups, and singers, most of whom pass into obscurity or become yesterday's news in an alarmingly short time. Those who manage to remain in the limelight for more than a brief moment, like Springsteen, Jagger, Diana Ross, and McCartney, must continuously change their titles and their styles. Perhaps this tells us more about love in today's world than do the lyrics of these songs—which are scarcely heard. Will two of today's adolescents be able to meet twenty years hence in some distant place, as we did, and as the children of the sixties do, and recognize one another by a shared musical heritage?

It is interesting to note the number of recent conferences that have "Love" as their theme, in contrast to those of the past few years that focused on narcissism, borderline disorders, and self psychology. In parallel fashion, popular recording artists such as Linda Ronstadt, Barbra Streisand, and Carly Simon have issued albums of popular standards of the thirties and forties, that are current top sellers. We speculate that this renewed interest in enduring love is a backlash against a culture of narcissism and consumption that emphasizes the primacy of the individual over the human need to relate in an interdependent way, which leaves its members feeling empty and alienated with nothing but the quick fix of a new sensation to provide temporary comfort. Just as the swing toward individuality was a reaction to oppressive romanticism and Victorian notions of sexuality, which often limited individual growth, we now seem to be searching for a balance that will enable us to express ourselves autonomously while still remaining emphatically connected to others.

NOTE

In its original, orally presented form, this chapter included the lyrics of a number of songs referred to in the body of the paper. Because of copyright restrictions, it has been necessary to paraphrase the verses.

REFERENCES

Carey, J. T. 1969. Changing courtship patterns in the popular song. *American Journal of Sociology* 74:720–31.
Fairbairn, W. R. D. 1952. *An object relations theory of the personality.* New York: Basic Books.
Gilligan, C. 1982. *In a different voice: Psychological theory and women's development.* Cambridge: Harvard University Press.
Jung, C. G. 1928. *Contributions to analytic psychology.* London: Routledge and Kegan Paul.
Kernberg, O. 1977. Boundaries and structure in love relations. *Journal of the American Psychoanalytic Association* 25:81–113.
Klein, M. 1964. Love, guilt and reparation. In M. Klein and J. Riviere, eds., *Love, hate and reparation,* pp. 306–343. New York: Norton.
Lomax, A. 1960. *Folk songs of North America.* Garden City, N.Y.: Doubleday.
Malcolm, J. 1981. *Psychoanalysis: The impossible profession.* New York: Alfred A. Knopf.
Money, J. 1980. *Love and love sickness: The science of sex, gender differences and pair bonding.* Baltimore: Johns Hopkins University Press.
Mooney, H. F. 1969. Popular music since the 1920's: The significance of shifting taste. In J. Eisen, ed., *The age of rock: Sounds of the American Cultural Revolution,* pp. 9–25. New York: Random House.
Palmer, R. 1985. What pop lyrics say to us today. *The New York Times,* Feb. 24.
Pauletika, A. 1980. *Sirens of song: The popular female vocalist in America.* New York: Da Capo.
Pessen, E. 1985. The great songwriters of Tin Pan Alley's golden age: A social, occupational and esthetic inquiry in American music. *American Music* 3:180–97.
Rodgers, R. 1973. Introduction to *Hundred best songs of the 1920's and 1930's.* New York: Harmony.
Sullivan, H. S. 1945. *Conceptions of modern psychiatry* (The first William Alanson White Memorial Lectures). Washington, D.C.: The William Alanson White Foundation.

4. Love in a Hall of Mirrors: Reciprocal Transference Relationships in Marriage

Walter Gadlin

In love, the most intense adult relationship, and in its therapeutic analog, the transference neurosis, the powerful effect of the relationship between two people is revealed. The nature of psychoanalysis requires that we concentrate on the feelings and meanings and transferences of our patient rather than include the lover, an unknown and unknowable other person. We can clearly see the effect of the lover but cannot clearly discriminate between the fantasy and reality components in our patient's perceptions and reports. Nevertheless, much can be learned about the way a patient has been loved and has loved from psychoanalytic exploration. The vicissitudes of the current relationship evoke old wishes, fears, frustrations, and conflicts that surrounded the patient's love experiences. In short, a person's love relationship can be utilized to shed light on aspects of his or her past psychic reality now transferred to the current love objects. Some analysts interpret this transference as displacements from the analyst while others interpret genetic origins directly.

This essay seeks to add a special perspective to the study of love by addressing the reciprocal changes in the transferential aspects of the relationship of the married couple as seen through the prism of couple therapy. The term *reciprocal* refers to how the transference of one spouse affects and is affected by the transference of the other. Transference is emphasized to underline the extent to which the marital interactions are determined by each partner's infantile and, to a lesser extent, later fantasies of relationships rather than reality. These past relationships make possible adult love by bringing warmth, depth, and meaning as well as difficulty to it.

It is necessary at this point to address the use of the term *transference* to refer to aspects of relationships in other than the analytic situation. Many psychoanalysts have restricted the term to the context of psychoanalytic treatment. For them it does not exist in other relationships, by its very definition (Macalpine 1950; Waelder 1956; Menninger 1958). Still others have held that while transference may be ubiquitous in human relationships it is best to reserve the term for the psychoanalytic situation as the sole relationship whose characteristics allow clarity in understanding and interpreting what the patient transfers. All other interpersonal situations bring some measure of provocation by "the other," thereby obscuring the target individuals' unconscious conflicts (Fenichel 1945; Greenacre 1954). Similarly, Stone (1967) affirms the presence of "latent transference" with or without therapy, as demonstrated in dreams and in neurosis, but differentiates this from "clinical transference which surges through defenses toward a real object of distinctive character; i.e., the analyst" (p. 85). He regards the latent, nonclinical transference in a restricted sense: it has as its object the "old intrapsychic representation." In this view, only analysis provides the special relationship that allows for the emergence of a clinical transference. It is unclear whether Stone would accept the notion of a transference that surges through defenses toward another real object of distinctive character, that is, the spouse.

Nevertheless, most psychoanalysts have regarded transference as too important a characteristic of human relationships to restrict the term. Freud (1909) notes that transferences arise spontaneously in all human relationships and do not differ in nature whether they are directed toward the analyst or to some other person (see Laplanche and Pontalis 1973) and that "it is a universal phenomenon of the human mind . . . and in fact dominates the whole of each person's relations to his human environment" (1925, p. 42). Accordingly, Hofer (1956) regards the analytic situation as a variant of human transference relationships. Brenner emphatically states, "The major conflicts—wishes, fears, defenses, guilt feelings and compromise formations—of early childhood reappear . . . in the patient's relationship with his analyst. . . . what has just been described happens in *every* adult relationship, not just in the relationship between patient and analyst" (1976, pp. 111–12). Recently, Loewald (1986) has even written about the analyst as having transference, not countertransference, reactions to the patient.

In order to account for this discrepancy in the use of such a basic term by members of the psychoanalytic community, we must acknowledge that not one but two distinct and nonparallel, albeit overlapping, concepts are being referred to by the same name. To this writer, the more central and important conceptualization refers to "a process of actualization of unconscious wishes. . . . In the transference, infantile prototypes re-emerge and are experienced with a strong sense of immediacy" (Laplanche and Pontalis 1973, p. 455). The second conceptualization of transference emphasizes not what is transferred from the past relationship nor the process by which this happens but the one specific target onto whom the *widest* possible array of material can be transferred, that is, the analyst. While this conceptualization is useful and necessary in understanding the unique aspects of the individual analytic relationships, it obscures, and can even be misused to deny, the essential role of transference in all other important relationships.

I regard the first conceptualization of transference as an apt and necessary paradigm for understanding many marital interactions. Although the analytic situation is the best arena for the expression of all of an individual's possible transference reactions, marriage tends to be the favored arena for the expression of a more limited array of primitive transference themes.

If marriage is suffused with primitive transference reactions, the couple therapist must differentiate the roles of transference and reality in any given interaction. When Freud first coined the term (1909) he used it in one restricted form, as transference *resistance,* and certainly did not believe it to be an essential part of the therapeutic relationship. Indeed, it was seen as an obstruction whose faulty interpretation was to blame for the premature curtailment of Dora's treatment. By the time he wrote his first general exposition of transference (1912), he had broadened the concept into a process that organized the treatment. Nevertheless, for Freud, transferences were living proof of the patient's neurosis and were to be differentiated from reality. Current psychoanalytic thought seems to have evolved away from that clear distinction. Sandler et al. (1969) believe that the transference is now used as a multidimensional phenomenon that must be conceptualized in terms of a metapsychology of object relationships, or, put more simply, that transference must be seen as present to some degree in all relationships. Brenner (1976) states plainly that transference is always present and that it is never completely analyzable.

I have found it impossible to conceptualize abstract guidelines to determine when an interaction is predominantly fueled by a transference fantasy and when by reality, because any given communication has elements of each. It is much easier to discern the contributions of fantasy and reality in the actual clinical situation because the couple therapist, like the analyst, is relatively free from enmeshment in the couple's transference-countertransference reactions. As in the individual therapy situation, the vital ingredients of the analyst's capacity to weigh the relative importance of fantasy and reality are analytic neutrality and objectivity, the constant monitoring of transference and countertransference, and an appreciation of the patients' developmental history.

But the manifestations of transference in marriage, as in psychoanalysis, are not static. What is expressed in a given moment of the "here and now" transference experience reflects different levels of the original infantile traumas and defenses. What is expressed is affected not only by each person's life situation and adaptation (as Erikson [1950] has detailed) but also by the specific reality and transference demands, frustrations, and enhancements provided by the specific others with whom one shares one's life.

Any marriage, then, is in part a reciprocal relationship between two possible transference and countertransference neuroses; the success of the marriage depends on the successful resolution of both sets of neuroses. The task of couple therapy is to help each partner reexperience and understand at least some of the genetic roots of his or her demands upon the other as well as the changes in their more recent lives that have led to the current dislocation.

It appears that all love relationships can be described through the analysis of a limited number of these mutual transference patterns. What follows is a description of one particular set of mutual transferences that dominates the relationship of some of our intelligent, ambitious, nonpsychotic and nonborderline patients.

This relationship may often begin with the young man falling in love with his future bride and wooing her assiduously and unambivalently. Among her other attributes, he is most attracted by her combination of neediness and attentiveness. Here, finally, is a woman whose needs he can satisfy and whom he alone can truly make happy. Simultaneously, he sees her as the only woman sufficiently attentive to him and supportive of him without his having to whine, demand, or even ask for her ministrations. He believes that this relationship will enable him to successfully tackle his life's work. Elements of a positive maternal transference dating from the mother-son relationship of very early childhood underlie his attraction to her. (These positive transferences are well disguised from consciousness, as these men invariably portray their mothers as shrill, controlling, manipulative, and impossible to please.) Additionally, the girlfriend is different enough from the young man's mother, and temporarily weak enough, so that with her he never feels at risk of losing his independence or his differentiation from his domineering mother imago.

At the same time, the future bride is much less sure of her passionate love for him but does feel that she has finally met the nice man who will love, provide for, and protect her. Although many of these women have previously achieved substantial academic, artistic, and/or vocational success, they are in the midst of a "crisis of confidence." Some have been scarred by one or more disastrous affairs, while others have refrained from dating because of the transferentially based conviction that they have nothing to offer the kind of man with whom they could fall in love. All have come to question the validity of their previous success: some feel that it was based on little-girl cuteness and that their fraudulence will soon be exposed; others, that it resulted from a fortuitous accident and that they've run out of luck; and still others, that they are unable to pass muster in the hard, cruel adult world. All feel that they've been trying too hard, that they're psychologically out of breath, that they are vulnerable to hurt and needy of a protector who will afford them a lengthy time-out from competitive life.

In the beginning stage of the relationship, the woman is secretly smitten by the man's love for her, and her reciprocal feelings are of gratitude to him, not love of him. Underlying this "crisis of confidence" and its temporary resolution with her new husband-to-be is a transference relationship that has both maternal and paternal elements. In essence, the young woman is unconsciously in retreat from a maternal accusation of worthlessness and is saved by a warm, loving Daddy for whom she is secretly the Princess.

Soon after the marriage, the negative aspects of his maternal transference, which the groom had not previously associated with his bride, begin affecting the relationship. He feels and complains about her controlling behavior, her anxieties, and her neediness. These complaints by her previously adoring husband serve as further fuel for her own transferentially induced self-accusation of unworthiness and incompetence, and she responds by trying harder to please him.

In the couples I am describing these attempts by the wife are never completely successful, but neither are they inconsequential. The couple "gets by," and even achieves occasional moments of happiness, by immersing themselves in family, career, and community and by gaining financial independence. Frequently, therapy for one or both is essential to facilitate these achievements.

As their family grows up, her time-out nears its end. As a result of successful maternity, vocational, and/or artistic achievement, social relationships, and frequently psychotherapy, she has, to some extent, worked through the original transference relationship to her husband. Now she feels basically competent and whole, in need of some support as she ventures further afield in search of her own growth and fulfillment.[1] (In terms of the transferential aspects of her relationship with her husband, she has moved from the original experience of herself as the four-year-old Princess needing to be rescued by Daddy to the more mature re-creation of her state as the adolescent girl hoping for Daddy's encouragement yet fearing his rejection.) But her husband is not ready to give up *his* transferentially tinged attachment to *her*. He still requires her devoted attention to him as the single most important part of her life. In his individual therapy, if any, he has dealt with the inhibitions against success induced by his "father transference" and the controlling and rejecting aspects of his mother. However, he has never worked on his ego-syntonic need to recapture the feelings of oneness with his mother. This unconscious transference demand is continuously enacted with his wife.

Couples of the type I am describing usually request a consultation, the wife threatening divorce or homicide unless changes are made and the husband declaring his innocence: after all, she has changed, not he. As the couple therapy begins, therefore, the wife feels increasingly stifled by the infantile demands of her husband and resents him more and more as he reminds her of the dependent aspects of her father; the husband feels increasingly betrayed by the latest rendition of maternal rejection.

The course of the therapy includes the reliving and the sharing of their feelings during the nodal points of their relationship: first meetings, decision to marry, the honeymoon phase, and so on. Many of these feelings and thoughts were never fully shared by the couple because they contained secret and sometimes shameful elements, such as her worries that she really didn't love him enough, or his feelings that he wasn't attractive to more vivacious women and therefore settled for her. Associations to similar feeling states in their families of origin are remembered, shared, and examined. This preliminary work allows the couple to recapture some loving feelings and to once again successfully work together.

The most powerful mutative moments occur with the explosive return of attitudes, feelings, and thoughts derived from unconscious infantile relationships now experienced with the spouse as the obviously inappropriate object. The aftermath of such an explosion is similar to the resolution of the transference to the analyst that is worked through in an individual psychoanalysis. The patient realizes that he or she has reacted with powerful feelings that derive from outside the current situation, but, unlike individual treatment, the "here and now" object of the distortion is the spouse, not the analyst. The couple therapist, like the analyst, provides the interpretations that facilitate the resolution of the transference. The couple therapist, again like the analyst, and unlike the spouse in their natural home environment, refuses to let the patient (or spouse) apologize for, excuse, dismiss, argue, or otherwise deny what just happened but instead utilizes this moment of primary-process confusion to elicit infantile memories and unconscious connections with the result that the neurotic demand upon the other is lessened.

Three technical points are worth noting. In couple therapy, the patient has much less resistance to involving him- or herself in the transference (to the spouse) than he or she has in psychoanalysis (to the analyst). The couple frequently begins treatment with a complaint of transferential attachment, for example, "He keeps making me feel like I'm supposed to be his mother," or, "She wants my approval for every new move she makes and then wants me to tell her how independent she is." The therapeutic difficulty lies in the adhesiveness of the transference resistance in its second meaning—the refusal to resolve the transference[2] and to surrender the demand for transference gratification, as each defends and justifies the correctness of his or her own perceptions and "reasonable" demands upon the other. Second, the couple therapist, unlike the individual analyst, has to take some care to not be the focus of transference reactions by either member of the couple. This can be accomplished by the quick interpretation of any such reaction as soon as it appears and by maintaining the couple's focus upon their perceptions of each other rather than upon the therapist. And third, the primary work is accomplished through the patients' associations and explorations and through the couple therapist's interpretations of transference and resistance—not through the negotiation of differences. Previous or concurrent individual therapy is therefore extremely useful in making these associations and understandings quickly available to the couple therapy.

I have chosen the following example to illustrate this particular set of reciprocal transferences because of the availability of data from each of their individual analyses, which were conducted by respected analysts and completed some time before the beginning of the couple therapy.

Mr. and Mrs. A. met at a prestigious university where each was enrolled in graduate training. Mr. A. was proud of his academic performance and was readying himself to begin a career in his high-pressured field. He did not feel as accomplished in the social realm. Although he had many acquaintances he had no close friends, and he had still not won the love of a woman of whom he could feel proud. Mrs. A. was just beginning to recover from the disintegration of her life. For the first time she had been unsuccessful in school and socially unpopular, living as a virtual recluse in her dormitory room. The uneasiness that she had felt all her life as a vague sense of unworthiness was now experienced as a full-blown conviction of failure.

Having stumbled upon each other at a university dance, they quickly found that they much preferred each other's company to anyone else's. Mr. A. felt powerful because she not only turned to him for advice but also made him feel that he was saving her life. She, on the other hand, felt for the first time that she could rest. She had finally found a man who loved her and promised to take care of her and did not care about her performance.

The above is a reconstruction of the thoughts and feelings they remember being conscious of during this initial period of the relationship. We can, however, piece together much fuller pictures of their psychic states at this time of their first meeting from data uncovered during and after their analyses.

Mr. A. was bored by women with less than superior IQs, but he was unconsciously afraid of bright women, regarding them as junior editions of his mother, whom he described as "shrill, controlling, manipulative, and impossible to please." From his later analysis we know of some of the more positive elements in his unconscious maternal imago that were operative at this time. Mother was the driving force that had single-handedly maintained the family through financial depression, repeated hardships, and tragic deaths; his very survival was attributable to her. Although she had expressed her faith in his ability to achieve in predominately negative and hostile terms, this faith became incorporated by him as the basis of his conviction that, unlike his father and older brothers, he could succeed in life. Also incorporated in this imago was a much-beloved aunt who had lived with the family until her death during Mr. A.'s adolescence. She was the uncritically loving, totally available, and appreciative mother substitute who provided the time, attention, and affection that his harassed and harassing mother could and/or would not afford him. At age nine, he had engaged in a sit-down strike, using total passivity in order to force his mother to care for him as she did his father and older brother. His demands were ignored, and in what he reconstructed as *the* turning point in his life, the young Mr. A. screwed up his courage, cast aside his yearnings to recapture the tenderness he had felt from his aunt, and decided that he could and would do it all by himself. This decision remained firm until he met this girlfriend and realized that he had found the woman with whom he could share his life. She seemed to have all of the virtues of the ideal woman—intelligence, inner strength, confidence in him, and the ability to love him without presenting the danger of overwhelming him.

Meanwhile, the future Mrs. A. had done poorly at school and had isolated herself from friends and family. She had been feeling desperate, believing that she could neither survive alone nor disgrace her parents by returning to them. Mrs. A. never felt quite right about her relationship to her powerful mother, whose love and approval she had always sought. For as long as she could remember, Mrs. A. had been the good little girl: poised, pretty, polite, cheerful, and charming. She had been a star student achieving high honors from kindergarten through graduation from an Ivy League college. Nevertheless, her mother had always seemed preoccupied with Mrs. A.'s brother, a school dropout three years her junior, knowing in her maternal heart that he was the best and the brightest and that this would be apparent to everyone as soon as he "found himself." Indeed, it often seemed that Mrs. A.'s most intimate relationship with her mother was as her special helper and confidante in the Sisyphean task of raising the son. Mrs. A. consciously felt her father to be her mother's devoted slave, and obsessively considered two possibilities to account for his disinterest in her. Her first hypothesis was that her mother was so perfect and so sufficient for her father that he had no need of his little daughter's affection. Her second hypothesis was that he too was afraid of the evil witch's jealous rage, which would be unleashed if he were to show his love for the daughter.

During her individual analysis, repressed memories of her father were recovered and disavowed feelings toward her mother were reintegrated. She remembered her "love affair" with her father when she was three and her brother was born. At that time each had felt abandoned by the mother who had become totally enmeshed with her infant son. In consolation, but also with excitement, father and daughter discovered each other and developed a deep bond of love partially based on their mutual identification as mother's discarded objects. This "love affair" ended when mother's total involvement with her walking and therefore separating one-year-old son decreased and she resumed her role as materfamilias.

The four-year-old girl was left with new feelings of abandonment, this time by her father, but at least with memory traces of having been his darling princess. She was also left with the hurt of having doubly lost out with her mother. First, of course, she lost the competition with her mother for father's love. Just as important, she lost the hope of ever feeling truly loved by mother or even appreciated for her own qualities and talents. Mother's view of her, Mrs. A. reconstructed, was a very nice but not at all special daughter who was fortunately able to be reliable and problem-free so that she, mother, could devote her full maternal love and energy to the development of her very special son.

Here was an almost perfect meshing of two people's transferences. With their relationship they could each unconsciously deny an important component of their infantile trauma and heighten a less threatening, and more adaptive, aspect of their defenses. He needed to be in an exclusive relationship with a bright and beautiful woman who loved him, but most who met this requirement were powerful enough possibly to overwhelm him. She proved her lack of dangerousness by unambivalently needing to feel preferred and exclusively loved by a smart, attractive, and ambitious man who in turn would present no danger of leaving her for another woman. He was therefore happy to love and protect her, and she was delighted to honor and cherish him.

Soon after the marriage the previously denied negative aspects of the groom's maternal transference began affecting the relationship, as his new wife began expressing needs and feelings that were not absolutely congruent with his priorities. For example, she expressed her feelings of loneliness, criticized his obsession with his work, and demanded his attention to domestic tasks such as the purchase of a living-room couch. What he had experienced as her adoration he began to see as neediness, her love for him became her wish to control him, and her desire for his love and attention he now understood as her unresolved anxieties. His complaints increased as she became more and more overwhelmed by the difficult task of caring for the household, with two babies in diapers, while discreetly managing her husband's bruised ego. His complaints were magnified as a displacement of his own failing sense of power resulting from his first occupational difficulties and setbacks. Mrs. A. was initially surprised by her heretofore loving and protective groom's complaints but then gloomily came to accept them as a natural consequence of her unworthiness. Just as his transferentially tinged love before the marriage (deriving from his earliest loving relationships and fantasies about his mother and aunt) had connected with her unconscious transference of being lovable and desirable (deriving from her fourth year with her father), so now his equally transferentially tinged anger and complaints (dating from his later and more frequent relationship and fantasies with his mother) connected with her more conscious transferential experience of unworthiness and guilt (dating from her later interactions with her mother).[3]

As it became clear to Mr. A. that he was failing professionally, he began a psychoanalysis, which resulted in rapid improvements in *both* of their lives. He began doing better at work, so that his complaints were less fueled by displacements and feelings of failure, and more psychic energy was funneled into the analytic transference, relieving the pressure on his wife and allowing her *almost* the room to successfully manage the family. Although their lives had much improved, Mrs. A. remained in a state of subacute depression, so when Mr. A. completed his analysis, she began hers.

In the analysis she quickly accepted the idea that it was legitimate for her to want something for herself as well as through her husband. She learned how these issues were derived from her relationship to, and fantasies about, her parents. The understanding of these transferences gave meaning to her lifelong state of never feeling quite right about herself or believing in her own worth as a successful woman. As she absorbed these insights she came gradually to feel entitled first to the analysis itself, which she now understood as having begun in envious imitation of her husband, then to another child and finally to a career.

After the conclusion of each of their analyses, the A.'s prospered as individuals and as a family until they began having trouble with their adolescent daughter, and were referred to me for family therapy. The sessions began with Mr. and Mrs. A. solidly arrayed against their daughter and seeking help to control her drug addiction, delinquency, and school failure. As we began to explore the family members' perceptions and distortions of each other, it became apparent that the parents' "solid front" was a translucent cover for their mutual accusations of failures and shortcomings. Also, their daughter began to resist coming to the sessions and with my permission ceased to do so. I continued to meet with the parents and urged them to continue to explore their own differences and the unfulfilled fantasies of their daughter and of each other. We used the ensuing material for two distinct activities. At first we concentrated on devising a successful plan for controlling and motivating their daughter so that she was eventually able to become drug-free, to cease her delinquent activity, to graduate from high school and proceed to college. From the beginning we also worked to analyze their hidden feelings and misconceptions about, and projections upon, each other. After several months, the successful management of their daughter required less time and planning, leaving us free to shift our primary concentration to the marital issues.

The first set of transference distortions to emerge began with Mr. A.'s long-standing complaints that the problems with their child (and almost everything else) stemmed from his wife's failure in her task as family manager. This led to the resurgence of Mrs. A.'s rage at him for demanding his unchallengeable primacy. Any attempts by Mrs. A. to reject her husband's appointment of her to the position of family manager and instead to talk of her individual needs and aspirations led to his reproach that she never fully appreciated his endeavors, which were solely on behalf of her and her children; that she was never satisfied and in fact was unsatisfiable; and that, above all, she should first take care of the family's needs before gratifying her own ego. In the face of this barrage, she withdrew in seething rage, feeling that she was being forced once again to surrender her claim to importance and that it would never be her turn to be first in anyone's heart and mind. Her father had wanted only his wife, her mother preferred her son, and her husband favored his work and his troubled child. The resurgence of these irrational and sadomasochistic attacks on each other despite a basically loving twenty-year marriage and fifteen years of combined analyses is testimony to the often intractable nature of the spousal transference neuroses. Nevertheless, the couple therapy was pivotal in blocking Mrs. A.'s withdrawal and helping her put her demands into words.

Although each stated it differently, the couple's difficulty in accommodating to Mrs. A.'s growing need for independent functioning became the central "surface" issue of our work. She would have said that they were working on whether she could finally have her own place in the sun or whether her needs were too much for him. He would have said that they were dealing with her difficulties in asserting herself in her career or with the children, and he would have added his complaint that, of course, the only one with whom she could assert herself was him. I formulated this standoff as being fueled by a reciprocal transference distortion, and I interpreted its elements. Mr. A. had reacted to the stress of their problem with their child with his usual set of accusations that his wife was to blame because she was uncaring and weak. The unconscious roots of these accusations were in his complex relationship with his maternal imago. He was blaming his wife because she was just as uncaring and not as strong as his mother. Mrs. A.'s response added her lifelong rage at her mother to her realistic anger at her husband. She unconsciously perceived her husband as making demands of her as though he were her mother. Her needs were again to be subordinated to those of her brother (daughter/husband).

Slowly but surely the fortunes of the marital war favored Mrs. A., and she found surer expressions for her needs. She proved that no one in the family suffered as a consequence of her attention to work, and her husband ambivalently came to delight in her recognition and success.

But old transferences die hard. Contemporaneous with his wife's success Mr. A. found that he had revived an old but precious dream of achieving nothing less than the pinnacle of his profession—a goal of public office that, if reached, would entail his frequent absence from home and a tremendous decrease in income along with a chance to "make a difference." He expressed righteous indignation in response to his wife's concerns about the financial side effects and the frequent separations that his ambition entailed. In his view, it was her responsibility to put aside petty needs and selfishness to support him in his quest, but, he continued aggressively, he really didn't expect her to do so for him as no one ever had, and he could and would rely on his own resources to meet this challenge. This was a re-creation of his transference state as the beleaguered nine-year-old boy, and again he resolved to succeed by himself against all odds. For Mrs. A., the transference experience as the betrayed four-year-old had returned. She was once again feeling cast aside and forced to surrender her own self-interest in the face of the needed object's demands. But this time she would not be a good girl, do as she was told, and give in without a fight. She could now stand up for herself, she continued angrily, and since she finally recognized that no one would ever provide the love she craved she too could and would rely on herself.

As they continued this debate, I interpreted their transferential distortions of one another and helped clarify reality for them. Mr. A. seemed to be deliberately provoking his wife's anxiety and transference by emphasizing the prospective decrease in their income when, upon closer observation, it turned out that they would still be able to vacation in five-star French hotels. On her part, Mrs. A. was unduly emphasizing her husband's ambitions as indicative of his dismissal of her importance when it had a more relevant meaning as the culmination of his life's dream that he was desirous of sharing with her. After a while, the issue became temporarily moot as he had failed in his first bid for the position. They lovingly shared their ambivalent reactions to this defeat, but when Mrs. A. talked about her wish to have had him succeed in the hope that he would finally be content with his accomplishments in life, she was interrupted by his explosion of rage. In a complete though momentary break with reality, he screamed at her, with a quaking voice, that she was lying to him, that if she had really wanted him to have the job she could easily have engineered it for him, that he had suffered all their lives together from her unwillingness to provide the attention and care that she had known he had secretly needed.

Mr. A. was simultaneously enraged and crying about how alone he had felt throughout his life while first his mother and then his wife had deliberately and selfishly withheld what they could have easily provided, their total gratification of his needs. He was most furious at his wife because when they had first met she had proved that she was capable of doing so and had fooled him into thinking that she wanted to as well. Mrs. A., instead of retreating into her usual guilty and conciliatory response, met this transference storm with her own fury. I prevented the development of an argument and asked for Mr. A.'s associations to what he also was beginning to regard as an inexplicable outburst. He responded with various childhood fantasies organized around the theme that his mother was being mean only to test him and to make sure that he was strong and that soon she would again love him, hug him, take care of him, and be satisfied with him.

As Mr. A. reported his recollections, his wife was able to share her memories of feeling forced to be responsible for her brother's happiness and well-being. She remembered not only her anger at having to care for him but her despair that she never would be thanked for her efforts, indeed never even explicitly asked to help—just expected to do so by her mother in a way that demanded compliance and foreclosed refusal, complaints, or even discussion.

In the aftermath of Mr. A.'s outburst we were able to uncover the residues of the couple's reciprocal transferences, which had evaded their individual analyses. Mr. A. had remained unconscious of his yearning to passively submit and rejoin his omnipotent and all-loving mother imago despite the many years of analytic attention paid to the sequela of this constellation of fantasies. Much of his character had been constructed around the need to repress and contain his unfillable, self-annihilating, but still powerful wish. Now we understood that his defensive structure represented this basic transference wish in less primitive form (he was just asking that his wife handle her responsibilities), opposite forms (she didn't have to, he could take care of the family), and symptomatic forms (his lifelong castration anxiety and its defenses, expressed as the need to dominate and not be vulnerable to potentially phallic women, most importantly, his wife). Despite the character armor and symptoms, enough of the original yearning "leaked" through to his wife throughout the years of their marriage to have augmented and maintained her own transferentially based sense of being worthless unless she took adequate care of him, but cheated and secondary, "selfless," if she did.

The couple therapy culminated with a thorough review of how this set of transferences had affected their lives throughout their relationship. Mr. A. became able, for the first time since his marriage, to hear a need or request from his wife without assuming that she was trying to dominate him, and Mrs. A. could hear an irrational or selfish demand from her husband without either becoming enraged or jumping to satisfy him.

SUMMARY

I have presented the idea that reciprocal transference neuroses exist and are enacted within a love relationship, evolving and developing over time, reflecting off of each other, and thus effecting their mutual expression through the phases of the relationship. I have described one such reciprocal set and have delineated how a psychoanalytic couple treatment can succeed in interpreting and resolving such transference neuroses. This essay demonstrates that transference is not a single unitary thing but rather a richly faceted gem whose full colors appear dramatically in the sequential events of a long and basically good marriage. Transference lies intertwined with objective reality. The husband, in the case cited, *was* demanding and self-centered, but his wife's reactions were equally determined by her prior object relationships. Similarly, the wife *had* changed from an absolutely supportive, frequently needy, and excessively worshipful girl into a much more independent and ambitious woman, but it was primarily the husband's unconscious insistence on recapitulating his early object relationships that prevented him from welcoming her metamorphosis. This essay has also demonstrated that when these reciprocal transferences are interpreted, relationships can improve and become more loving and rewarding.

NOTES

1. This capacity to feel basically competent and whole, and to constructively act upon this feeling is what differentiates her from other women with a borderline personality organization, who the same kind of men often marry by mistake.
2. See Gill (1979), Gill and Hoffman (1982), and especially Richards (1984) for elucidation of the clinical and conceptual basis of this important distinction between the patient's resistances to: a. the awareness of the transference; b. the involvement in the transference; c. the resolution of the transference.
3. The form of Mr. A's second and negative transference to his wife follows Racker's (1968) description of the transference that places the object of the current recapitulation in the place of the self in the past relationship. Just as his mother had nagged, complained and found fault with him so he now did the same with his wife.

REFERENCES

Brenner, C. 1976. *Psychoanalytic technique and psychic conflict.* New York: IUP.
Erikson, E. 1950. *Childhood and society.* 2d ed. New York: Norton, 1963.
Fenichel, O. 1945. Neurotic acting out. In *The collected papers of Otto Fenichel* 2:296–304. New York: Norton, 1954.
Freud, S. 1909. Five lectures on psycho-analysis. *Standard edition* 11:1–55.
———. 1912. The dynamics of transference. *Standard edition* 12:97–108.
———. 1925. *An autobiographical study. Standard edition* 20:1–70.
Gill, M. M. 1979. *Analysis of transference, vol. 1: Theory and technique.* Psychological Issues, Monograph 53. New York: IUP.
———, and I. Z. Hoffman. 1982. *Analysis of transference, vol. 2: Studies of nine audio-recorded sessions.* Psychological Issues, Monograph 54. New York: IUP.
Greenacre, P. 1954. The role of transference. *Journal of the American Psychoanalytic Association* 2:671–84.
Hofer, W. 1956. Transference and transference neurosis. *International Journal of Psycho-analysis* 37:377–79.
Laplanche, J., and J. B. Pontalis. 1973. *The language of psychoanalysis.* Trans. D. Nicholson-Smith. New York: Norton.
Loewald, H. W. 1986. Transference-countertransference. *Journal of the American Psychoanalytic Association* 34:275–87.
Macalpine, I. 1950. The development of transference. *Psychoanalytic Quarterly* 19:501–39.
Menninger, K. 1958. *The theory of psycho-analytic technique.* New York: Basic Books.

Racker, H. 1968. *Transference and countertransference.* New York: IUP.

Richards, A. 1984. Transference analysis: Means or ends. *Psychological Inquiry* 4:355–66.

Sandler, J., A. Holder, M. Kawenoka, H. A. Kennedy, and L. Neuroth. 1969. Notes on some theoretical and clinical aspects of transference. *International Journal of Psycho-analysis* 50:633–45.

Stone, L. 1967. The psychoanalytic situation and transference: Postscript to an earlier communication. In Stone, *Transference and its context,* pp. 75–117. New York: Aronson, 1984.

Waelder, R. 1956. Introduction to the discussion of problems of transference. *International Journal of Psycho-analysis* 37:240–43.

5. Sibling Relationships and Mature Love

*Judith F. Lasky and
Susan F. Mulliken*

The purpose of this essay is to explore the impact of childhood sibling relationships on later love relationships, with respect to both the dynamics and the structure of the mature love relationships.

It is frequently said that the sibling experience is neglected in the classical literature, and the fact that "sibling" does not appear as a topic heading in the 404-page index of the *Standard Edition* is cited as evidence. Yet Freud's case histories, dream reports, and interpretations offer examples where the presence of the sibling is often a crucial factor in the dynamic picture.

In the case of Little Hans (Freud 1909), where the birth of a sibling is a precipitating factor of a nascent neurosis, the importance of siblings is indirectly noted. A more direct example, both structurally and dynamically, is the case of the Wolf Man (Freud 1918), where the object choice of maturity is seen as a reversal and displacement of an early traumatic sexual object relationship with a sibling which was causal in the formation of the later neurosis. One example indicating Freud's awareness of the importance of siblings is the statement that "Transference is not necessarily bound to mother or father images, but may also proceed from the 'brother imago' " (1912, p. 100). While one might ask where the sister is, his attention clearly is to the point.

Colonna and Newman (1983) present in more detail a review of Freud's writings that relate to the sibling experience. These are based on both analytic material and observations of his own and colleagues' children. Findings include acknowledgement of rivalrous feelings towards the sibling; the significant impact of the birth of a sibling on sexual curiosity, and on the experience of parental affection; and the effect of the sibling on future object choice.

Freud's autobiographical statements, as well as biographical comments by Jones and others, provide evidence of his interest in sibling relationships. A fascinating insight into Freud's impact on his siblings is revealed in a personal vignette by Freud's sister, Anna Bernays, who wrote in a book dedicated to the memory of her recently deceased brother (cited in Soulé 1981):

> In spite of his youth the regulations and desires of Sigmund were respected by each member of the family. Before I was eight, my mother who had been very musical, permitted me to study the piano, and I began my hourly exercises. Since the piano was not far from Sigmund's room, it disturbed him. He told my mother that the piano would have to be moved or he would certainly leave the house. The piano disappeared, and with it, any possibility for his sisters to become musicians. (p. 52)

Jones (1953) described the impact on Freud of his close and sibling-configured relationship with his nephew John, who lived under the same roof during part of Sigmund's childhood. In speaking of the significance in Freud's early life of this nephew John, who for all practical purposes was raised as a brother during early childhood, Jones states,

> When Freud came to review his childhood he repeatedly indicated how his ambivalence towards John had conditioned the development of his character. (p. 8)

Freud's consideration of this early relationship with John is quoted:

> Until the end of my third year we had been inseparable: we had loved each other and fought each other, and as I have already hinted, this childish relation has determined all my later feelings in my intercourse with persons of my own age. My nephew John has since then had many incarnations, which have revivified first one and then another aspect of a character that is inerradicably fixed in my unconscious memory. (cited in Jones 1953, p. 8)

It may be most accurate to say that Freud treated the sibling experience in an implicit manner, but this does not imply neglect or lack of awareness. Even recently, only a few studies have had the sibling experience as their main focus. The following review of the literature is meant to be not exhaustive but rather illustrative of some different emphases on sibling relations and outcomes in adult object relations.

The reactivation in the transference of the sibling interaction was, to our knowledge, first studied in depth by Lesser (1978), who points to the fact that siblings spend at least as much time together as each does with their parents. She speculates that the analytic setting, as well as some theoretical biases, have left little room for awareness of "the recapitulation in the transference of relationships to one's siblings," and she suggests a systematic exploration of the transference possibilities with each sibling in order to free rigid life patterns. (Some of the later case histories will illustrate the power and endurance of these patterns of object relations and the difficulty of extricating oneself from them.)

The general impact of the sibling relationship on personality development and object relationships is discussed by Holmes (1980), Bank and Kahn (1982), Provence and Solnit (1983), and Rossner (1985). Holmes (1980) presents cases illustrating three ways in which the sibling relationship may influence adult personality: (1) the birth of the sibling may become a point of fixation, particularly for depressive concerns; (2) the sibling relationship may affect character formation and sexual identity; and (3) the sibling relationship may become intertwined with the oedipal relationship in such a way that the individual feels doubly defeated.

Bank and Kahn (1982), in *The Sibling Bond,* review both general clinical and theoretical material in their attempt to delineate the form and strength of attachment between siblings over the life span. Their material is too extensive to be detailed here, but they agree with the previous authors that the sibling experience may affect object choice and identity. Of particular relevance to this essay is their description of three conditions necessary for the development of a strong sibling bond: (1) a high degree of accessibility between the siblings, (2) insufficient parental presence or influence, and (3) use of the sibling as an influence in the search for personal identity. From a more psychoanalytic perspective, it appears that in certain instances, if accessibility is lacking or impossible (because of separation or death), fantasies of contact may take the place of real contact as a contributor to a strong bond. A case to be discussed later will illustrate this point.

Provence and Solnit (1983) emphasize the development-promoting aspects of the sibling experience rather than the rivalrous and negative ones. They make the point that the sibling experience forces one to realize that one is not singular and unique. They are suggesting that this healthy shaking of the narcissistic bubble is a positive part of the adaptation in a normal sibling relationship:

> . . . one can examine the advantage of a partially shared development space . . . [but] . . . such a theoretical or potential advantage is realized only if the parents reactions and the nature of their attachments to each child are supportive of the advantage. (pp. 342–43)

Healthy sibling attachments may favor establishment of capacity for subtle empathic communications and may foster the ability to share indirectly in the experience of the other. One does not need to extend this far to appreciate how these capacities may build and benefit later love relations.

Rossner (1985) focuses his attention on the impact of the sibling on ego formation, personality structure, and object relations.

Turning more specifically to adult object choice, Abend (1978) suggests that although it may most often be appropriate to view erotic interest in a sibling as a displacement from the parents, this is not always so. He presents two brief case vignettes illustrating erotic involvement between siblings that is more than a reflection of their oedipal relationship and that is sufficiently powerful to affect later object choice. What these cases seem to have in common is the presence of an opposite-sex parent with a quality that made them hard to admire.

Kris and Ritvo (1983) state that the sibling relationship is

> . . . always a factor in the choice of a marital partner because it involves overcoming the incest barrier against the peer generation which derives from the sibling relationship, and thus ultimately from the oedipal incest barrier. (pp. 322–23)

A contribution that crosses the lines between literary commentary and psychoanalytic observation, Kiell's *Blood Brothers* (1983) is concerned with the drama of the relationship between famous writers and their brothers, including some dyads in which both brothers were writers (the Huxleys, the Jameses, the Stracheys, the Singers, the Durrells). And along the way we are treated to some significant examples of interactions between sibling formations and later object relations.

The question as to whether the implicit rather than explicit attention in the literature to date reflects the lesser significance of the sibling relationship has been raised by all of the above authors, and all agree that it does not. Both our reading of the literature and our clinical work have led us to agree with the opinion so eloquently stated by Kris and Ritvo (1983):

> . . . although the sibling relationship is not essential for normal development and many do not have it . . . for those who do, it has a profound influence on psychic life throughout their lifetime. (p. 311)

Two major areas where this influence comes into play are identity and object choice; the latter is the focus of this essay.

When sibling relationships have been examined, the emphasis has more frequently been on rivalry, jealousy, and envy than on love. Yet libidinal feelings, ranging from concern through attachment and including the most intense love, are among the spectrum of feelings that siblings can arouse in one another. Which feelings come to predominate in the childhood sibling relationship and the ways in which this relationship will come to affect later relationships will vary with the individuals and circumstances. Many factors will play a part in the emotional tone, structure, and cumulative impact of the sibling relationship: age of siblings, presence or absence of parents, family constellation, parental fantasies about each sibling, and the specific endowments of each family member. So, for example, as Bank and Kahn (1982) and Abend (1978) discuss, an intense and ultimately addictive sibling relationship may be more likely to develop in the presence of an emotionally and/or physically unavailable parent.

Having accepted the importance of the sibling experience, the task of separating what is attributable to the parent-child relationship and what to the sibling relationship remains. Several possibilities present themselves. The sibling relationship may be a new edition of the oedipal relationship, but this time with a less dangerous, more available, yet still taboo object. Or a defect in the parent-child relationship may give the sibling contact heightened significance. It may be that in most cases the sibling relationship and parent-child relationship are so inextricably intertwined that their threads may be described but not disentangled.

Our focus is on the sibling of childhood as an often neglected contributor to the form and dynamics of adult love relationships. We see this focus as having particular clinical usefulness in the excavation and elucidation of hidden recesses of repetitive neurotic behavior in intractable contemporary love relationships that might not otherwise be explicable. It has been our experience that these dynamics often have a more "ghostly resonance" and are less apparent than parentally derived dynamics. Our focus will be on the adult analytic patient, and the childhood sibling references will be those which emerge in the course of the analytic work.

Sibling material emerges in treatment in variations that correspond to the ego organization and defensive structure of the patient and to the nature of the material. As with other associative material, thoughts concerning siblings and love will be presented most readily either when there is little conflict about it because its meaning is not apparent (as exemplified by the patient who describes his girlfriends in terms of their dissimilarity to his younger sister, and so assumes that he is describing his independence from her) or when the conflict is close to the surface (as when a younger sibling refuses to date people whose sibling position was the older sibling because of a wish never to be bossed around again). It is often the case, when the sibling situation is most directly replicated in the contemporary love relationship, that the patient is generally unaware, denying, or manifesting total repression of the earlier derivation of the current relationship. Often the sibling will be left out of the associative material and will emerge only through disassociated, displaced, and dream references. Thus, it behooves the therapist to develop a listening ear for the parallel elements. As always, when there is more to listen for, the listening process becomes yet more complex, but our findings are that this pays off in the uncovering of formerly denied and inaccessible repetitive parallels.

We will now present a number of case examples. Each will represent a different aspect of the dynamic impact of the sibling relationship. We will be presenting material that is most germane to the sibling situation. Even then, it may well be possible to propose other interpretations of the clinical material. We intend to say not that sibling factors are the only relevant ones but, rather, that they are often critical.

In their broadest outlines, the first three cases illustrate two differing effects of a deep (although not always conscious) attachment to a sibling: repetition of aspects and qualities of that relationship in the adult love relationship, or interference with the development of a new love relationship because of the power of the old one.

Mrs. L., a thirty-five-year-old woman, had been married for twelve years to a man who was highly competent outside the marriage but who maintained with his wife a needy, passive, and demanding dependent relationship, in which she consistently felt impotent rage and unmet wishes for equality. Mrs. L. spontaneously mentioned her sister, four years younger, only twice over a year of treatment. When inquiry about the sister occurred, her significance in the patient's contemporary life was dismissed. She was able to maintain this indifference without difficulty because the sister lived at a great distance. The sister visited once, staying with the patient and her family. In short order, the patient was in a rage, a rage familiar to her in its qualitative likeness to the anger she chronically and less consciously felt toward her husband. Describing her reactions to the visit, Mrs. L., ordinarily extremely well spoken, said, in reference to the sister, "Before she camed," rather than "Before she came," stopped herself, and inquired of herself, "Why did I say 'camed'?" An interpretation was hazarded that she had been thrown back into her four-year-old grammatical forms, her age when the sister was born. The patient listened attentively and went on to tell, in detail, of her sister's infractions on the recent visit. "It reminded me of when we were children. She got angry at me and smeared feces on my towel. I had the feeling she was going to do what she wanted to do, going to defy me and be destructive just as she was when we were children." This impotent feeling, the inability to change, confront, or be satisfied in the relationship, it was noted, was precisely paralleled in the marital relationship. The husband was the child who did what he wanted, offered her no gratifications, and constantly expected her to adapt to his needs. Her impotence in dealing with the sister was dictated by the parental edict "You are the older sister," with the implication that she had to take what the sister dished out. This paralleled her external rage and impotence in deriving satisfaction from the husband. This was the first successful clue, both for the patient and the analyst, to her experienced inability to change, fight, or restructure the unsatisfying elements of her martial relationship.

A significant aspect of the second case was an almost delusional attitude on the part of the patient, an older sister, that her younger sister was her child. It is not possible to enter into the complicated vicissitudes of life that created this experience. No matter what the twists and turns of her own life, the fact that Mrs. N. represented for the younger sister a strong and maternal figure was an anchor of her identity. This image of herself interfered, for many long years, with her establishing an independent and long-lasting relationship with a man of maturity. Her relationships were terrible, tempestuous, and always terminated. But she remained an anchor for her baby sister. Her sister then married. After a period in which Mrs. N. predicted that the marriage would come to no good, the baby sister had a baby. It was at this point that Mrs. N. entered treatment. Her equilibrium was truly shaken. Her baby could be her baby no longer; her present marriage was terrible; and she had no longer the anchored position of guide to her baby sister, who was obviously making it without her. She was wretched. Interpretations focused on her reactions to the dissolution of this established, though illusory and outdated conviction that her well-being was dependent on her sister's need of her—and stressed that this conviction had robbed her of the ability or need to establish an independent and lasting object relationship, external to the sisterhood. With greater urgency, she turned to her husband more and more, finally working out, with more attention and concern than ever before, the sexual inhibitions and aggressive stands that interfered with making her marriage truly viable. She terminated treatment when her own married life became sufficiently full and rewarding and when the vicissitudes of her sister's life became issues of more distant concern.

Mr. P. was born late in his parents' life, four months after the accidental death of a teenaged sister. Another sister, age twenty, was already out of the house at this time, and he did not recall much of her from his childhood. He had always felt that he came too late to have his parents at their best. At age twenty-eight, he saw his friends marrying and he felt that, once again, he was late. But despite his wish to form a long-term relationship, he found himself frustrated by his failure to meet other than boring, everyday women, and he could not understand why his luck was so different from that of his friends.

Mr. P. believed that he had not learned about his dead sister until he was a teenager. She did not enter into his attempts to understand the past, and he did not even mention her in treatment until several months had passed. But it soon became apparent that she was very much a presence in the household. In time, he began to recall unclear allusions to her in conversations, or family photos in which not everyone was clearly identified. It became evident that his parents were trying to hide their grief from him by keeping his sister a partial secret, but that he knew something. In childhood he attempted to make sense of all this by imagining an angel hovering over the household. It was this angel that he was unconsciously looking for, as a way to bring peace to his still-mourning parents and because no one else was so worthy of his love. Also, lack of interaction with a real live sibling (since his older sister was out of the house) made natural contact with women of his own age even more difficult to attain.

Although these are unusual circumstances, they are enlightening because they illustrate not only unconscious attachment to a sibling but also how that can take place in the absence of real contact with that sibling.

Although object relations and self-concept are always interrelated, the following two cases provide vivid illustrations of the way that self-image, as affected by the sibling position and relationship, may strongly influence the qualities of adult love relationships.

Miss V. had been talking about the one good and authentic relationship of her thirty-year life, one in which she didn't choose a lame duck, or a psychopathic character, or a man with some obvious flaw to which she remained oblivious until it was too late and until she had lost some valuable sense of herself. She was the youngest of seven children of a dynamic family, with various disturbances among the members. She came into treatment because she was the baby of the family, unable to make judgments without advice from older sisters or brothers. Her next oldest sister suggested she begin therapy, wanting a way out of the dilemma of the younger sister's dependency on her.

In contemplating her trends toward flawed men, Miss V. said meditatively,

> All my siblings knew more than I did so I probably feel less intelligent. So I'm thinking of the flaws in the men I choose, I'm thinking maybe I accept them either because it lessens their imperfections . . . or maybe it's not their problem; it's my imperfections . . . what I'm trying to say is by being the youngest and having the idea that other people know more than me . . . therefore, I'm not smart . . . or imperfect . . . or maybe I'm more comfortable . . . or maybe imperfections are okay with me because I'm not that smart.

In the instance above, the sibling-dominated experience of the world is that one always has to be youngest, therefore last, therefore the loser; or, projected onto another, that the love partner has to be the loser, the reject. She identified herself with reference to the men in her life within a structure that repeated the position she had experienced as one of many children within the family, less able and, by unconscious extension, flawed. Interventions and interpretations here focused on her seeking out or repeating processes of experience in the "mature" love relationship that were instances of the felt, sensed, primary experience as sibling. In this example, the dynamic repetition was from "baby," to "not as able," to "flawed," to "choosing the flawed one."

Mr. J., the younger of two sons, sought treatment in his twenties because of loneliness and isolation. He reported a series of relationships with older women, which began with their being impressed with him and ended with their expressions of dissatisfaction with him as a boyfriend, although they wished to remain his friend. He could never understand why this happened. In exploring the beginnings of these relationships, it became clear that he presented himself in a way that led potential dates to assume that he was older, more accomplished, and wealthier than he was. As the truth began to emerge and the women expressed their disappointment, he felt deeply humiliated by their unwillingness to treat his plans for the future as the equivalent of accomplishments. The women of his own age, who would probably have been more sympathetic to his achievements to date, he saw as mere girls.

Since he had emphasized his closeness and importance to his mother in the face of his father's inadequacy, the oedipal elements in his pursuit of older women was explored in depth. It was not, however, until he mentioned in passing the coincidence of a former girlfriend's and his brother's sharing a birthday (both day and year) that the importance of his sibling relationship (which he had previously dismissed) become more apparent. His quest for older and more accomplished women could be seen as an attempt to turn himself into his brother's peer, who could both compete successfully for his brother's women and be his brother's friend. This dynamic is not in competition with, but rather in addition to, his brother as oedipal substitute for father. As he learned more about his attachment to his brother, and as he arrived at more accurate perceptions of himself and his position in the world, he was able to move in the direction of more appropriate and, therefore, available love objects.

The final example, from the history of psychoanalysis, nicely illustrates how sibling attachment may be reflected in the range of one's adult relationships, as well as in a primary love relationship.

Lou Andreas-Salomé, in her correspondence with Freud (1966), noted that having been a younger sister, with several older brothers who adored her, had the effect of making her feel deeply and profoundly that all men were her brothers. This may well have had a significant influence on her well-known capacity for profound love relationships and friendships with men throughout her life. In her correspondence with Freud, they both made references to her "brothers" within the psychoanalytic circle and her "special" place among them. The experience and expectation of the world as being a place full of loving brothers may lead to a role in life as a woman who is the lover of many men and the sister of many men—a striking example of the potential for forming object relations out of the parameters of the earliest sibling constellations and affects.

We have made a preliminary attempt to represent some variations on the theme of sibling impact on the mature love relationship, variations that are extreme in broadest outline, thus simply reminding us that we may profitably attend to such matters.

We believe that these examples are not unique to our practices but that similar ones could be found in other analysts' practices. It is our hope that by focusing on them, we will be contributing to a further understanding of the historical roots of love in general and of our patients' conflicts in the area of love in particular.

REFERENCES

Abend, S. 1978. Sibling love and object choice. *Psychoanalytic Quarterly* 47:660–61.

Bank, S., and M. Kahn. 1982. *The sibling bond*. New York: Basic Books.

Colonna, A., and L. Newman. 1983. The psychoanalytic literature on siblings. *Psychoanalytic Study of the Child* 38:285–309.

Freud, S. 1909. Analysis of a phobia in a five-year-old boy. *Standard edition* 10:3–149.

———. 1912. The dynamics of transference. *Standard edition* 12:97–108.

———. 1918. From the history of an infantile neurosis. *Standard edition* 17:3–123.

Freud, S., and L. Andreas-Salomé. 1966. *Letters*. Ed. E. Pfeiffer. New York: Norton.

Holmes, J. 1980. The sibling and psychotherapy: A review with clinical examples. *British Journal of Medical Psychology* 53:297–305.

Jones, E. 1953. *The life and work of Sigmund Freud*, vol. 1. New York: Basic Books.

Kiell, N. 1983. *Blood brothers*. New York: IUP.
Kris, M., and S. Ritvo. 1983. Parents and siblings: Their mutual influences. *Psychoanalytic Study of the Child* 38:311–24.
Lesser, R. 1978. Sibling transference and countertransference. *Journal of the American Academy of Psychoanalysis* 6:37–49.
Provence, S., and A. Solnit. 1983. Development-promoting aspects of the sibling experience: Vicarious mastery. *Psychoanalytic Study of the Child* 38:337–51.
Rossner, S. 1985. On the place of siblings in psychoanalysis. *Psychoanalytic Review* 72:457–77.
Soulé, H., ed. 1981. *Frères et soeurs*. Paris: Les Editions ESF.

6. Perversion: The Terror of Tenderness

Leanne Domash

Martin Bergmann (1985) speaks of love as a wish to find the past and a wish to find what the past did not give. Love can contain some optimal proportions of these two aims: the person gravitates to a partner who embodies many of the qualities of the parent but also has qualities that improve on old impasses in the original love relationship. Yet love can also primarily embody *only* the wish to find the past, and when that past object was abusive, the love becomes perverse. Stoller (1975) writes that perversion, the erotic form of hatred, is a fantasy that is usually acted out. Perversion is a habitual, preferred aberration necessary for full satisfaction, which often includes the expression of hostility in sexuality, taking the form of a fantasy of revenge. It serves to convert childhood trauma to adult triumph. Stoller hypothesizes that a perversion is the reliving of actual past sexual trauma, which had been aimed precisely at a person's sex or gender identity. In the perverse act, the original trauma is momentarily overcome. Essential ingredients are a sense of risk and a dehumanization of the object.

Obvious examples of the perverse need for revenge range from murder that sexually excites to other physically sadistic acts such as whipping or cutting a person, defecating or urinating on him or her. More disguised acts of revenge may be expressed by the promiscuous person who has sex mainly for the fantasy of degrading or conquering the partner. Another disguised example is the masochist who endures punishment in order to enjoy a fantasy of revenge on the tormentor.

This essay addresses the group of narcissistically impaired patients who are perverse and who have a need to refind the old, abusive object.

Further, they have a terror of a new, empathic object or of finding any "repair" of the past. This group belongs to the more broadly defined category "narcissistic personality disorder," in which preoedipal determinants, including disorders of the separation-individuation phase of development, are the major factor of the perversion. There are other patients in whom oedipal factors may be primary or who show an interaction of the two. An extensive discussion of these latter factors is beyond the scope of this essay, although the interaction of preoedipal and oedipal factors will be referred to in the clinical example.

The nature of passion and sexual excitement are areas rarely discussed by psychoanalytic investigators. In the case of perversions we are exploring "passionate hate"; in the latter part of this essay we move to "passionate love," including an exploration of the many layers of symbolism involved in the act of intercourse. Aspects of perversions, such as infantile sexuality and the preponderance of aggression, are universal. However, rather than being the central features, as in perversions, they become only one ingredient of many, in mature love. As Fenichel (1945) wrote, observers before psychoanalysis stated that perverse acts are a one-sided, exaggerated distortion of acts that in a less exclusive and definite form can also occur in the sexual behavior of normal persons, especially in the introductory acts before intercourse. Freud (1920) added the observation that perverse tendencies or occasional perverse acts, or at least fantasies, occur in the life of every single individual, in the normal as well as the neurotic. Recently, Stoller (1976) has emphasized that the mechanisms of perversions hold true for an understanding of sexual excitement in normal people as well, but that these mechanisms would be only one ingredient of a mix rather than the main feature.

DYNAMICS

This group of patients who engage in perverse acts fear a tie to a more positive or empathic object because it threatens the tie to, or partial fusion with, the abusive object. They are blocked in their access to the preverbal, empathic bond as a transitional form of mental representation, which is needed as a means to a deep self-object restructuralization in psychoanalysis. To allow a connection to an empathic object would inevitably release rage and then cause a traumatic separation from the abusive object. This separation would bring about a mourning process. According to Gorkin (1984), narcissistic patients are unable to mourn and relinquish the past. Mourning would bring into consciousness their rage at the abuse and then their pain at the loss of the positive tie inherent in their connection to the abusive object. The perversion permits both a denial and a glorification of the rage and a magical reconnection.

Put slightly differently, Reich (1953, 1954, 1960) describes the tie to an old object as one of magical identification resulting in a fused attachment. Rather than going through the separation process that could be required for them to become like the same-sex parent, they follow the path of imitation. Imitation means *to be,* magically, the envied parent and not necessarily *to become* the parent. As they *are* the parent, and do to others what was done to them, there is a sense of revenge and triumph.

The perversion then becomes a haven to protect them from overwhelming rage and separation anxiety. Further, it provides multiple secondary gains: a fulfillment of erotic needs as the pain is libidinized as well as satisfaction of the wish for revenge, an illusory triumph of the grandiose self. It is a reversal of the past and statement of survival, and, in that sense, represents hope. From a different perspective, the repetitive nature of the perversion can be likened to play in children that is ritualized and lacks creative spontaneity. At best, it is blunted creativity.

The focus of this essay is on the preoedipal element in the resistance to forming a positive transference. Yet there can also be oedipal determinants, as well as a frequently powerful interaction of oedipal and preoedipal factors. If there is a self-object tie to an abusive object, the oedipal crisis is fraught with difficulties. For example, one female patient is unable to form a positive father transference because she fears her mother's fury. This failure then causes a regressive defense because of the fear of the mother. At the same time, this patient is partially fused with her abusive mother and unwilling to let the analyst come as a wedge between her and her mother. This partial fusion with the mother makes her less willing to weather the anxieties of the oedipal struggle, fueling her use of a regressive defense. It is clear that oedipal as well as preoedipal factors are operative in the resistance to forming a positive transference.

TREATMENT SITUATION

The treatment situation presents a formidable task for these patients in that it fosters a tie to an empathic analyst. With narcissistically impaired personalities, treatment optimally provides the basis for the development of a mirror or idealizing transference. It is specifically the perverse patient's resistance to forming a narcissistic transference that presents a problem.

In the treatment situation this resistance manifests itself as a need to ward off the empathy of the analyst, who is paradoxically "too good" for them to accept. The tenderness or empathy must be repudiated as the patient clings to the abusive object, either in fantasy or real life. The attitude toward the analyst may range from derisive contempt to bored withdrawal. Kohut (1980) discusses briefly the resistance to forming a narcissistic transference and the importance of analyzing the intense vulnerability of the patient. In addition to extreme vulnerability, I would emphasize the patients' intense need both to preserve the original self-object tie with the abusive object and to ward off the treatment as it directly threatens the maintenance of the original tie. This tie is sometimes preserved by splitting, where a defensive idealization coexists with marked perverse aspects.

Free association severely threatens this psychic structure. It is a danger both to the conscious experience of the self as well as to the experience of the idealized object. If the associative process is attempted prematurely, it can be experienced as a not-me experience. Free association here is being referred to in its relatively pure form, as the patients' being able to report whatever enters his or her mind without prior formulations, agendas, editing, and so on. In this sense, free association, which Bergmann has described as a "love gift" to the analyst, is difficult, if not impossible (1985). In sum, these patients cannot "give" the loving gift of free association to the analyst, nor can they accept the therapeutic love of the analyst: empathy.

Free association also is a threat because it begins to effect separation. As one verbalizes and associates, one begins to give shape to an amorphous, partially fused self and object representation, beginning the separation of self and object. The patient senses that free association would begin to clarify and define his relationship with the old object and foster separation from it, because it both helps mobilize the normal push for growth and individuation and would also force the patient to clarify the abusive qualities of the object, and perhaps shatter the idealization. The patient is less and less able to deny the abusive or inhibiting effects of the "bad" object and can no longer deny the rage. The experience of the rage aids in further separation and allows for the experience of tenderness and also greater choice in finding a new love object. Of course, many diagnostic groups have difficulty with free association and, in some broad sense, the ability to associate freely is the *goal* of analysis. The point of this discussion is to highlight the problems in free association relevant to this group.

Viewed differently, to associate is to sublimate some of the libidinal needs, which helps release the patient from the tie. Sublimation involves desexualization of goals. Sexual and aggressive drives are deflected from direct expression. The associative process is an example of sublimation, the transformation of sexual and aggressive impulses. Clearly, to those with a perverse aspect to their sexuality, this is a threat because it is a request to direct the expression of the sexual and aggressive impulses verbally in the therapy, that is, to deflect their aims more rather than to express them directly in the sexual act. Sublimation is work. Frequently, this patient does not want to give up the magical identification with an object or feel the pain of separating, which is preparatory to normal identification. The sublimatory process of free association begins to foster the processes of separation, mourning, and genuine identification.

Related to the views of Reich expressed earlier, Chasseguet-Smirgel (1974) discusses the relationship among creativity, sublimation, and perversion. She writes that when sublimation does not occur, it is because of certain faults in identification. True sublimation, eventually resulting in creativity, is not possible without good and proper identification. She goes on to say that the sexual pervert is frequently more of an aesthete than a real artist, his work having been hindered by the impossibility of making the paternal identifications necessary to the process of sublimation. Since introjection of the paternal attributes, which normally accompanies the resolution of the Oedipus complex, has not occurred, and the desires linked to this process have been repressed and countercathected, the subject does not possess the necessary sublimated libido to construct his work. She suggests that the work that is produced is frequently more of an imitation or a copy than truly creative. She also notes, however, that the patients described are not always devoid of the capacity to sublimate. The gaps in identification are of varying magnitudes, and there are those who manage to produce authentic and outstanding works.

CLINICAL EXAMPLE

Mr. S. is a thirty-year-old, very intelligent, creative man, who became, over the course of treatment, a highly successful musician. He was beaten as a young child by his father for any demonstration of sexual curiosity, sex play with young children, or masturbation. His mother watched the beatings, in which he was naked, and then comforted him immediately afterwards. His father would also have eruptions of psychotic rage at his mother, including throwing and destroying furniture, while the patient watched in terror. Understandably, fears of castration as a child were intense, and he remembered many dreams from this period in which his penis was cut off and thrown into a pail full of blood.

For the first few years in treatment, contrary to what one would expect given his high intelligence, this patient exhibited a "pseudo" free association where he became tangential, circumstantial, and autistic-like in his productions. At times these associations seemed psychotic. Seemingly unaware of his confusing presentation, he continuously accused me of misunderstanding him. He clung to various perverse activities, including self-flagellation, an addictive involvement with pornography, and a sadomasochistic relationship with his wife. Analysis made it clear that in his frequently belittling, derisive manner toward me, he was, in effect, beating me up as well.

Eventually Mr. S. began to free-associate in the treatment and to feel some measure of being understood. However, the terror at the loss of the abusive object became overwhelming. His wife, who also represented his sadistic father, was threatening that she would leave him if he continued analysis. He fled precipitously from treatment, giving no notice, after having spent a six-month period finally feeling understood and having real hope about the possibility of change.

In this case, some of the dynamic issues include his tie to his abusive father, which he maintained in his perversions, and his fear of forming a positive mother transference to me on an oedipal level because of the retaliation of this feared father. Therefore, for a long time, he was "stuck" in the perversion. To move forward was to both court the father's fury regarding sexuality and to lose whatever self-object connectedness he experienced with him—and, therefore, to be frighteningly alone. He was also convinced that he would permanently lose any erotic pleasure if he gave up the perverse activities. Finally, the perversions gave him a chance to mask his vulnerability by a triumphant expression of his grandiose self as he denied the pain, especially in the acts of self-flagellation.

The analysis of these anxieties and gratifications is a powerful challenge to the analyst. In this patient's case, discussion of his intense vulnerability and his fear of being understood (or his need to be *misunderstood*, hence, his psychotic-like associations) finally helped permit the development of a therapeutic alliance. After he accepted this, he worked with me to help analyze his tendency toward self-destructive behavior in his music work and related business activities. He was able to work more effectively and creatively and to allow powerful sublimation of some of his drives. In a sense, this working through was a rehabilitation of his ego ideal in which I became an authority who was finally not beating him but rather helping him to move forward. Further, empathic reconstructions of the dynamics of the perversion also helped him move ahead. He was able to go through some mourning regarding the loss of the tie to his father. This permitted a more mature identification with the father, who had been very successful in a field allied to the patient's.

Countertransference feelings were intense with this patient, and needed to be continually monitored. I feared I did misunderstand him and felt very alienated at times. At times I experienced different degrees of horror and pity, particularly at his self-flagellation. For a long period, I also felt a certain amount of impotence in his continual destruction of one of the most powerful analytic tools: empathy. It was my sense that the self-analysis of the countertransference provided rich understanding of the parallel processes in the patient. He felt alienated, misunderstood, impotent, pitiful.

DISCUSSION

These patients, especially early in treatment, manifest some aspect of a negative therapeutic reaction in response to the empathy of the analyst. As described by Kohut (1982), the empathic ambience can be overstimulating for patients with abusive histories. Deprived of empathy for so long, the rich diet of the analytic experience is upsetting. For such patients the ability to tolerate care and empathy is a major step in relatedness and is frequently then paralleled by an increasing ability in the self to understand others, especially the analyst.

I want to relate the problems of these patients, their inability to experience empathy and the amount of hostility in sexual excitement, to the nature of mature love. Tenderness is one ingredient of mature love. Passion and sexual excitement are others. Stoller (1976), one of the few writers who have explored this subject, makes the point that some hostility and mastery of hostility is present in most sexual excitement. He writes,

> hostility, overt or hidden, is what generates and enhances sexual excitement, and its absence leads to sexual indifference and boredom. This dominance of hostility in eroticism attempts to undo childhood traumas and frustrations that threaten the development of masculinity and femininity. The same sorts of dynamics, though in different mixes and degrees, are found in almost everyone, those labelled perverse and those not so labelled. (1975, p. 903)

The word *mix* is important, and Stoller does state that for those in the normal range, the overcoming of hostility coexists with affection and closeness. He continues by stating the factors, present in perversions, that he believes contribute to sexual excitement in general: hostility, mystery, risk, illusion, revenge, reversal of trauma or frustration to triumph, safety factors, and dehumanization (fetishization).

Like many others, including Freud, Stoller could not find a precise point on the continuum of sexual behavior that separated normal from perverse. He does suggest that as one proceeds along a continuum toward less use of mechanisms of hostility, one is proceeding from the bizarre (psychotic) through the character disorders diagnosed as perversions and into the range of the normative, where the mechanisms propelling the excitement are energized by hostility but where affection and capacity for closeness also thrive. At the far end of the continuum is a small group of people who enjoy loving, unhostile relationships with someone else and who are not so frightened by intimacy that they must fetishize the other person. And for many, the amount of anger may be of such a minimal degree that the word *hostility* is too strong. Stoller views sexual excitement as a re-creation in fantasy of the traumas of childhood, which everyone experiences at some point as hurt and humiliation, and a subsequent mastery of it through the pleasurable act of intercourse and orgasm.

The notion of hostility in normal sexual excitement makes sense. Given the hurts and humiliation all people endure in the maturing process, it is not surprising that in lovemaking these would be recalled and overcome in a powerfully condensed, pleasurable manner. The hostility is overcome through orgasm within the context of powerful feelings of closeness and affection.

While Stoller emphasizes the mastery of past trauma in sexual excitement, Horner (1985) asks, when is passionate love a manifestation of a new synthesis that creates heightened potential for a mature and intimate relationship? Freud (1914) and subsequent writers have linked falling in love with a sexualized version of his or her own ego ideal. Horner suggests that in individuals with developmental arrests, passionate attachments are more narcissistically determined and have as their aim a completion of a part of the self. This is the distinction Bergmann (1980) makes between *needing*, based on an inadequacy in any one of the subphases described by Mahler (1968), and *loving* in the more evolved individual. Horner suggests that mature passionate love does not involve the defensive idealization of the individual in need but the ability to idealize in the positive sense. She writes,

Such love is, indeed a state of disequilibrium, but one in which there is a potential for re-organization, a re-organization that allows either for the repair of felt deficit, or for a new synthesis in which a widened and enriched sense of self may emerge. (1985, p. 2)

She quotes as an example from Iris Murdoch's *The Sandcastle,*

He wondered for the hundredth time what it was that he wanted from her. . . . He wanted to be the new person that she made of him, the free and creative and joyful and loving person that she had conjured up, striking this miraculous thing out of his dullness. (1978, p. 238)

Horner comments how Murdoch describes the reintegration of repressed aspects of the self of her character within an interpersonal context. In these instances Horner stresses the progressive, creative aspects of passionate love and likens it to the passion of the creative process. In stressing the role of positive idealization, Horner is linking mature love to the maturity (and creativity) of the ego ideal. Previously, we discussed the obverse, namely, Chasseguet-Smirgel's (1974) view of the relationship between perversion and certain distortions or failures in the development of the ego ideal.

With Stoller's concept of sexual excitement and Horner's of mature love comes an additional possibility that may further explicate the power of the experience of intercourse, since it is likely an intense condensation of a myriad of psychological and physical events. In sexual excitement and orgasm, there is an analogy to Winnicott's notion of the path the infant traverses from object relating to object usage. Initially, in object relating, mother and child are merged, and the mother is perceived only subjectively. As part of this process, the infant goes through an experience of faith in the transitional area of illusion. He experiences a sense of freedom linked to a limitless feeling of wholeness prior to raising the question of absolute limits. Attempting to make the object real, the infant then tries to destroy her, and she must survive his attack. The mother becomes the object of the infant's instinctual desires. The destructiveness creates the externality, and the mother is finally a presence no longer taken for granted but appreciated as coming through the potential destruction. This is termed "object usage" by Winnicott (1969).

This process involves a simultaneity of love, destruction, and survival. The infant feels grateful that he can destroy and love the object and that the object survives. He feels that integrity is possible without destroying self or other. Love is strong enough to use destructiveness creatively.

The analogy to intercourse is as follows: The original physical and emotional merger is replicated, and each person goes through a dual feeling of faith (an exultation, a limitless feeling of wholeness, a sense of freedom), a need to destroy (a cataclysmic feeling of violent excitement sometimes coupled with destructive or hostile fantasies of harm or revenge), and finally a need to make the other real and still survive the instinctual attack (the gratitude and affection expressed in afterplay). All these feelings contribute to the sexual excitement and are condensed in the pleasurable act of orgasm and afterplay. Part of the motivation for the afterplay is the renewed appreciation of the otherness of the partner and the gratitude that the partner has both helped one participate in the healing area of faith and survived the instinctual attack. I am postulating these feelings as present in normal, mature loving.

In summary, then, mature love, is a combination of tenderness and passionate sexuality. I would like to offer my definition. *Love* includes the choice of a sexual object in which genital arousal and excitement and capacity for orgasmic pleasure, on the one hand, and feelings of tenderness and caring, on the other, are experienced with a partner in a mutually acceptable manner. The experience is as much a new, creative synthesis as a re-creation of past experiences with original objects. The sexual excitement includes the elements of risk, illusion and mystery, the reversal of childhood traumata, and the original creation of the objective mother by the infant. The aspect of hostile mastery is but one ingredient of a mix in which positive feelings of tenderness and concern predominate.

REFERENCES

Bergmann, M. S. 1980. On the intrapsychic function of falling in love. *Psychoanalytic Quarterly* 49:56–77.
———. 1985. Transference love and love in real life. Colloquium, New York University Postdoctoral Program, Jan. 11, 1985.
Chasseguet-Smirgel, J. 1974. Perversion, idealization and sublimation. *International Journal of Psycho-analysis* 55:349–57.
Fenichel, O. 1945. *The psychoanalytic theory of neurosis*. New York: Norton.
Freud, S. 1914. On narcissism: An introduction. *Standard edition* 14:67–102.
———. 1920. *New introductory lectures on psychoanalysis. Standard edition* 22:1–182.
Gorkin, M. 1984. Narcissistic personality disorder and pathological mourning. *Contemporary Psychoanalysis* 20:400–20.
Horner, A. 1985. Falling in love and the idealization and sexualization of the power attributed to men. Annual Meeting of the American Psychological Association, Los Angeles, Calif., Aug. 25, 1985.
Kohut, H. 1980. Reflections on advances in self psychology: Summarizing reflections. In A. Goldberg, ed., *Advances in self psychology*, pp. 473–555. New York: IUP.
———. 1982. *How does analysis cure?* Chicago: University of Chicago Press.
Mahler, M. 1968. *On human symbiosis and the vicissitudes of individuation*. New York: IUP.
Murdoch, I. 1978. *The sandcastle*. New York: Penguin.
Reich, A. 1953. Narcissistic object choice in women. *Journal of the American Psychoanalytic Association* 1:22–44.
———. 1954. Early identifications as archaic elements in the superego. *Journal of the American Psychoanalytic Association* 2:218–38.
———. 1960. Pathologic forms of self-esteem regulation. *Psychoanalytic Study of the Child* 15:215–32.
Stoller, R. 1975. Sexual excitement. *Archives of General Psychiatry* 33:899–909.
———. 1976. *Perversion: The erotic form of hatred*. New York: Dell.
Winnicott, D. W. 1969. Use of the object and relating through identification. *International Journal of Psycho-analysis*. 50:711–17.

7. Differential Roles of Narcissism in Healthy and Pathological Love Relationships

Michael P. Varga

The narcissistic component of love, the idealizing aspect, which causes us to feel that we are "in love," can work in either of two ways. It can supplement and enhance the "caring," "loving" dimension of love, as it does in healthy love relationships. Or, in pathological love relationships, it can serve to defend against awareness of underlying anger and hostility. Often, in such relationships, there is the experience of being "in love" but there is little actual caring or loving. In this essay, I will explore this dual role of narcissism in love relationships from the perspective of object-relations theory. I hope to show how this perspective may help move our patients' love relationships in the direction of increased mutuality of "caring."

THEORETICAL FORMULATION

In his *Three Essays on the Theory of Sexuality* (1905), Freud states that a person may choose his love object on the basis of either an anaclitic model or a narcissistic model. When the choice follows the anaclitic model, the love object symbolizes, and is chosen because it resembles, the person's parent. When the narcissistic model dominates, the love object symbolizes, and is chosen because of some resemblance to, what the person is, was, or would like to be.

In both healthy and pathological love relationships the love object may be selected (often unconsciously) on a narcissistic basis. Thus, the person reenacts the parent-child relationship, but with the roles reversed: the person unconsciously identifies him or herself with the parent, identifies the other with his or her childhood self, and loves the other as he or she was and would like to have been loved by the parent. The same love object may also, simultaneously, be selected on an anaclitic basis, with the person reenacting the parent-child relationship directly, loving the other as he or she loved the parent. However, I focus on instances in which the love-object choice has a narcissistic basis because we are thereby better enabled to grasp the role of defensive idealization in love relationships. This heightened understanding, in turn, facilitates our psychotherapeutic work in helping the patient's defensive idealization give way to normal idealization, leading to greater mutuality of caring in the patient's love relationships.

My basic theoretical paradigm, based on a predominantly object-relations perspective, is as follows: In healthy love relationships, given that there was a preponderance of object-related love or caretaking in the parent's rearing of the person, the person, in turn, is predominantly loving or caring toward his or her love object. The idealizing component is a necessary but subsidiary aspect of the healthy love relationship. It reflects the narcissistic investment that the parent had made in rearing the person, the idealizing sense of ownership, pride, and aspirations surrounding desirable qualities in the person, which the person, in turn, invests in his or her love object. This idealizing component provides the "in love" dimension to supplement the "loving" dimension of the healthy love relationship. The erotic, passionate component of the healthy love relationship embodies the drive to unite sexually with the love object, experienced both as the cared-for self and as the embodiment of idealized qualities of the self.

In pathological love relationships, it is assumed that there was a deficiency of object-related love or caretaking in the parent's rearing of the person, in some form of neglect or overt hostility. The person in turn is preponderantly neglectful and hostile in the caretaking aspect of his or her relationship to the love object. It should be noted, however, that the negative parental representation identified with may not be entirely veridical with the actual parent, since elements of the person's reactive rage may be fused into the representation as well. Since the person strives to love the love object as he or she would like to have been loved, however, there is a need to defend against this reenactment of neglect or hostility in the relationship to the love object. This the person does by relating to the love object predominantly in terms of the idealizing component, loving the other as an embodiment of idealized qualities of the self, and splitting off or repressing the negative caretaking aspects of the love relationship as much as possible. In such pathological love relationships, the person tends to be "in love" with the love object when very little loving or caring is present in the relationship. The erotic, passionate component of the pathological love relationship embodies the drive to unite sexually with the love object, experienced as an embodiment of idealized qualities of the self, but with the warded-off meaning of discharging aggression against the neglected or hated self.

Before turning to case material, let me briefly place the paradigm within the context of existing theory. The role that idealization plays in pathological love relationships has been discussed from a similar point of view by Reich (1953). She describes women whose narcissistic object choice largely serves a defensive function in relation to the underlying anger and hostility that these women feel towards their love objects. My formulations, in addition, include an object-relations perspective wherein both a projective identification of idealized self-representations onto the love object and a concomitant identification of the self with the parental object representations, a form of reverse transference, are seen as underlying the narcissistic object choice. Kernberg (1976) and Volkan (1976) have documented the prevalence of reverse transference in borderline and narcissistic character pathology. Racker (1968) has described working with reverse transference processes as a major aspect of psychoanalytic treatment at all levels of psychopathology. We may note the presence of reverse transference in healthy individuals in the frequent observation that becoming a parent brings to the surface formerly unconscious identification with one's own parent. As for the prevalence of the idealizing, "in love" aspect of healthy love relationships, the psychoanalytic literature on this extends back to Freud's observations in *Group Psychology and the Analysis of the Ego* (1921) regarding the projection of one's ego ideal onto the love object, leading to the idealizing quality of normal love relationships. Blos (1962) has described such a relinquishment of one's contrasex ego ideal to the heterosexual love object as a necessary step in the formation of heterosexual identity.

CASE ILLUSTRATIONS

The first case is of a clearly pathological love relationship, the second of a less disturbed relationship.

Ms. A., a thirty-three-year-old physician, came to treatment in crisis around a very turbulent love affair, which had extended over the past year. Her lover, a painter with a bohemian lifestyle, had initially been strongly attracted to her, delighting in her extremely articulate, witty, and knowledgeable manner. Although at first not very attracted to him, she had felt quite gratified by his intensely adoring attitude toward her, and so entered into an affair with him. The first few weeks of the relationship were ecstatic, with passionate, prolonged periods of lovemaking, resulting in her feeling that all boundaries were down between the two of them. After several weeks, he abruptly began to withdraw from her, looking for opportunities to be away and acting coldly toward her. He talked of past affairs and implied that one of them, in particular, had been more meaningful to him than his relationship to her was, and that given the opportunity he would choose to return to the previous relationship.

Ms. A. began to develop severe panic at the thought of losing him. On several occasions when he expressed reluctance to specify future dates for their getting together she threw scenes in public. On another occasion she showed up at an exhibition of his work, to which she had not been invited, in order to see him, and then pressured him to take her to a bar afterward, in order to plead with him to revive their relationship. As they saw each other less and ended their sexual relationship, Ms. A. came to feel more and more isolated and desperate. She came into treatment for help with her feelings about this relationship, which obsessed her to the point of interfering seriously with her capacity to function at work and vitiating her motivation to keep up relations with friends and colleagues.

Examining the psychodynamics of this pathological love relationship, Ms. A. was most readily aware of the transference meaning of her lover as a frustrating, unavailable father figure, modeled after her own father, who had been away from home for extended periods while she was growing up, and was frustratingly unavailable to both Ms. A. and her mother. Ms. A. was also readily aware of her identification with her mother, which showed itself in the desperate way in which she attempted to cling to her lover as her mother had to her father, by behaving in an extremely intrusive, controlling fashion, which, she felt, drove away her boyfriend as her mother had driven away her father. Ms. A. was much less aware of the extent to which her lover embodied her own ego ideal, modeled after the roving father, of being an independent, free spirit. She was also not in contact with the parallel between her lover's reaction of withdrawal and coldnesss to her controlling intrusiveness and her own cold, indifferent reaction to her hysterical, intrusive mother.

We may note that Ms. A. further defended against expression of her underlying object-related hostility in this relationship by splitting it off into relationships with other men. With a series of would-be and intermittent lovers, seen over this same period, she was aware of adopting a cold, manipulative, depriving attitude, which she readily identified as similar to the attitude she had taken toward her younger brother in growing up. At the same time, she also identified this attitude as that of her mother toward her, in treating her as a doll-like object to be fussed over out of the mother's needs but cast aside in terms of Ms. A.'s own needs. Ms. A. was also in touch with the fear that if her idealized lover were not so fiercely independent, she might dominate him in a manipulative fashion as well, so that he would be as worthless to her as her other exploitable lovers.

The second case, Ms. J., a thirty-year-old secretary, also came into treatment around difficulties in her love relationship. For the previous four years, she had been exclusively involved (although living apart from) a man she very much loved, who was rather critical toward her and begrudged showing her physical affection. She saw him as being like her father, who had been critical toward her while she was growing up, largely, she felt, because of his disappointment over not having a son. She also readily identified her difficulties in standing up to her boyfriend as parallel to her mother's domination by her father, in both cases because she saw the man as far more intelligent than the woman.

The idea of looking for a reverse transference hidden beneath Ms. J.'s masochistic posture vis-à-vis her lover was first suggested by a review of Ms. J.'s abortive first love relationship. She had ended this short-lived marriage because she had felt too much the "man" in the relationship, too much in control, and critical toward her husband, so that despite his being more supportive than her current boyfriend she could not love him.

The assumption was made that Ms. J.'s masochistic posture with her current lover defended against awareness and expression of her underlying identification with the dominant, critical father. Her difficulties in self-assertion with her lover were interpreted along the lines of her concerns that to have her way with the lover made her into the kind of cruel domineering person that her father was. Ms. J. began to get in touch with how much she did in fact identify with her lover's underlying vulnerability and how much she feared hurting him, because she knew how devastating it felt when she had been hurt by her father's cruelty toward her. Concomitant with her increasing awareness of this underlying reverse transference, Ms. J. began increasingly to assert herself with her lover: she requested and received more consistent and attentive lovemaking; she ceased letting him browbeat her in verbal exchanges over his lack of consideration toward her; she ceased centering her personal life totally around him and his schedule, balancing her time with him against the pursuit of independent interests, despite his insecurities over her doing so. As Ms. J. increasingly asserted herself, the love relationship began to shift away from one-sided idealization of and caretaking devotion to the lover on her part toward increasing mutuality of respect and caretaking. Although still admiring her lover's intelligence and verbal facility, Ms. J. no longer felt hopelessly outclassed by him in these regards and increasingly reported evidence of her lover's growing admiration of her own cleverness in handling various social situations. In response to her decreased toleration of inconsiderateness on his part, the lover began also to show sensitivity for her needs consonant with her sensitivity to his needs. As she moved in the direction of health in her love relationship, Ms. J. became increasingly comfortable with self-assertion in her work and began preparing herself for a career in editing by returning to college.

In summary, I have attempted to show how both highly pathological and relatively healthy love relationships may exhibit an aspect of the relationship dominated by a reverse transference, in which the person loves the other as he or she was loved by the parent. Further, to the extent that the person felt uncared for or hated by the parent, the person defends against awareness or expression of this neglect or hostility by defensive idealization of the lover. The neglect or hostility is then split off into other relationships, as in the love relationship of the first case, or repressed and acted out through masochistic reaction formations, as in the neurotic love relationship of the second case. A significant aspect of treatment in these cases consists of bringing to awareness the underlying identification with the hostile or neglectful parent, thus diminishing the compulsive reenactment of hostility or neglect. This enables the love relationship to move in the direction of increasing mutuality of caretaking. Also, the one-sided idealization, which had served as a defense against underlying hostility, becomes increasingly mutual and subsidiary to the caretaking aspects of the relationship, thus providing the "in love" dimension of a predominantly "loving" or caretaking relationship.

REFERENCES

Blos, P. 1962. *On adolescence.* New York: Free Press.
Freud, S. 1905. *Three essays on the theory of sexuality. Standard edition* 7:123–243.
———. 1921. *Group psychology and the analysis of the ego. Standard edition* 18:65–143.
Kernberg, O. F. 1976. *Object relations theory and clinical psychoanalysis.* New York: Aronson.
Racker, H. 1968. *Transference and countertransference.* London: Hogarth.
Reich A. 1953. Narcissistic object choice in women. *Journal of the American Psychoanalytic Association* 1:22–44.
Volkan, W. 1976. *Primitive internalized object relations: A clinical study of schizoid, borderline, and narcissistic patients.* New York: IUP.

8. Fantasies of Love and Rescue in Fatherless Adolescent Boys

Patrick R. Lane

This essay is concerned with aspects of love of fatherless adolescent boys as it appears in the transference. Before focusing on this special population, it makes sense to look at adolescence in general and specifically the adolescent's developmental task of confronting and dealing with "this thing called love." Teenagers have the awesome responsibility of mastering the maturational forces of heightened libidinal urges and desires at a time when important physical as well as psychic changes are emerging. Their egos and self-identities are in the process of consolidation and integration, and final adaptation is taking place.

Adolescence has two primary aspects: the revival of the Oedipus complex and the disengagement from primary love objects (Blos 1962). It is the task of adolescence to give up the oedipal objects, gradually mourn them, establish a new object love, and fall in love. The state of loving a new object is marked by a heightened sense of completeness, sentiment, and a sense of belonging. Adolescent boys' earlier roughhousing sex play is gradually replaced by a sense of tenderness and concern for a particular love object. The resurgence of fear of dependency and emotional surrender and struggles with ambivalence often accompany this phase. Earlier attachment history to the mother (parents) can serve as the source of repetitive conflict in adolescence as well as in adult life.

Preoedipal forerunners of the oedipal resolution are reawakened. In the classical view adolescents are once again drawn to and repulsed by earlier feelings and conflicts in the context of their current social and psychological milieus. Preoedipal experiences that may have involved trauma and narcissistic injuries, particularly if faced with narcissistic and frustrating parents, can ultimately be the frame for further resolutions involving love and object choice in adolescent and adult life (Miller 1986).

The most important attachment figure for a child is usually the mother. The importance of the father cannot be minimized, however, as research reported later in this essay suggests. If conscious or unconscious aggression and sexuality is sensed in interactions with parents, the adolescent may become insecure, frightened, and confused and acquiesce to their wishes rather than face rejection. This drama can often be the underlying theme in the adolescent quest for finding and experiencing love. It is therefore crucial to have a thorough understanding of an adolescent's developmental history with accompanying conflicts present in the current clinical picture. The tendency to repeat what was initially experienced will undoubtedly resurface in relatedness and attachment behaviors during adolescence.

The history of the adolescent's relation to and separation from the mother including pleasure and distress of self-body boundaries, object constancy, and inner representation of self and object and more sophisticated development of object relations, ego organization, and development of defense (Pine 1985) are crucial to their adaptation to these instinctual cravings as they intensify during adolescence.

The phase-adequate adolescent ego can only develop appropriately if the previous phase of the latency period has been more or less successfully experienced. The pre-adolescent with a scarred latency period will not be able to deal with tasks required in puberty and will revert to preoedipal and infantile phases of conflict. To cope with puberty, the ego needs the achievements of the latency phase (Blos 1962). These include an increase in inner self and object representation, a tendency away from regression, a more sophisticated superego and self-critical ego, an increase in verbal interactions through higher language acquisition, and finally mastery of the environment through the use of secondary-process thinking.

Early adolescence highlights the ego in transition. The ego ideal gradually takes over during a time when early object ties and detachment from the oedipal parent occurs. Sexual identification heightens as adolescents become interested in members of the opposite sex. Boys tend to be predatory in approaching girls at this age. Awkward play often precedes actual experimentation.

In middle adolescence love emerges which consists of heightened eroticism and sentimentality leading to tenderness, devotion, and a special idealization of the love object that must be preserved at all costs.

The late-adolescence phase-specific task is the consolidation of the self. Self-representation and integrity become stable and fixed as consolidation occurs. A period of homeostasis takes place as infantile conflicts are tamed. Ego identity takes its formal shape (Erikson 1974). The ability to love and hate becomes particularly set. The late adolescent is able to put to rest earlier oedipal and preoedipal conflicts, and his self-identity becomes stable and syntonic. Failure to accomplish these developmental tasks leads to possible breakdown with accompanying borderline and psychotic conditions.

In this chapter, I present a description of three fatherless adolescent boys who have failed to meet these phase-specific tasks in preadolescence. Actual experiences of abandonment by their fathers play an almost irreversible role in their acting out and the reenactments of earlier traumas color their search for identity, love, and trust.

THE ROLE OF THE FATHER

The impact of fathering on child development has been a controversial issue. Many theorists have assumed that the mother-infant interaction is unique and vastly more important than any other subsequent relations. In fact, Bowlby (1951) and Freud (1923) explicitly see the mother-infant relationship as the prototype of all later love relationships.

More recently, however, research has been carried out on the role of the father as an attaching figure with the infant. It is beginning to be recognized that fathers have always had a significant impact on children, whether they function as single parents or within the nuclear family. Father absence or inadequacy clearly has deleterious effects on children, although specific data about the effects of fathering or lack thereof on children is still unavailable. Research thus far has been limited both by scope and inadaquacies of measurement instruments and by biases on the part of social scientists.

K. Alison Clark-Stewart (1978) states, "Fathers are no longer forgotten—but the nature of their role and their contribution to children's development remains uncharted and unknown" (p. 466). Clearly their absence can produce lasting and permanent reactions in their children.

Therefore, fantasies of love and rescue by the father appear frequently in the treatment of these three adolescent boys. The fantasies often manifested themselves through and became an integral part of the transference and were used in facilitating change in the patient's pathology. It is important to describe these fantasies in depth and to understand them in the context of current analytic theory. Examination of specific transference interventions aimed at producing change and growth in acting-out and severely disturbed adolescent boys will be explored. Particular attention will be paid to transference love, idealization, and development of an ego ideal.

Fantasies about rescue by the biological father or the therapist have many meanings and implications. There are, however, certain underlying universal dynamics relevant to these fantasies. The wishes of these patients to identify with a father figure in order to strengthen their inner sense of male identification, as well as to gain a more cohesive self, are prominent. Their need to identify with their unknown fathers also represents a wish to emulate these men as they struggle against strong recurring preoedipal wishes and emerging sexuality.

Rescue fantasies can also be interpreted as defenses against strong abandonment rage and depression resulting from actual desertion and isolation from a much-needed male figure. These defenses often manifest themselves masked in overidealization of the missing parent and denigration of the present one.

When these fantasies appear in the transference the therapeutic alliance can be reinforced. The emergence of a particular transference love and idealization is necessary for the continuation of deeper and more intensive work with these difficult cases.

The fantasy to be rescued by the biological father was revealed in statements such as, "My father can help me get out of this mess—I wish I could find him." "I wish I could be like him." "Could you help me find him?" Often the fantasies, when further explored, encompassed the therapist in idealizing transference statements such as, "I wish you could be like my father and come to school and get me out of trouble." "You are good for me." "I wish I spent more time with you—things would be better for me." One patient stated rather directly, "Can I go home with you?" "Do you have a son my age?"

Clearly these statements express the patient's overt wish for contact with a male figure as well as wishes for a male ego ideal necessary for the establishment of a more consolidated and integrated core self.

The allowance and encouragement of this kind of transference love is a necessary technique for the establishment of a positive working alliance and will be emphasized in the presentation of each of the three cases.

The need for rootedness and identity have been recognized as important variables and forerunners in the development of a healthy self-concept, adult maturity, and satisfactory object relations. Recent investigations have recognized the need for adopted children when adults to seek out their biological parents, and even legal barriers once preventing this from becoming a reality have since been revised. The studies have revealed mixed and varying outcomes. Some adults who found their biological parent reported a greater inner sense of historical connectedness, which they had previously experienced as missing. Many adults, however, were terribly disappointed and actually came away from the experience bewildered and psychologically harmed.

All three patients were in conflict with their mothers and the school at the time of admission to the clinic. Each mother was in collusion with her son's acting-out behavior. All three mothers overtly identified their first-born son with the denigrated missing father, constantly making negative remarks such as, "He's no good—just like his father; he seems just like him—he even walks like him." Two of the boys had a stepfather in the home with whom they were in conflict. Their mothers often gave mixed messages as to her allegiances. All three boys felt confused and ambivalent about their mothers and exhibited a marked underlying depressive core to their personalities. These patients, however, were able to develop strong transference reactions and were able to benefit from analytic therapy. This was partly due in two of three cases to good maternal care in phase-specific early developmental stages. Their family patterns, developmental history, their perception of acceptance and rejection from parents and significant others, and resolutions are four factors considered by Nielsen (1983) to be predictive in adolescent acting-out and borderline conditions. No one factor can explain the adolescent behavior.

Peter Blos (1962), in a paper on predelinquency in adolescence, points to actual or emotional desertion as a predisposing and necessary element in acting-out or delinquent behavior. He dismisses the instinct gratification theory as well as the theory of the missing superego as outdated descriptions for delinquent-type behavior in favor of more contemporary considerations of ego pathology. Blos further reports that the puzzling elements of the adolescent's acting-out behavior result from an incapacity to internalize conflict and its projected alloplastic outcomes in conflict with the outside world. Jacobson (1964) suggested the presence of strong masochistic trends in acting-out adolescents. Their need to act out is punished by a punitive superego, which provides its own form of gratification. Boys cling to an ego ideal—father—and he is seen as a wish-fulfilling force to help them with the painful experience of the reality of their lives.

Contemporary theorists (Kernberg 1978; Masterson 1982; Nielsen 1983) explain the acting-out behavior in adolescence as a developmental failure in which good and bad self-representations are not integrated into a total self-concept. They attribute this to a failure in integrating idealized and sadistic forerunners of the superego, thereby not allowing realistic images of the parents to emerge. These images become distorted by powerful projective processes and foster primitive identifications and a lack of differentiation and integration. They can often result in depressive conditions of a borderline nature.

The object-relations view of the acting-out tendency is similar. Winnicott (1965) suggested that there is a severe emotional deprivation in acting-out patients and that the trauma was experienced during the early toddler stage. Winnicott further noted that the acting-out patient perceives his environment as failing him in ego support and that the ensuing acting-out tendency is in a sense an attempt at a cure for this lost internal object and experience.

These patients often have lacked empathic understanding and have experienced only the ambivalent side of love which can result in a lack of intimacy in their adult lives. These attachment difficulties and the incapacity to experience love in a phase-appropriate manner reflect serious developmental failures with ensuing conflicts signified by anxiety, guilt, aspects of shame, and pathological character traits affecting the self-identificatory process.

It is this author's intention to show how these three patients' lack of impulse control and acting-out tendencies are a result of early emotional desertion, lack of appropriate male figures for healthy identification, and the mother's identifying the patient with the denigrated missing male who acted out as well. In a sense, one way of retaining or recapturing an idealized connection with father is to be just like him. One patient revealed such merger fantasies on projective material in which he and his lost father would go off acting out together against a perceived sadistic society.

CASE I

Max is a thirteen-year-old black male born out of wedlock to a fourteen-year-old mother and a fifteen-year-old father whom he never knew. He was brought to the clinic because of stealing and alcoholic abuse in junior high school. He revealed in the intake that drinking made him feel better—less lonely and less depressed. He stated that he hated school and felt bored despite above-average potential and that he was very unhappy at home with his stepfather, mother, and four younger siblings. The patient reported he had few friends and that he joined gangs as a way of establishing contact with peers.

Although his mother was supportive of him, she often identified the patient with his acting-out biological father who was in jail for robbery. She subtly encouraged conflict between her current husband and her son as a way of acting out her own anguish in the marriage. The patient was seen in individual and family therapy for seventeen sessions and revealed strong wishes to find his biological father and to live with him. He actually made attempts to make this a reality. Psychological testing results revealed an adolescent with psychopathic trends, with strong depressive/melancholic features, poor superego development, and anxiety around identifications.

Max explicitly stated in sessions that he had been able to find out where his father was. Further exploration of the fantasy revealed Max's hope that his father could provide sustenance, a needed sense of connectedness and relatedness with a male figure. He stated that circumstances prevented his father from rescuing him but that he would never desert his family when he became an adult and parent. He thought that the most important thing a father can do is to stay with his family and make them feel loved and wanted, something he had not experienced with his stepfather.

There were clear rivalrous oedipal feelings between the patient and his stepfather over his mother's primary allegiance. She admitted feeling torn between both, with ambivalent feelings toward her current husband, and even admitted that she encouraged the patient to act like a substitute father/husband. This threw the patient into further conflicts heightening his confusion around sexuality and identification. He found necessary release in acting-out behavior.

His rescue fantasies were clear wishes for alleviation from these contradictory and conflicting feelings towards mother as he entered adolescence. His rescue fantasies can be viewed as wishes for security and comfort—to make up for his abandonment by his father and heal his depressive trends.

CASE 2

Daniel is an appealing, light-skinned thirteen-year-old Puerto Rican black youngster who was referred for behavioral and conduct problems in school and at home. One of his first remarks during the intake interview was, "Why do people have children if they don't know how to raise them?" The patient lives with his mother who gave birth to him at age sixteen years. His father was twenty-one years old. Both parents had lived in foster homes and had had rather turbulent backgrounds.

The patient's parents divorced when Daniel was a young child. For the previous year, the mother had been living with a boyfriend and reported Daniel and the boyfriend to have many conflicts. Daniel described his mother as very withholding and as not knowing how to care for him.

He came to my office one winter night, panicked and tearful. He had received a bad report from school, and his mother was furious. Daniel did not want to go home for fear of severe punishment from his mother and boyfriend. The patient suggested that I call his father. He had not seen him in many years, but said he knew where he lived. With the mother's agreement I contacted the father, who came to my office and "rescued Daniel."

After staying with the father for approximately four months, Daniel slowly revealed that his father was abusing him sadistically. At one point, his father in a rage beat the youngster with a metal pipe and locked him in the closet for several hours. Daniel was then immediately returned to live with his mother. His behavior improved somewhat in school and at home with only occasional outbursts.

During the course of treatment Daniel's fantasies of love and rescue were revealed in the sessions. Prior to his placement with his father, he continuously verbalized his wish to live with him. He idealized his father and thought he would be able to satisfy his wish for the love and care he was not receiving from his retentive mother. Often he would set up situations in treatment (by staying outside my door after the session was over, bringing me gifts and asking if I could see him on the weekends, soliciting other staff and personnel) to get me to rescue him from his bleak life. Strong countertransference feelings, namely, my wish to rescue him, were, in part, induced by the patient.

Daniel is an angry youngster with strong masochistic trends brought on by rather severe abandonment. His acting out reflects his yearning for attention as well as his rage at the kind of treatment he was receiving from his parents.

CASE 3

José was twelve years old when brought to the clinic by his mother and grandmother. He was acting out at school and at home. He was described as hyperactive in school, with attention and concentration deficits. At home José was described as disobedient. He lived with mother, grandmother, and a sister four years older. The parents were divorced, and the father lived with his new family in Brooklyn. He visited and supported José and his mother. José's mother openly identified José with his father, denigrating both, and projected onto José the angry feelings she had toward her husband. José, in turn, idealized his father and viewed him as a kind of superman, making statements such as, "My father could help me calm down and straighten out," and "He's a great guy and I hope I can turn out like him." Obviously strong, unconscious resentment toward the father's rejection was masked by such idealizing feelings. As the treatment proceeded, the patient formed a close attachment with me and was quite open about his need to see me more often, perhaps on weekends. He would ask me if I had a son his age, and exploring this fantasy he named my son "José" and developed a fantasy that barely masked his strong wishes to be rescued by me.

At one point during the treatment José's father asked to see me, and we discussed José's dilemma. The patient's father, obviously experiencing guilt, requested that I see José on weekends and that he would pay extra for it.

José was able to develop some controls through his experience in treatment and identification with a positive mirroring self-object from which he could gain internal control of ambivalent feelings toward both parents and toward his dilemma in life.

Countertransference again involved rescue fantasies on my part, partially induced by the patient's strong wishes. Discussion with colleagues and self-analysis helped me to see clearly that José's wishes for my saving him were masking angry resentful feelings he had toward his father for the impossible situation he was placed in, reflected in his abandonment-depressive feelings.

In summary, fantasies involving the wish to be rescued by the biological father have important meanings and repercussions. In all three cases the boys' rescue fantasies represented an identificatory wish for a father figure to help the adolescent deal with an identity crisis. The need for security, rootedness, and belongingness, to offset long-term depressive feelings, were clearly present in the wishes. Interestingly, in two patients, there were partial to full rescues by the biological father with immediate symptom alleviation. However, long-term effects were less optimistic, and the prognosis for repetition of pathological attachments in adulthood is extremely high. Finally, and most noteworthy, these rescue fantasies are deep yearnings for comfort, closeness, and that special relationship each boy needs with a loving and caring father. Through the evolution of a therapeutic loving relationship, both real and transferential, their treatments were greatly enhanced.

REFERENCES

Bowlby, J. 1951. Maternal care and mental health. World Health Organization Monograph. Series #2.
Blos, P. 1962. *On adolescence.* New York: Free Press.
Clark-Stewart, K. A. 1978. And baby makes three: The father's impact on mother and young child. *Child Development* 1:466–78.
Erikson, E. H. 1974. *Dimensions of a new identity.* New York: Norton.

Freud, S. 1912. The dynamics of transference. *Standard edition* 12:97–108.
———. 1923. *The ego and the id. Standard edition* 19:12–66.
Jacobson, E. 1964. *The self and the object world.* New York: IUP.
Kernberg, O. 1978. The diagnosis of borderline conditions in adolescence. In S. Feinstein and P. Giovacchini, eds., *Adolescent psychiatry* 6:298–319 Chicago: University of Chicago Press, 1978.
Masterson, J. 1982. *Narcissistic and borderline conditions.* New York: McGraw-Hill.
Miller, A. 1986. *Thou shalt not be aware.* New York: New American Library.
Nielsen, G. 1983. *Borderline and acting-out adolescents.* New York: Human Sciences Press.
Pine, F. 1985. *Developmental theory and clinical process.* New Haven: Yale University Press.
Searles, H. 1979. *Countertransference and related subjects—Selected papers.* New York: IUP.
Winnicott, D. W. 1965. *The maturational processes and the facilitating environment.* New York: IUP.
———. 1969. *The child, the family and the outside world.* Baltimore: Pelican.

9. Falling in Love and Being in Love: A Developmental and Object-Relations Approach

Eileen J. Setzman

Michael Balint said that the "aim of all human striving is to be able to love in peace" (1965, p. 67). Yet the experience of being in love eludes many individuals. What have our patients told us about what prevents them from "loving in peace"? How can psychoanalytic theory inform us about what prevents love relationships from maturing? These are the issues I will address in this chapter.

There is a qualitative, meaningful distinction that can be made between falling in love and being in love. Almost all individuals have experienced the kaleidescope of feelings that they call "falling in love." Consciously these are experienced as excitement, rapture, fantasy, and idealization. Unconsciously, there is often a tantalizing and unobtainable aspect to the love object. The lover tends to be seen through the perspective of one's own needs, arousing the fantasy that this person will meet all the unfulfilled needs from childhood.

The capacity to be in love—an enduring, object-related, and satisfying relationship—is more difficult to achieve. The reality of a relationship requires a reconciliation of the good with the bad and the pleasurable with the unpleasurable aspects of the lover. When a person is in love, the needs of the other become more important.

Several analytic theorists have described the difference between falling in love and being in love. According to Heinz Kohut, "Our relationships with others can be understood in terms of whether we are actually loving them as others or loving them as parts of ourself. . . . There is no love relationship without mutual mirroring and idealization" (1977,

p. 122). Freud said that love is built on the quality of the love which is reciprocated: "Loving in itself, in so far as it involves longing and deprivation, lowers self regard; whereas being loved, having one's love returned, and possessing the love object raises it once more" (1914, p. 99).

Winnicott defined falling in love as "the fantasy of finding someone who has the time and inclination to know what is needed and fulfill it" (1976, p. 72). Meissner defines being in love as "having the capacity within the self for engaging in, maintaining, and gaining meaningful gratifications from object relations" (1981, p. ix). From an object-relations perspective the emphasis is on "the distinction between love which recognizes the needs and reality of the other and that which fails to, which usually is made by contrasting object-love and infantile or dependent love" (Rycroft 1968, p. 85).

Being in love and falling in love are in large part two different forms of love and styles of relating. I believe they are outgrowths of early object relations that occur during crucial stages of development. Falling in love in no way suggests pathology in and of itself. It is part of normal development. Crushes or puppy love, which can occur at any age, may include a search for a mate or a period of experimentation; they are ways of learning about oneself in an intimate dyadic relationship outside the family. When a person falls in love repeatedly without its ever maturing into a state of being in love, or when the love relationship remains stagnant or nonevolving, it does indicate pathology.

Many people who present themselves for treatment have experienced considerable difficulties in maintaining a satisfying, enduring love relationship. Often they have had some experience falling in love sometimes compulsively, but rarely staying in love. From an object-relations perspective their love relationships are based on a defensive style of relating—a relationship with split-off objects in their inner world that prevent them from developing and maintaining real relationships in the external world. This defensive style, which evolved during childhood to protect the self from intolerable pain or frustration, forces them to live in the outer world with the emotions generated from the inner world.

One patient, Ms. E., came to treatment in distress that her love life seemed stagnant and repetitive. She described finding fault with every man she dated. After several sessions I hypothesized that she had come into treatment because of the conflict between the idealization of her father and, by extension, all men, and the reality of her unfulfilling relationships.

Since the age of fifteen, Ms. E. had had several intense, long-lasting love relationships, ranging from two to three years to her current affair, which has been on going for seven years. From multiple and detailed descriptions of these relationships a pattern emerged. Initially, Ms. E. began each relationship assuming that she had met "Mr. Right". In her words, "he had the right chemistry." These men adored her, took her out to exciting places, and bought her expensive presents. After several months of this kind of courtship, she would perceive the relationship as "dead," and yet she would remain with this man until she encountered the next Mr. Right. Each new relationship brought with it new hope, the fantasy that this new boyfriend would make her alive. Her ideals and expectations were, of course, never met, and she would experience total and complete despair and disappointment.

In the therapeutic exploration of her relationships with her parents, two central insights emerged. First, her father, who presented himself as charming and superior to everyone, consistently found fault with every man she dated. No one was good enough for her. He was a greedy man who had "captured" her for himself and chose not to share her with anyone. Second, her mother, a distant, beautiful, and compliant woman, did little to encourage her daughter's independence and exploration of the world. The overbearing father and passive, enveloping mother effectively stifled and crushed the young girl's individuation. These perceptions were followed by a growing awareness that she was still maintaining her relationships with the parent imagos. The insight that her interaction with men mirrored a child with its parents helped Ms. E. to look more realistically at her current relationships and to decipher how she felt about them.

In the case of another patient, Ms. D., we can see an aspect of love that Freud described, how longing and deprivation can be wounding to self-esteem. As will be seen in the following description, Ms. D.'s self-esteem was directly related to the other person's response to her.

Ms. D., age forty-one, had recently attended a convention in Montreal. While there she said she fell in love with a chemist. They spent the week together, with both of them attending professional meetings during the day, and socializing every evening. When Ms. D. returned, she passionately reviewed every word they had exchanged and marveled at the ecstatic feeling of being in love again after five years of feeling hopeless and alone. Some of her fantasy comes alive in her words: "He was so wonderful; I felt he could fill in all that I had ever lacked. We had no barriers between us. He was my Prince Charming . . . and I was his Sleeping Beauty waiting to be awakened. We vowed never to be separate from one another." When this man did not write or return her calls, Ms. D. felt abandoned and was devastated. She became withdrawn and depressed, and experienced an enormous decrease in her self-esteem. The loss of this idealized perfect relationship dealt her an excruciatingly painful narcissistic injury. Her longing for the good mother went unabated.

In this first section I have explored some of the difficulties in loving that patients present in therapy. In the next section, I will discuss some of the theoretical approaches which guide my clinical work, and then present some additional case material.

A DEVELOPMENTAL AND OBJECT-RELATIONS PERSPECTIVE ON LOVE

The distinction between falling in love and being in love requires an understanding of the importance of the satisfactory completion of certain tasks during age-appropriate stages of emotional development, including the quality of the object relationship with the primary caretakers. There is a maturational timetable for normal psychic development as well as for physical development. The psychological developments include specific developmental sequences. These sequences consist of a momentous journey out of oneness with the mother, to separation, followed by individuation (Mahler 1968; Mahler, Pine, and Bergman 1975), the formation of internal structure (A. Freud 1965), and a capacity for and specific style of object relations (Winnicott 1958). Most patients have experienced difficulties with one or more of the normal developmental stages, or some of the essential tasks in a stage.

According to Kernberg, object relations,

is a psychoanalytic approach to the internalization of interpersonal relations, the study of how interpersonal relations determine interpsychic structure and how these intrapersonal structures preserve, modify, and reactivate past internalized relations with others in the context of present interpersonal relations. Object relations theory deals with the interaction between the internal world of objects (the internalized relations with others) and the actual interpersonal relations of the individual (1970, p. 1).

It is important to note that the word *object* "refers to the whole person . . . not to connote an inanimate object or person treated as inanimate" (Kosseff 1975, p. 213). Guntrip had indicated to Kosseff his preference for the term *personal relations theory* rather than *object relations theory*. This chapter will follow the more common practice of using the term *object relations*.

At the beginning of life the newborn requires an environment that adapts to it. If the environment fails to adapt, it is experienced as an intrusion or impingement to which the infant must react. This impingement disturbs the development of the new individual and produces a split between psyche and soma. This split results in either an overemphasis on the intellect or feelings that can only be experienced somatically through physical illness. Splitting of the object world occurs because of the infant's immature ego and its inability to tolerate excessive frustration, which eventually turns to anger.

The infant "accommodates" by splitting the object world into "good" and "bad," so that aggression/anger will not destroy what is good and loved. The massive structural splitting results in the formation of a self-created world and an emotionally isolated individual. Splitting is thought to begin as a normal inability of the immature ego to integrate good and bad, but by three to four months (following symbiosis), it is considered to become a defense mechanism. In theory, splitting gradually disappears during the third year; for most of us, however, it persists in various degrees throughout life.

When splitting of the object world is excessive and the person is unable to unify the good and bad object into one single image, the person cannot love. When angry, he or she is incapable of holding onto the loving feelings (the stage of object constancy has not been reached). Often he or she falls in and out of love and feels disappointed and betrayed by the lover.

The concept of splitting is illustrated by a patient, Mr. F., both in his self-perception and his relationships with women. Mr. F., a twenty-five-year-old cabinet-maker, presents himself to the world as a "macho guy," a real "ladies' man." When he entered treatment he was dating three women concurrently. Each of these women was unique in her own way. Not one, however, had all the necessary attributes to satisfy his image of the ideal woman. He enjoyed dating these women until they became involved and expressed their needs, at which point he would grow terrified of being "trapped and consumed." This fear of being consumed or devoured may be a reflection of his own neediness. Feelings of dependency are unacceptable to him, they are denied and projected. These feelings only appear in the transference after some break in treatment, such as a vacation, or when he feels a woman is losing interest in him. My vacation and the lover's loss of interest are experienced as rejections. The little boy, hated because of his neediness, is split off and projected onto the woman; thereby the little boy is never acknowledged in himself.

About one year into treatment, Mr. F. dropped two of the three women and intensified the relationship with the third. He began to tolerate some degree of intimacy. This action followed a growing awareness and acceptance of his having some needs. The little boy within him was now less frightening to Mr. F., and the macho man played less of a role. Even though Mr. F. stayed loyal to one woman, he was terrified of a commitment. It took two more years before he was ready to say, "I love you." The terror of commitment had two aspects: that the woman would be able to see his inadequacies and that he would have to confront the split between superman and the deprived little boy in himself. In treatment, the little boy came into focus. Mr. F. recognized that some of the pleasure he experienced in woodworking and sculpting the wood came from feelings of tenderness towards his mother. "I love working with the wood, following the lines of the grain; it really is quite sensual." The wood could always be molded to his own specifications. As he slowly became more tolerant of his own needs he was more able to learn how to accept the woman's needs.

Another aspect of object relations theory is the belief that "the schizoid position is the ultimate base dynamic in all psychopathology, and must be reached and worked through if full reconstructive change in the psyche is to be effected" (Kosseff, 1975, p. 214). Like Guntrip (1969), Fairbairn (1952), Kosseff (1975), and others, I am using the term *schizoid* to refer to a psychopathological undercurrent rather than to a particular diagnostic entity. The connection to objects in the inner world rather than to personal relations is the sine qua non of the schizoid style. Often, other schizoid symptomatology is present, such as fear and flight from external reality, which appears as a fundamental detachment; a preoccupation with inner reality; an in-and-out oscillation where the individual is impelled into a relationship by needs and driven out by fear of consuming the other or being consumed; an overwhelming sense of despair with no hope for love; excruciating loneliness and weakness; an attitude of omnipotence; and a sense of futility.

THE COMPOSITION OF THE INNER WORLD

Several theorists have conceptualized the inner world in a schematized manner, evoking metapsychological imagery not dissimilar to the Freudian model of id, ego, superego. In function, however, it is quite different because the inner world is inherently object-related. Fairbairn theorized the inner world as being composed of split-off objects (good, actually idealized, and bad) part objects, and subselves that develop around the objects (1952). Kosseff describes the inner world "as being composed of split objects, a split object ego fragment and the affect associated with this splitting process" (1975, p. 220). In essence, the inner world of objects assumes the form of a complex composite structure. As a result of the multiple internal relationships with split-off selves and the concomitant overemphasis on the inner world, external relationships are limited. In the case of individuals with severe pathology they are totally lacking.

The inner world distorts the individual's perception and experience with real objects. "Archaic, internal, dissociated object relations are projected to the outside world and are imposed on the human relationships existing there" (Kosseff, p. 221). These objects in the inner world are bits and pieces of an early relationship with an exciting and/or rejecting love object. Good experiences are stored into memory. The bad experiences are neither digested nor absorbed but rather retained as foreign objects. Thus the bits and pieces are split-off pieces of the bad or unsatisfying object, which is internalized to gain control. The unsatisfying object has two facets: "it frustrates and it tempts or allures." It splits further to become the "needed or exciting object and the frustrating or rejecting object—all repressed" (Fairbairn 1952, p. 138). It is not unusual for the exciting objects to be concentrated on one parent and the rejecting onto the other.

In infancy the primary object was essential for psychic survival or even life itself. In adulthood, when the connection to the internal object is disrupted through an analytic interpretation (or perhaps other, less benign disruptions), maintenance of personal identity is felt by the patient to be threatened, as though an indispensable section of the self is being demolished.

In the following clinical vignette it is possible to see the patient's intense need to cling to her flagrantly contemptuous yet idealized lover. Ms. S. is a twenty-nine-year-old teacher who, according to her perception, unknowingly fell in love with Mr. J., her school's principal. She entered treatment in a panic that her lover was about to leave her, and she wanted support so she could leave him. Mr. J.'s wife had discovered their affair and had come to the school to confront Ms. S. publicly. Mr. J.'s deceitfulness and his wife's threats provided sufficient incentive for her finally to give up the relationship. Yet within days she resumed the affair. Clearly, she believed that she needed him and that leaving him would prove even more painful.

Every time she attempted to leave him, he would entice her with presents, make himself more accessible, and promise to leave his wife. When Ms. S. succumbed to him he would once again become unavailable, pleading his wife's suspiciousness as the cause. Why was Ms. S. bound to this exciting and rejecting object? Why could she not separate from him to search for a more pleasurable love relationship? Based on the thinking of Fairbairn (1952) and Guntrip (1969), Greenberg and Mitchell have theorized "that the emptier the real exchange (mutuality of the relationship) in the external relationships, the greater the devotion to the promising yet depriving features of the internalized parent" (1983, p. 173). For Ms. S., the childhood terror of abandonment is still operative: if she disengages herself from the lover (a transference figure and tie to the internal object) she will find herself totally alone—inside and out.

In their analysis, some patients literally describe the presence of a "guard wall" or facade within themselves. These patients indicate that they have walled off a part of the self (Winnicott's true self/inner world), in order to maintain their self-identity and self-esteem. I understand the wall to be a reification of an unconscious pattern of withdrawal established during a very early age, possibly when there was little differentiation between mother and child.

Most likely, this shield was developed to protect the immature, fragile, developing ego from impingement or frustration. Unfortunately, instead of protection it makes the individual feel isolated, removed, and detached from human contact. This walled-off quality is evident in the case of Mr. M. who describes himself as an observer rather than an active participant in the world. His reason for keeping himself aloof is the belief that the world is filled with what he calls sharks, people who relate to him only when they need something. In his personal relationships he is concerned that he will be taken advantage of. These relationships both drain him and leave him feeling unsatisfied. He never really makes contact with others, and they never touch him emotionally.

Mr. M. is able to maneuver his way through the day because he walls the "sharks" up in a glass cage, which he calls the aquarium. It is he, however, who is actually walled off, out of touch with himself and with any human being, and therefore cannot have a relationship. Nobody has been able to get though the glass cage.

Recently, while relating a dream, he described an embryo image. "It was so minuscule, I can't imagine anyone could possibly know of its existence." I have understood this embryo image to be the "true self" that never matured and was split off and frozen years ago.

In treatment, the split-off objects are gradually brought into awareness and the accompanying affect is also recovered. As the attachment to the inner objects is lessened, the need for a shield is also reduced. There is an evolving inner feeling of increased security that stems from the consolidation of the self. As the quality and complexity of relatedness to others increases, newer, richer relations become a real possibility.

Sensitivity to our own internal world can quickly alert us to the patient's area of conflict. We must also "act in the encounter as a real person; true experience has little chance of emerging in a false setting" (Lomas 1973, p. 12). "If we really are to understand our patient's deepest anxieties, we must accept the reality of our own corresponding anxieties . . ." (Little 1981, p. xvii). Theory used correctly, as an aid to organizing the patient's material, can provide a route for the journey together. If theory is used merely to understand the patient intellectually, we will never be allowed to see beneath the conforming false self, nor will the patient be able to gain access to the true self. There may be some behavioral change, but without reexperiencing the emotion the patient knows it only intellectually, not emotionally.

We can offer our patients a safe holding-environment in which to grow by acknowledging their unaccepted feelings and unmet needs—which had been put aside or frozen. As the cut-off feelings or splits emerge, they find expression most clearly in the transference, and because of their primitive nature are often felt first by us in our countertransference. A patient who feels "held" (Winnicott's concept of the "holding environment") will begin to experience these formerly unheard or denied infantile needs. If the needs eventually can be accepted as legitimate, the splits will be healed.

Therapy provides awareness and insight. When the patient finally discovers the unmet infantile need, this must be followed by an acceptance of the needs as legitimate. The acknowledgement by the patient that the old primary object will never satisfy the needs, involves the final confrontation with what was not and can never be. The first feelings to accompany this recognition are those of loss and mourning. "If a sense of hopeful possibility is lacking, if the patient feels that the renunciation of his/her infantile attachments to his/her parents and internal objects may not result in new, richer relations but in an isolation and lack of contact, the attachments remain" (Greenberg and Mitchell 1983), and genuine relatedness cannot occur. At this point it is essential that the analyst be hopeful and believe in the possibility that some of the patient's needs can be met in the real external world, as well as in the patient's newly developed ability to care for the deprived part of the self.

One patient, Ms. L., described two dreams that convey the quality of the mourning. She has just separated from a very idealized and fascinating lover. In the first dream, she goes to buy a dog. "They are all top-class, beautiful, and alert. Off to the side, and slightly behind the others is one far from perfect but very friendly dog." She leaves the others and, without really understanding why, chooses the less than perfect one. She has given up the idealized perfect object. That same night she had a second dream.

I arrive at an apartment, enter and walk towards the bathroom. I can hardly hold the diarrhea. Everything is drained from my body. I fear that I am dying. I hear someone in the next room . . . she is talking to someone else. . . . Will she know that I need help? . . . will she reach me in time? I am crying . . . I cannot stop.

When the two dreams were understood as a mourning reaction not only to the loss of her lover but also to the loss of the idealized object, Ms. L. felt a tremendous sense of relief.

The healing of the splits is a slow and painful process, but as the person begins to feel genuinely alive with access to the true self, the full range of feelings becomes available, the person feels empowered, more satisfied and competent. The individual is now ready to love another.

Love that is freed from primitive needs and fantasies can give birth to tremendous feelings of creativity, productivity, and mature dependence or mutuality.

REFERENCES

Balint, M. 1965. *Primary love and psychoanalytic technique*. New York: Liveright.
Fairbairn, W. R. D. 1952. *An object relations theory of the personality*. London: Routledge and Kegan Paul.
Freud, A. 1965. *The writings of Anna Freud,* vol. 4. New York: Basic Books.
Freud, S. 1914. On narcissism: An introduction. *Standard edition* 14:73–102.
Greenberg, J., and S. Mitchell. 1983. *Object relations in psychoanalytic theory*. Cambridge: Harvard University Press.
Guntrip, H. 1969. *Schizoid phenomena, object relations and the self*. New York: IUP.
Kernberg, O. 1970. *New developments in psychoanalytic object relations theory*. Topeka, Kans.: Menninger Foundation.
———. 1976. *Object relations and clinical psychoanalysis*. New York: Aronson.
Kohut, H. 1977. *Restoration of the self*. New York: IUP
Kosseff, J. 1975. The leader using object-relations theory. In Z. Liff, ed., *The Leader in the group*, pp. 212–42. New York: Aronson.
Little, M. 1981. *Transference neurosis and transference psychosis*. New York: Aronson.
Lomas, P 1973. *True and false experience*. New York: Taplinger.
Mahler, M. 1968. *On human symbiosis and the vicissitudes of individuation,* vol. 1. New York: IUP.
———, F. Pine, and A. Bergman. 1975. *The psychological birth of the human infant*. New York: Basic Books.
Meissner, W. 1981. *Internalization in psychoanalysis*. New York: IUP.
Rycroft, C. 1968. *A critical dictionary of psychoanalysis*. New York: Basic Books.
Winnicott, D. W. 1958. *Collected papers: Through pediatrics to psychoanalysis*. New York: Basic Books.
———. 1976. *The maturational processes and the facilitating environment*. London: Hogarth.

10. Trust and Testing in Love Relations

Peter Lawner

This chapter focuses on testing, a type of communication often used by neurotic[1] individuals to structure their relationships to others. I view testing as the emotionally troubled person's unconscious provocative mode of assessing the degree of his or her safety in intimate relationships. In everyday life, responses to such testing tend to cause relationships to labor under the burden of dissatisfaction and conflict. I contrast this with what can occur in treatment when the experienced therapist responds to such communications with a recognition of the motivation behind them. As a result of such therapeutic responsiveness, the troubled individual tends to develop a greater inclination to trust others.

Testing is not a new concept and has long been part of psychodynamic understanding and practice. For example, many patients will test the limits of such issues as the maintenance of time parameters at the end of sessions or test the therapists' patience about late payments. When these issues appear in the literature on adult analysis, they tend to be regarded as of occasional occurrence and of limited dynamic significance. The testing to which I refer occurs frequently and is of signal dynamic and therapeutic importance. It is my contention that the patient is testing the analyst in the expression of many more issues than have been previously acknowledged, and it is in response to these invitations that the analyst performs much important work.

Such dynamically significant communication may be used by psychologically troubled individuals in love relationships in everyday life but is rarely heard or acknowledged as other than antagonizing and disjunctive by the recipient. Let me give three brief examples.

A college student on a "drug trip" urgently summoned a fellow student to whom she was attracted and who was engrossed in studying in the library to come to her room without delay to hear about her "fantastic" experiences while on the trip. He evinced less and less interest in her.

A man reports in his analysis unremittingly asking the woman with whom he had been involved whether she loved him, observantly remarking: "I think I would have kept that up more and more until I drove her away."

A woman who had had a falling out with her female lover, who had taken up with someone new, arranged a morning meeting between her and her lover. She "did not remember" until the time of their assignation that she had a temporally conflicting therapy appointment, which, on brief deliberation, she elected to attend. Upon hearing from her by telephone at the last minute "apologetically" canceling their get-together, her (former?) lover flew into a rage.

This chapter will explore testing as it emerges and is dealt with in psychoanalytic therapy.

Trust, the prevailing assumption that one's significant others will appreciate and support one's fulfillment and growth, may be viewed as at the core of harmoniously developing relationships (Benedek 1938; Erikson 1950). I believe that testing comes from both a lack of trust and from *a typically masked wish and striving to reopen the issue of trust.* That is, it arises not only from mistrust, from the unconscious (and often conscious as well) expectation of disappointment by the other but also from a wish to question whether one's pessimistic expectation in this relationship could be mistaken.

Many neurotics suffer from the incapacity to integrate lasting relationships, or, if they do succeed, are unable to establish relationships other than predominantly hurtful, disappointing, and otherwise emotionally deficient ones. Notwithstanding the lack of mutuality, intimacy, and commitment as well as active sadomasochism (Lawner 1979) characteristic of a large proportion of such pairings, I nevertheless follow Freud (1912, 1915; see also Schafer 1977) in regarding them as *love relations*. I do this in recognition of the beloved (e.g., adored, depended upon, cared for) status of the prototypic figures of infancy and childhood upon whom such contemporary partners are unconsciously modeled. One of the established goals of psychoanalytic work is the unearthing of such prototypes and identification of the motives for their perpetuation, so as to free the individual to integrate more genuinely loving and fulfilling relationships.

For approximately the first two decades of Freud's psychoanalytic explorations (i.e., 1897–1920), the infantile and childhood prototypes for later pathologically discordant relationships were understood principally in terms of their predominant psychosexual drive patterns. Whether from an object-relational perspective, emphasizing the neurotic's idiosyncratic unconscious attachments to figures of early life, or from a drive-structural viewpoint, focusing upon his pregenital drive patterns (Greenberg and Mitchell 1983), the adult neurotic was regarded as a closed system, enlisting the world about him as a "stage" upon which to compulsively enact his unconscious strivings. Thus the patient's daily pattern of self-defeating extra-analytic love relationships was understood as intrapsychically generated and the analytic situation, regarded as the arena for the emergence and resolution of the individual's transference neurosis (Freud 1914a), as a faithful replica of his or her inner world. From this perspective, the exploration of the patient's intrapsychic world was understood to be fostered principally by the analyst's removal of himself from interaction with his patient through abstinence, surgeonlike commitment to technique, silence, neutrality, and lack of self-revelation.

However, scant attention was paid to the critical role of the extra-analytic love object's responses in perpetuating the neurotic's self-defeating modes of relatedness (Wachtel 1980). Nor was the significance for fruitful personality evolution of the analyst's provision of a "manifestly active" therapeutic relationship properly credited. In what follows, I contrast the effects of responses by the love partners of the neurotic in everyday life with those of the analyst, especially as these differentially promote the patient's tendency to integrate future love relationships on the basis of trust or testing.

Before we go further, some changes in Freud's thinking from 1920 onward are worth considering. As long as his instinctual-drive psychology was ascendant, Freud tended to view the individual as rather automatically seeking pleasure in characteristic ways. However, with the recognition of the power of the impulse to destructiveness toward oneself and others, independent of considerations of libidinal pleasure, and of the need to master traumatic situations through ceaseless repetitions of them, Freud (1920) was well on the way toward formulating his ego psychology. Since those who chronically engage in testing of their loved ones manifest considerable destructiveness toward themselves and their partners and seem to be seeking mastery of a relationship that, at least in terms of its past prototypes, has proved intolerably painful, Freud's (1920) insights from *Beyond the Pleasure Principle* are directly relevant to our theme. The manifest hurtfulness and strivings for mastery reflected in such testing may usefully be viewed as two sides of the same coin brought to light in that work. In *Inhibitions, Symptoms, and Anxiety* (1926), Freud further illuminated the character of the ego, the postulated agency of self-protection and adaptation. He showed how we regularly involve ourselves not only in mastering old traumas through repetition but anticipating new ones through internal self-signaling, once again in the effort to turn a familiar variety of passively experienced helplessness into an actively initiated state of security. Since in the developmental hierarchy of feared traumatic situations Freud outlined in that work—loss of the object, loss of the object's love, castration anxiety, and superego anxiety—each bespeaks attachment as well as fear of traumatic helplessness in relation to loved others, he clearly understood that the principal threats to our security occur in relationship to significant others.

There is some disagreement among contemporary observers of the psychoanalytic scene, however, as to whether Freud and his successors have fully appreciated that the individual is, in everyday life, as in analysis, an open system involved in crucial interactions with others, whose responses in turn vitally affect his or her sense of security and safety, as well as growth or psychopathological stasis. Theorists such as Loewald (1960) take this understanding among contemporary Freudians for granted. Others, such as those in the Mt. Zion Psychotherapy Research Group (Gassner et al. 1982; Sampson et al. 1972; Weiss 1971; Weiss and Sampson 1986a) suggest that this understanding is far from well established within the Freudian mainstream. This group has proposed that during psychoanalysis, to the extent that defenses against a particular anxiety-laden theme have been substantially resolved and the analysand is able to move toward openly voicing it, he or she becomes particularly vigilant as to the analyst's response to its expression. Unconsciously, the analysand scrutinizes the analyst's responses to increasingly direct expressions of this theme (e.g., sexual wishes toward the analyst), as well as often provocatively inviting an excited response (e.g., a reciprocally erotic or perhaps punitive one) to its open expression. The latter of these two efforts at anticipatory control of the analyst's response to expression of an anxiety-laden theme are what the Mt. Zion group and I, following their lead, refer to as "testing." This group further maintains that the patient's primary motivation for such testing is to sway their analyst to reveal his or her attitude toward their open expression of the threatening, emerging theme. The analyst's continued neutrality and imperturbability at such junctures are viewed as serving to reassure the analysand of their safety to openly express this theme, free of the danger of its being mutually and traumatically acted out. Of course, such a result does not occur through conventional verbalizations of reassurance, which lend themselves to being experienced as shallow and hypocritical. Rather, this group proposes, it is mediated by the analyst's abstention—neither praising nor condemning, neither being available to be seduced, intimidated, nor provoked to retaliate, and so on—which truly reassures the patient of her or his safety to bring forth hitherto warded-off themes. While I concur with these researchers' emphasis upon the decisiveness of the atmosphere of safety within analysis, particularly when dealing with patients' tests, I depart from their proposal regarding the manner in which the crucial ambience of security is most effectively achieved. I emphasize the desirability of the analyst being explicitly active in identifying and, where possible, elucidating such tests.

Far from restricting the vital unconsciously inspired activity of testing to the analytic situation, psychologically troubled individuals engage in such testing throughout their extra-analytic love relationships. As a rule, the neurotic's extra-analytic love objects consistently "fail" those tests, contributing to the lack of satisfaction in his or her relationships. By contrast, the analyst may pass. When the analyst fails such tests, these failures tend to reflect what Edgar Levenson (1972) has described as the patient's "transforming" his therapist. Joseph Sandler (1976) has assayed this in terms of the analyst's "role responsiveness." Ultimately and predominantly, the analyst must pass them. Passing these tests may be viewed as freeing the analysand to express and thereby better integrate his or her strivings and feelings toward the analyst, while internalizing a "background of safety" (Sandler 1960; see also Lawner 1984; Ogden 1979; Strachey 1934).

The trusting person tends to live life relatively uncomplicated by self-initiated provocations, and in far more mutually satisfying open exchanges with others. Living out of a trusting, supportive inner world, modeled after an appreciative "holding environment" of early life or fruitful analytic treatment (Winnicott 1965), this individual tends to experience loved others as safe, trustworthy, and fulfilling. The trusting person experiences him- or herself as though a good human environment for the other with whom possibilities for intimacy exist. Perhaps most relevant for our theme is this individual's maintenance of the capacity to tolerate feelings of anxiety, frustration, ambivalence (Klein 1935), sadness, and loss (Loewald 1962; Zetzel 1970), which are part and parcel of satisfying love relations. The analyst may or may not predominantly have achieved this level of self-evolution outside professional life. However, the success of his or her analyses largely depends upon having integrated such a capacity to trust, and correlated openness to depth interpersonal experience, exemplified by the ability to be aware of, process, and therapeutically capitalize on countertransference experiences (Searles 1979) as part of his or her analytic "work ego" (Fleiss 1942; Lawner 1981).

By contrast, among those whose love relationships are sadomasochistic, a wide range of potential experiences with others and their accompanying emotions are feared as unbearable (Lawner 1979). These individuals repetitively and unconsciously test their loved others to assess whether it is safe to communicate or engage with them regarding such vital matters. To whatever degree the neurotic's provocations are motivated by such unconscious testing, the partner tends not to recognize them in their functions as queries concerning the possibility of developing a new and more fulfilling relationship together, but rather tends to take them "personally"—that is, as hurtful and inflammatory—and to respond counterprovocatively. In brief, this other fails such tests.

Before illustrating my proposal with a clinical example, I should like to clarify it in two respects. One is in sharpening my meaning of the term *active* in regard to the therapist. The second is in locating the concept of testing in relation to the pivotal psychoanalytic concepts of transference and resistance.

Applying conventional descriptive standards, psychoanalysts at work have often been derogated as "passive" (Lawner 1984). From a dynamic standpoint, I do not believe this to be, or indeed ever to have been, true. However, I believe that in abjuring open response to their patients' tests in a theoretically buttressed maintenance of silence and "neutrality," they sacrifice critical therapeutic opportunities. Analytic patients are, I believe, misunderstood if viewed principally as seeking to verbalize new themes. Rather, they may better be understood as seeking opportunities for a new type of relationship. In this light, their testing represents neither a passive transferential reenactment alone, nor merely a quest for greater self-disclosure, but also a provocatively disguised *questioning* of their analyst concerning the character of their potentially attainable mutual relationship. Further, patients, as a rule, experience increased safety with and trust in their analysts (and potentially others) to the extent the analysts are not just dynamically but also *"explicitly active."*[2]

I propose that such explicit responsiveness exercises its therapeutic action on at least two grounds. First, it consistently promotes the analysand's awareness of the presence and the nature of the anxiety to which he or she responds by testing (with the questioning implicit in it), thereby tending to render such testing less automatic and peremptory. Second, it suggests the analyst's relative comfort and clear conscience about what the analysand is asking concerning their relationship. The analyst's nonanxious responsiveness implies readiness truly to engage and potentially deepen their exploration and relationship, as well as suitability for fruitful internalization (Strachey 1934).

In summary, not only am I recommending that analysts attune themselves to the frequent occurrences of their patients' tests, I am further suggesting that whenever possible they make a point of commenting on these tests in such a manner (depending upon their dynamic context and transparency) as to identify their probable function as tests, distill and reflect back the particular question(s) of foremost urgency implicit within them, and/or respond to their analysands' successive associations as elaborations upon the questions implicit in their preceding tests.

These tests may be presented in forms as varied as rebuttals, questions, statements, threats, seductions, entreaties, ultimatums, and so on, and may assume configurations as pervasive as moods or extended associational trends, underscoring the subject of testing as a broad one indeed. Some phenotypes of these tests will doubtless suggest themselves by means of the vignettes I shall offer.

The relationship of testing to the key analytic constructs of transference and resistance deserves consideration. While the reiterative character of transference is well known, routinely embedded within transference are inquiries concerning the potential for the current love object to provide a different and more salutary human environment than that provided by the prototypic caretakers of childhood. Thus, the analytic transference includes a desired relationship to a "new object" (Schafer 1983). Testing is, I believe, a critical and oft-traveled avenue for assessing the character of this would-be new object. While the inexperienced or untrained practitioner is disposed to "fail" patients' tests by reacting to their provocative testing in a non-self-correcting counterinflammatory manner, the classically restrained and silent analyst also, I believe, sacrifices a significant opportunity. By not explicitly responding to such veiled overtures and thereby not declaring their view of them as particularly significant communications, analysts often unwittingly invite the analysand to interpret them as uncaring, covertly out of control, or otherwise unsatisfactory according to the model of problematic childhood prototypes. Labeling tests, by contrast, identifies the analysand's search for the more soundly loving other, which is cloaked by provocative self-presentation.

While resistance in analysis is commonly expressed transferentially (Freud 1912)—that is, in the form of an intense, one-sided emotional striving or avoidance in relation to the analyst—it is also considered in its own right. In either case, it may be viewed not only with regard to intrapsychically propagated anxieties, and consequent obstruction of the free-associational, self-revelatory, and correlated self-integrative process. It also deserves consideration in actual (not just fantasized) interpersonal terms, both with regard to the analysand's apprehensive assessment of the analyst's attitudes and feelings toward him or her as well as to the analyst's response to this assessment. The analysand is most likely to test the analyst in a variety of ways when moving toward expressing a new theme, as the Mt. Zion group view it, or, as I stress, when awakening to the possibility of a new type of relationship with the analyst. It is my view that since testing is far more prevalent in our work than is implied by the Mt. Zion group, these junctures are likely to occur much more frequently. An analyst's apparently unmoved response (e.g., silence or verbally unelaborated adherence to the "frame") by omission typically supports resistance in its traditional sense of "that which interferes with analytic progress" (Schafer 1976). By contrast, overt response, such as verbal clarification, reflection, or emphasis upon subsequent implicit associational reference to that with which the test was concerned, tends to confirm the presence of the concerns about the relationship so often embedded within patients' apparently resistive and disjunctive activity. In turn, it heightens their awareness of the particular fears they have of relationships, as well as the manner in which they simultaneously express these fears, mask them, and strive for a more trusting relationship.

CLINICAL ILLUSTRATIONS

For the purpose of clarification, I shall intertwine the clinical illustrations in this section with further observations of a more conceptual nature. My first observation is that the data of dynamic psychotherapy and psychoanalysis are multifaceted and multidetermined. Many may be fruitfully understood from the vantage point of testing but nevertheless are properly considered as well in relation to their possible function as traditionally conceived resistances, transferences, and so forth. One of these perspectives thus is taken to supplant the others only at the cost of oversimplification. Secondly, the Mt. Zion group is exploring extensively and delineating the phenomenon of testing in dynamic psychotherapies, including psychoanalysis (Weiss et al. 1986b), in a major research program. They have at this point extended their view of testing to encompass the individual's broad, unconscious idiosyncratic aims with regard to achieving a sense of safety and security in his or her dynamic psychotherapy, and this person's ongoing unconscious assessment of the congruence of the therapist's responses with these aims ("plan compatibility"). In distinction, I am concerning myself here with a narrower band of communications than they, those which tend to be identifiable in terms of their provocativeness, their effect of (at least briefly) flustering the therapist, and their decipherability as questions concerning the therapist/analyst's "true" attitudes.

Further, I would like to distinguish my account of testing from Loewenstein's (1957) concept of "seduction of the aggressor." While Loewenstein has deepened our comprehension of sadomasochism by highlighting the interpersonal enlistment of the other unconsciously in the attempt to master feared painful relational possibilities, he views this principally as in the service of perpetuating the psychopathological status quo. While similarly noting the covert invitation to interpersonal participation intrinsic to testing, I emphasize, in contrast, the progressive striving available for discovery within it.

I will now illustrate some occurrences of testing, and the productive or nonproductive uses to which they are put within psychoanalytic psychotherapy.

Toward the beginning of a session, Mrs. R., a chronically bitter and often provocatively disappointed woman with whom her therapist had been struggling to surmount an impasse, said: "I don't find people in general interested in me, nor do I think you are either.'" At this juncture, her therapist found himself emotionally immobilized and withdrew. He had at this point "failed" her test.

In her query was an implicit provocative assertion, namely, "Are you interested [i.e., still my emotional ally], despite my provoking you?" Even without verbally responding, had her therapist remained emotionally related and attuned to her testing, he could well have referred back to this earlier interchange. This would, however, have constituted foregoing an opportunity for therapeutic engagement and permitting the continuation of a nontherapeutic disjunction between them. This incident illustrates the value of explicit intervention by the analytic therapist.

Paradoxically, the most vital context for the therapist's response to testing has to be an internal one. The key response is the private one registered. Perhaps the therapist feels flustered and provoked, and will see this experience as a signal of the possibility that the patient is testing. This can then stimulate a search for the dynamic context for the apparent test, such that an appropriate and explicit therapeutic response can be made. However, some tests are best passed, even if verbally, without interpreting them as tests.

Miss B. had recently moved and was beginning a new analysis with me. She was emphatically unenthusiastic about me and one day asked, as she was just about to leave my office at the end of a session, my reaction to her extolling her previous therapist—which indeed she had in abundant detail in our preceding sessions. I felt sure that she was testing me, although unclear about the meaning of the test. The fact that she had suffered traumatic abandoments by both parents, most continuously by her narcissistically preoccupied mother, will suggest to the reader—and did later to me—hypotheses regarding the meaning of and query implicit within her test. At the moment, however, I was aware principally of feeling off balance, "on the spot," and of being tested, and replied, "It's clear that he [i.e., her prior therapist] was, and continues to be very important to you, else I take it you wouldn't be telling me so much about him and your relationship to him." The fact that she returned and increasingly became involved in a fruitful therapy, I interpret as tending to validate the value of this response. By contrast, I assume she would have heard my labeling her query as a test at this point, probably correctly, as narcissistically defensive.

In other situations, often better analytically secured, explicitly identifying one's patient's proffering of a test and, if feasible, the nature of this test as well, tends to be therapeutically productive. For example, in response to one's analysand's being gratuitously nasty, it has in my experience proved helpful to say something like, "I have a feeling right now you are testing me," to be followed by, if appropriate, "What might that have to do with?" Often, the analyst is quite clear about the underlying question in these tests. The anecdote of Mrs. R. presented earlier, concerning the patient's saying to her therapist "people are not interested in me . . . nor do I think you are either," constitutes a clear illustration of a juncture in which the therapist could fruitfully respond, "You seem to be wanting to know if I care about, and am interested in you, even at times, like now, when you're critical toward me."

An analogous instance occurred in work with an analysand who was also in the mental health field and spoke to me about her own work with patients. She reported in our session having been troubled by her work with a patient who had urgently and repeatedly asked on what street her office window looked out. When she twice received no reply to her inquiry regarding the source of the question, and her patient once again importuned a reply, she then gave the demanded information; whereupon the latter fled to get her car, which was parked there. In considering this, I implied the value of persisting in her questioning despite her patient's demands for an answer. At the beginning of our following session she excitedly and conspiratorially asked if the other person in the waiting room was from the same training center with which we were both affiliated. After I twice queried her question, entreated a reply a third time, I said, "Could it be that you're wanting to know if I really meant what I said last session concerning the value of persisting in the inquiry?"[3]

The final form of testing I wish to discuss is one in which the appropriate response to the question implicit in the test is a psychodynamically informed response to the associational material.

Mr. G. came in one session and agitatedly reported, as he had at times before, that his son was regularly throwing temper tantrums in response to the least frustration. This time, however, he also asked if I could recommend a child psychologist for his son. I responded that I felt that we had to understand better what it meant to him before I would feel justified in offering him such a recommendation. I knew my analysand strongly identified with his son, whom he viewed with disfavor as compared to his daughter, and had felt deeply rejected by his own father. In the ensuing weeks, I had repeated occasion to interpret to him his feeling uncared about and unloved by me. At the end of this period, he reported to me with surprise and pleasure that his son was behaving much better and more maturely. His son was also sleeping better as well, reflecting an amelioration in this hitherto chronic difficulty. This welcome change might well, my analysand surmised, have to do with the bedtime stories he had recently taken to telling his son before he went to sleep. It did not seem likely to be profitable at that juncture to interpret to him what I believe had occurred between him and me, and between him and his son. I believe he had tested me concerning whether he should ship his son off to a psychologist rather than provide the crucial "therapy" only he himself could at that point provide for him. By not colluding in what would have represented a rejection of his son, and by interpreting to him what, in identification with his son, he was feeling with me, I was able to pass a crucial test, allowing him to be more truly loving in this one of his most vital love relationships.

I hope I have conveyed ways in which those who experience their inner worlds in peril are disposed to engage others through testing, and how analytic responses, implicitly or explicitly expressing recognition of such individuals' tests, assist them to achieve greater trust in their love relationships.

NOTES

1. I employ this term in the sense that Freud (1914b) typically did, i.e., to refer to those across the broad range of functional psychopathology.
2. In connection with interpretation of resistance to awareness of the transference, Gill (1982; Gill and Muslin 1976; see also Lawner 1985) similarly stresses the value of consistent explicit analytic activity.
3. I do not intend to imply here that the implicit suggestion I made to her in the first of the two sessions reported is generally desirable, but rather the

general applicability of the type of intervention I record in the second. Also, it will be observed that for other purposes, this vignette could be taken to illustrate the principles of my analysand perhaps counteridentifying with her own patient or turning passive into active, identifying with the aggressor, or engaging in parallel process in relation to her patient and me.

REFERENCES

Benedek, T. 1938. Adaptation to reality in early infancy. *Psychoanalytic Quarterly* 7:200–14.
Erikson, E. H. 1950. *Childhood and society.* New York: Norton.
Fleiss, R. 1942. The metapsychology of the analyst. *Psychoanalytic Quarterly* 11:211–27.
Freud, S. 1912. The dynamics of transference. *Standard edition* 12:97–108.
———. 1914a. Remembering, repeating, and working through. *Standard edition* 12:147–56.
———. 1914b. On narcissism: An introduction. *Standard edition* 14:73–102.
———. 1915. Observations on transference-love (Further recommendations on the technique of psychoanalysis III). *Standard edition* 12:157–71.
———. 1920. Beyond the pleasure principle. *Standard edition* 18:7–64.
———. 1926. Inhibitions, symptoms, and anxiety. *Standard edition* 20:87–174.
Gassner, S., H. Sampson, J. Weiss, and S. Brumer. 1982. The emergence of warded-off contents. *Psychoanalysis and Contemporary Thought* 5:55–75.
Gill, M. M. 1982. *Analysis of transference,* vol. 1: *Theory and technique.* New York: IUP.
Gill, M. M., and H. L. Muslin. 1976. Early interpretation of the transference. *Journal of the American Psychoanalytic Association* 24:779–94.
Greenberg, J. A., and S. A. Mitchell. 1983. *Object relations in psychoanalytic theory.* Cambridge: Harvard University Press.
Klein, M. 1935. A contribution to the psychogenesis of manic-depressive states. In *Love, guilt, and reparation and other works, 1921–1945.* New York: Delta, 1975.
Lawner, P. 1979. Sado-masochism and the imperiled self. *Issues in Ego Psychology* 2:22–29.
———. 1981. Reflections on the unknown in psychotherapy. *Psychotherapy: Theory, Research, and Practice* 18:306–12.
———. 1984. Protecting the psychoanalytic situation. *Contemporary Psychotherapy Review* 2:97–114.
———. 1985. Character rigidity and resistance to awareness of the transference. *Issues in Ego Psychology* 8:36–41.
Levenson, E. 1972. *The fallacy of understanding.* New York: Basic Books.
Loewald, H. 1960. On the therapeutic action of psychoanalysis. *International Journal of Psychoanalysis* 41:16–33.
———. 1962. Internalization, separation, mourning, and the superego. *Psychoanalytic Quarterly* 31:483–504.

Loewenstein, R. M. 1957. A contribution to the psychoanalytic theory of masochism. *Journal of the American Psychoanalytic Association* 5:197–234.

Ogden, T. 1979. On projective identification. *International Journal of Psychoanalysis* 60:357–73.

Rapaport, D. 1953. Some metapsychological considerations concerning activity and passivity. In Rapaport, *Collected papers*, pp. 530–68. New York: Basic Books, 1967.

Sampson, H., J. Weiss, L. Mlodnosky, and E. Hause. 1972. Defense analysis and the emergence of warded-off contents: An empirical study. *Archives of General Psychiatry* 26:524–32.

Sandler, J. 1960. The background of safety. *International Journal of Psychoanalysis* 41:352–56.

———. 1976. Countertransference and role-responsiveness. *International Review of Psycho-analysis* 3:43–48.

Schafer, R. 1976. *A new language for psychoanalysis*. New Haven: Yale University Press.

———. 1977. The interpretation of transference and the conditions of loving. *Journal of the American Psychoanalytic Association* 25:335–62.

———. 1983. *The analytic attitude*. New York: Basic Books.

Searles, H. 1979. *Countertransference and related subjects: Selected papers*. New York: IUP.

Strachey, J. 1934. The nature of the therapeutic action of psychoanalysis. *International Journal of Psycho-analysis* 15:127–59.

Wachtel, P. 1980. The relevance of Piaget to the psychoanalytic theory of transference. *Annual of Psychoanalysis* 8:59–76. New York: IUP.

Weiss, J. 1971. The emergence of new themes: A contribution to the psychoanalytic theory of therapy. *International Journal of Psycho-analysis* 52:459–67.

———, and H. Sampson. 1986a. Testing alternative psychoanalytic explanations of the psychotherapeutic process. In J. Masling, ed., *Empirical studies of psychoanalytical theories* 2:1–26. Hillsdale, N.J.: Analytic Press.

———, ———, and the Mt. Zion Psychotherapy Research Group. 1986b. *The Psychoanalytic process: Theory, clinical observation, and empirical research*. New York: Guilford.

Winnicott, D. W. 1965. *The maturational processes and the facilitating environment*. New York: IUP.

Zetzel, E. R. 1970. *The capacity for emotional growth*. New York: IUP.

11. The Struggle to Love: Reflections and Permutations

Joan O. Zuckerberg

"Side by side with the exigencies of life,
love is the great educator."
                    (Freud 1916, p. 312)

In this essay, I will explore some of the permutations that love's struggle may take, discussing particularly certain salient psychodynamic configurations. A basic underlying assumption is that patterns of early bonding and subsequent mothering, the degree to which the mother can both empathically meet and engage the phase-appropriate natural and biologically determined needs of her child, will determine in large part the individual's ability to love over time. These configurations will at times resemble familiar clinical diagnostic entities and will at other times remain phenomenological descriptions that cross over many diagnostic categories. In addition, I will attempt to draw inferences from the clinical material presented here and point to implications in terms of treatment dynamics, intrapsychic concerns, transference and countertransference issues.

Freud asserted that happiness is contained in the fulfillment of our childhood wishes. Further, if we are to understand subsequent individuation and growth, the solidity of the early symbiosis is a requirement. Winnicott reminds us the mother provides a "holding environment" within which the infant is both contained and experienced: "an infant who has had no one person to gather his bits together starts with a handicap in his own self-integrating task" (1945, p. 150).

From birth on, the human being seeks out love, be it in the form of a nursing embrace, a cooing dialogue, or a sweet smile. Touching, sucking, holding, laughing are illustrative expressions of the attachment and the nonverbal language of bonding. When the interaction between mother and child is solidified by sufficient empathic attunement on the part of the caretaker, and when developmental needs are accurately read, a solid foundation for subsequent emotional development has been built. This provides the basis for the infant's internal readiness to incorporate and hold on to a complex image of the caretaker(s). Gradually this image takes on qualities of a self differentiated from the other. Memory then becomes suffused with the sights, smells, sounds, the rhythm of the parenting one(s) and object constancy, the capacity to maintain object relatedness irrespective of frustration or satisfaction, the final resultant of this rich intrapsychic process, becomes established. This process of self-object differentiation and solidification begins in pregnancy on a nonverbal, intrauterine level and continues throughout the life cycle, and is, in fact, a prerequisite to any form of mature love and attachment.

After birth, the mother's urgent wish is to bond with the child, motivated in part by the desire to reinstate the symbiotic physical unity she has had with the fetus child (Zuckerberg 1984). As Lorenz reminds us, the infant, too, is equipped from birth to elicit caretaking behavior through a complex network of communicative gestures (1970). The survival of the human species rests on this preprogrammed object-seeking interaction. The infant is a seducer par excellence: his "babyness," his special appeal—a unique blend of fleshy responses, irresistible smiles, eye brightening, open curled-up mouth, head-back tongue thrusts—are dramatically evocative (Stern 1977). It is this evocativeness, together with the mother's wish to respond to and fulfill the infant's needs, that sets the stage for the capacity to love and to be loved.

Mahler underscores the interactive quality of this partnership:

It is the specific unconscious need of the mother that activates, out of the infant's infinite potentialities, those in particular that create for each mother the "child" who reflects her own unique and individual needs. This process takes place, of course, within the range of the child's innate endowments. (1967, p. 750)

In 1950, René Spitz attempted an etiological classification of psychogenic diseases in infancy. In his work we find powerful evidence of the psychological need for adequate maternal empathy, the foundation of love. Infants deprived of sustained, "good enough" mothering went into a coma in response to what was called "overt primal rejection"—a coma that can eventually bring death in the absence of nurturant intervention. Others may develop colic in response to primary anxious overpermissiveness. When mothering oscillates between pampering and hostility, there may be hyperactivity in the form of rocking (Zuckerberg 1984). Patterns of early mothering were demonstrated to result in early structural deficits in children, from the organic-physical to the emotional.

Essential to man's survival is the need and capacity to attach. Bowlby's (1973) naturalistic observations of nonhuman primates reminds us of the deep-rootedness of this biological imperative. He talks of the "lost piping" of young ducklings who have temporarily lost a mother figure, the bleating of lambs, the yelping of puppies. When left alone, patas monkeys screamed with wide open mouths and distorted faces (p. 57). When separated from our loved ones, protests are biologically intense and powerful; when reunited, we cling. An ongoing wish then in human adulthood is to be reunited in symbiotic harmony with the mother, perhaps the foundation of love.

Bowlby argues for a "primary object clinging" theory. There is in infants an "in-built propensity" to be in touch with and to cling to a human being. In this sense, there is a need for an object independent of food, which is as primary as the need for food and warmth (1969, p. 180). Added to this search is the very early realization that all is not perfect. Balint (1965) discusses the infant's experience with maternal rejection: the infant's mother is unique and irreplaceable, whereas the child *is* replaceable—by another infant, by other people, and by other activities—and this discrepancy provides an introduction to reality. (In analysis, this is represented by the idealized analyst who sees other patients, has a personal life, and may have other professional activities.)

Turning to the clinical data, I have selected situations that can occur in early childhood and may contribute to severe problems in loving in later life. The psychodynamic configurations are (1) insufficient loving and attachment, which can result in subsequent character pathology, impoverishment in object relations and narcissistic issues; (2) early psychic abandonment or separations that can lead to chronic rage, clinging, and so on, covering a host of diagnostic entities, but particularly borderline pathology; (3) overinvestment in a parenting figure, which can take the form of neurotic idealization, erotization, chronic oedipal competition, problems with envy, covering again a host of diagnostic entities; (4)

overexposure to a severely disturbed parent, which can lead to special sensitivities in object choice, vulnerabilities in object relations and problems in identity formation, again, diagnostically inclusive; and (5) a traumatic climate that was chronically invasive, examples being holocaust, early death of a parent, mental or physical illness, rape, incest. Clearly these configurations are not inclusive or mutually exclusive, but they illustrate certain early conditions that may contribute to persistent struggles in the capacity and ability to love in adult life. These struggles are often further compounded by difficulties in experiencing pleasure without guilt, a dynamic that colors all of the above configurations to be discussed later in this essay.

The patient who has been insufficiently loved, who has suffered early maternal deficits in bonding and subsequent negligence, rejection, or emotional abuse is particularly vulnerable. For Ms. S., a world of fantasy, a world of dehumanized objects and things, of romanticized people took the place of genuine object relations. Idealized notions about life and living, "grandiose" schemes of success and mastery became flimsy constructs and guiding principles. Her introjects and internal life were generally impoverished; her sense of self was experienced as in a perpetual state of psychic emptiness. This patient became an artist, "a perceptual realist," whose canvas was filled with an almost photographic realism; still lifes devoid of humans, in whom she claimed she was not interested, objects without motion and certainly without emotion. Character pathology, characterized by rigidity, black-and-white thinking, and impoverishment in the ability to empathize led to ongoing stressful family relations. Therapy for this individual has consisted of using the person of the therapist as an emotional educator, a teacher of the basic human alphabet. The relationship was central, and emotional responsiveness, empathic clarification, the elicitation of attachment behavior, including smiling, laughter, crying, were all essential elements in what constituted a therapeutic and healing emotional experience. Genuine countertransference concern, care, and devotion were salient features in the treatment.

Another patient, Ms. P., reported in the first minutes of her therapy that her mother was "sick on the subject of her." In dreams, mother was the "bear chasing her around the table with a knife." She remembered multiple caretakers, a passive, inconspicuous father, a protective older brother, a mother who only wanted the patient to reflect narcissistically her own personal needs, wishes and perfectionistic image. Ms. P. became homosexual in her object choices early in adulthood, and after a series of traumatic betrayals, became both people and place phobic. When she started therapy, Ms. P. was stiff with rage and unable to establish eye contact, unable to reach out to people in the most basic ways. Terrible fears of being buried alive got translated into numerous unyielding phobias in real life. The suffocating, raging mother from whom she could not escape made loving and emotional commitment nearly impossible. No one was allowed to penetrate. A life of isolation seemed better than a life of torture, which is really what relationship meant to this patient on an unconscious level. Ms. P.'s residual feelings went into poetry, and it was through poetry "shared" in therapy that human contact was established and grew.

In both these patients, the ability of the therapist to accept the art as a gift in the course of treatment, as gestures of love, as demonstrations of humanness, was essential. Gradually over time and through the therapeutic alliance and benevolent attachment, the person and the art slowly changed, both in depth and emotional complexity.

Closely related to insufficiency of attachment is early psychic abandonment or separations. At times other attachment figures were available for these patients, though clearly early and chronic abandonment colored the degree and quality of any subsequent attachment. A patient, Ms. T., recently stated: "I feel like a nonperson, an empty shell. I feel cheated, ripped off. I gave him everything and I am left with nothing to offer anyone. There's nothing left. Maybe I've always been this way. . . . I hate him. He stopped loving me; he's spineless, no backbone." This patient, whose mother died early in her life and who remembers a close sibling-cousin network, described her memory of her mother in a dream image as an "empty picture frame." Her problems in loving had to do with trusting and psychic drainage. Getting close meant self-body dissolution and loss of inner supplies. Current relationships were marked by friendly, siblinglike ties, avoiding deeper, more interdependent ties. Instrumental to movement in treatment was the therapist's facilitating the ventilation of rage toward the abandoning mother and the patient's fear of the devouring monster-mother inside her who was evil and damaged. Critical was the therapist's insisting that all transference feelings, object hunger, homosexual cravings, be expressed and understood so that further intimacy could be established. What appeared as a narcissistic and rigid arrestation gradually gave way to a more assertively alive individual who sought others more actively and who attempted to be more open about her ambivalences.

Another patient, a divorcée, who had a close, binding attachment to her daughter, had suffered a series of painful and damaging love affairs. Ms. N.'s father had left her when she was seven. She remembered him as abusive to her mother and sexually rejecting; her mother had slept with her for years after the desertion. Ms. N. never forgot this abusive, abandoning father or the overly intrusive, seductive mother. She constantly tested men to demonstrate and to prove love, to recognize her "givingness," to guarantee commitment, to provide a safe future, to make up for all she didn't have and more. This hunger, colored by anger and clinging, burdened her object relations terribly. Unrealistic demands, stemming from unresolved and powerful needs, doomed relationships from the start. In this case, the analysis of the negative transference to men vis-à-vis the father and the subsequent seductive, impulsively dangerous maternal behavior was critical. Through the clarification and working through of the traumatic events, perverted libidinal ties were loosened, thereby gradually freeing attachment seeking in healthier directions. The ability to love was reborn. In this patient, the transference was immediately idealized. Both my love for her and hers for me constituted core conditions of restitution for lost love, partly serving as a vehicle to reenact past events and evoke past memories, partly as a way of mastering trauma through repetition. Her ability to sustain loving feelings for the therapist, without the therapist's setting any conditions, helped her to form healthier object ties in the real world.

Love's struggle can be contaminated by an overinvestment in a parent who becomes overly idealized, erotized, a chronic competitor, an oedipal rival, an omnipotent caretaker to whom the individual is forever indebted and grateful. Mr. B.'s marital harmony was from the beginning disrupted by a series of love affairs. Mr. B. had experienced his mother as all-invading, all-knowing, all-powerful, seductive, stiff and critical. Her psychic presence and influence was more imposing than the father's. Mr. B. married a woman who clearly echoed the maternal introject. The transference love to the wife smacked of incestuous fixations and paved the way for an ongoing repetition-compulsion of a classically oedipal variety. Wife-mother was madonna, untouchable, encapsulated, protected from "out of control" libidinal drives (both aggressive and sexual). She was feared and perceived as castrating. The sexual partner was to be sought outside the home—"whore," sexual object, an unattached woman, away from children, a partner in lust and play. Complicating the resolution of this madonna-whore syndrome was the unconscious complicity of the wife, who also sought sexual love outside the marriage. This woman was searching for a "real man," a perfect man outside, a man who could rescue her from the rejecting, preoccupied, and hurtful husband in the home, a clear reminder of her rejecting, distant mother. Oedipal interpretations during the initial and ongoing erotic transference were crucial in revealing the nature of these overdetermined patterns of acting out. A classical neurotic core conflict with obsessive-compulsive features emerged. The therapist's flexibility, acceptance, neutrality, and constancy were clearly important here.

Love's struggle can be influenced by an overexposure to a single parent, in which the mother becomes idealized and the absent father denigrated. Ms. M. came into therapy as a young adult, a senior in college, and a virgin, complaining of difficulties with a jealous boyfriend, who she feared might be "crazy" like her father. Ms. M. feared intercourse, in part because of the change it might mean in her self-representation— "pretty, good girl, virgin, perfect daughter." Her mother was idealized as the poor martyr who took care of her psychotic father until he was institutionalized. Mother's approval, love, and acceptance were critical to this patient's feelings about herself. She was to be a virgin, an A student, a helper, and a therapist to her boyfriend. Critical to treatment was work on separation, including differentiating, distancing, and boundary structuring, eventuating in a psychic disengagement from the mother, and individuation, the evolution of intrapsychic autonomy, a separate sense of self over time. This patient had to use anger and experience disillusionment to finally separate internally from an overly protective and intrusive mother in order to sort out her own psychic direction, her own object choices. Genuine loving had to be preceded by disengagement and delibidinization of the mother-daughter complex. The availability of the therapist as a maternal, loving, giving human figure (imperfect, too) facilitated growth and helped fill the "void" experienced in psychically moving away from archaic and overly binding introjects.

A final dynamic configuration is of the patient traumatized by some significant aversive pattern in childhood or by a series of events that were clinically overwhelming. One patient, Ms. I., a child of Holocaust survivors, had trouble trusting in the continuity of family, happiness, and loyalty. Could good feelings and attachment continue in time, and further, was she entitled to them? Her expectations in life, her projections onto others were typically cast in "doom." This chronic malaise, despair, and pessimism were experienced by others as burdensome, rejecting, and clearly negative. It was critical that therapy provide a nurturant, steady, predictable, and healing base from which to separate and individuate from an unconscious, saturated with death, loss, broken family ties, horror, and hopelessness. It was essential that the therapist be hopeful and affirming of life, a catalyst for positive growth through modeling and empathic interpretation, aimed particularly at understanding the painful difficulties inherent in "embracing" a life following chronic trauma.

Another patient, Mr. J., was an orphan who had spent most of his childhood being transported from one home to the next. His first dream reported in treatment depicted a "space cadet"—literally a man encapsulated in a space uniform, afloat, "no strings attached" and "rootless." This was clearly a metaphor for the unattached individual, defended and bound. Now the father of two daughters, married, owning a home, a dentist, he was very much earth-bound and struggled to find enough free-floating space for himself to unwind. His conflicts remained centered on the balance between the compelling and often appealing tendency to draw back and "suit up" again when interpersonal demands to relate became too intense. Diagnostically this classically schizoidal picture required gentle interpretations on the part of the therapist and active efforts to promote attachment in the form of a reliable, consistent, continuous, and openly warm therapeutic alliance. My ability to be there for him was a powerful ingredient and facilitated "his being there for me" in terms of introspective honesty and emotional vulnerability.

Central to these dynamic patterns is the struggle that individuals have in experiencing pleasure, suffering from a kind of irrational guilt and anxiety that goes beyond "survivor guilt" and its attendant emotions (Why was I saved? Why do I live?). Though this kind of emotional constellation can be caused by a host of factors, it often has to do with deep-seated ambivalent wishes in the parents regarding their children's success in love or happiness and the parents' ability to carry through, emotionally, the empathic support required. A patient reported a dream recently:

> I remember a family that was murdered and I had escaped. And the murderer came after me. I was guilty and he was coming back to get me. I felt I had done something wrong. I had left them. I was responsible. He wanted me, too. I asked myself: "Did I set them up?" I wrestled the gun out of his hand. I had to save myself, not give in or give up.

His general associations had to do with his family of origin, his father's car accident and subsequent death when he was four, his oedipal wishes at the time, his complicity, guilt, rage. He spoke of his mother's death and his anger regarding her emotional negligence and limitations, and her ambivalence toward his growing up and being successful. He described his sister's need for gurus and her unresolved infantile dependancy ties at age forty-five. He revealed his wish to be happy and loving with his current family, his desire to give and to be a successful and strong man, free of handicaps. He believed that his ability to love, to give, and to experience pleasure was historically contaminated by the intrusion of unconscious guilt and murderous impulses. He felt that despite it all, he had to survive and go forth.

A woman patient had turned fifty, and described to me a birthday celebration that was full of good feelings. In fact, she had even written a prose poem, which she read aloud to a small group of friends and family. The poem spoke honestly of her life, full of loving and being loved, of children growing, of life's nonmaterial riches. Her mother, who was there, called her the next day and said: "What you said was really something. I looked at their faces and they were all so envious. What you have achieved is rare—nurture it." My patient thought about this maternal message and it bothered her. The poem was set on fire in a subsequent dream. Though the mother's words were in part true, her focus was on envy and loss, clearly in part a projection. What it aroused in the patient was old feelings of fear and guilt—fear regarding her mother's rage (remember the Queen in Snow White who out of envy abandons Snow White to be killed?); guilt about achieving and having, an archaic, irrational guilt regarding her wish to be separate from her mother and to have a very different life, and existential guilt because her happiness was thought to arouse longing, hunger, and anger in her mother, who was currently feeling particularly deprived.

The individual that can be happy and loving is one that feels that his parents deeply wished that for him or her and could, beyond the wish, empathically guide him or her toward a satisfactory life. Problems in loving can so often be traced to ambivalent wishes in the parents that result in the inability to allow the course of individuation to take place. As therapists, it is important to be in touch with our feelings regarding our patients' wellbeing. If there are deep-seated ambivalences in the form of jealousy, envy, competition in relation to the patient's success in loving and being loved, it will be felt in the transference-countertransference. If not recognized, albeit privately by the analyst, these feelings can be insidious and exert an influence on the course of treatment or limit the extent to which it can go. If left unanalyzed, these feelings and subsequent therapeutic action may cause a reenactment of the narcissistic parent who cannot tolerate, because of pathological envy and deprivation, the child's growth, success or happiness. Such a reenactment can cause in turn an empathic block in treatment—a barrier hindering subsequent growth.

Empathic blocks are often experienced in different ways in treatment and can, if unrecognized, interfere with our ability to care for our patients in a nurturant manner. Patients who can make us feel inordinately impotent, envious, guilty, frustrated, angry, and despairing, among other affective states, are typically called "difficult." In fact, what is difficult are the feelings they engender in the therapist. Our task is to work through these feelings creatively and with insight. Among the more powerful feelings engendered are love and intimacy. How do therapists, as people, receive love? How comfortable are we with intimacy? The degree to which we are, the degree to which our self-object boundaries are firm, allowing flexibly both benign symbiosis and benign empathic separateness, will determine in part the extent to which our patients will grow in intimacy. Bellak (1970) referred to the intimacy index as the "porcupine dilemma," inspired by the Schopenhauer parable of two porcupines huddling together on a wintry day for warmth: too close meant pain from the quills, too far meant that there was insufficient warmth. This index certainly applies to life and, in a microcosmic form, to the world of psychotherapy.

In facilitating our patients' ability to love, we are models. We are analysts, self-objects, parental figures, objects of transference, projective screens and mirrors, *and* genuine, imperfect human beings. In treating patients who have been emotionally deprived from early childhood, we respond empathically and flexibly to developmental needs, parameters of treatment being creatively modified according to individual requirements. What is needed is the flexible use of the self from neutral analyst to friend, to counselor—from opaque screen to an existential partner in life's struggle, and finally, as coparticipants in the human condition.

SUMMARY

The struggle to love is a natural part of each individual's unique historical legacy and psychic inheritance. It is made more complicated by the current cultural climate of shifting values. In understanding the individual dynamic configurations of our patients and in sculpting out unique pathways to health, we remain embedded in an age marked by much questioning and much acting out. As therapists, it is important to be clear, at least within ourselves, as to what we consider essential qualities of healthy love and attachment. The ultimate tool in therapy is the analyst—what we believe *will* shape what happens—and who we are, loving, unloving, steadfast, wavering, nurturant, unyielding, will facilitate or limit the growth of a "human" being. In loving our patients, I believe we are healing. Therapeutic cure rests on a unique human connection, one that is accurately empathic, accepting, and reliable.

REFERENCES

Balint, M. 1965. *Primary love and psychoanalytic technique.* New York: Liveright.
Bellak, L. 1970. *The porcupine dilemma: Reflections on the human condition.* New York: Citadel.
Bergmann, M. S. 1982. Platonic love, transference love, and love in real life. *Journal of the American Psychoanalytic Association* 30:87–111.
Bowlby, J. 1969. *Attachment and loss,* vol. 1: *Attachment and loss.* New York: Basic Books.
———. 1973. *Attachment and loss,* vol. 2: *Separation anxiety and anger.* New York: Basic Books.
Freud, S. 1916. Some character-types met with in psycho-analytic work. *Standard edition* 14:311–33.
Kohut, H. 1977. *The restoration of the self.* New York: IUP.
Lorenz, K. 1970. *Studies in animal and human behavior,* vol. 1. London: Methuen.
Mahler, M. S. 1967. On human symbiosis and the vicissitudes of individuation:

Infantile psychosis. *Journal of the American Psychoanalytic Association* 15:740–63.

Spitz, R. A. 1950. Anxiety in infancy: A study of its manifestations in the first year of life. *International Journal of Psycho-analysis* 31:138–43.

Stern, D. 1977. *The first relationship: Infant and mother.* Cambridge: Harvard University Press.

Stone, L. 1961. *The psychoanalytic situation.* New York: IUP.

Sullivan, H. S. 1953. *The interpersonal theory of psychiatry.* New York: Norton.

Winnicott, D. W. 1945. *Through pediatrics to psychoanalysis.* London: Hogarth.

Zuckerberg, J. 1984. Empathy: A fundamental aspect of healing. In P. Olsen, ed., *Comprehensive Psychotherapy* 4.71–91. New York: Gordon and Breach.

12. The Self and Loving

Harold B. Davis

Throughout the history of psychoanalysis the concept of love has rarely been directly addressed. A review of the literature shows a relative paucity of articles on love as compared to any other topic in psychoanalysis. Lust, passion, and sex appear more frequently than love and loving. Perhaps love is assumed to be covered under topics such as psychosexual stages and libido. Yet that it is subsumed under other concepts may well express anxiety about a direct reference to a concept of love. This anxiety may be related to the fact that Freudian concepts might have to be altered if love were considered a process independent of the sexual. Other psychoanalytic writers have seen love differently. Reik (1944), for example, considers love a process separate from the sexual drive that may nevertheless overlap with the sexual drive. By so doing he considers love as more than the sublimation of sex, and he implicitly questions drive theory altogether in relation to love. Analysts who have given up drive theory, such as Fromm (1947, 1956) and May (1969), have written directly about love, particularly as it relates to issues of identity and the self. Kohut (1964, 1977), who also has given up drive theory, comes close to Fromm (1947) and May (1969) in his concept of self as it relates to narcissism, with its implications for the capacity to love. This essay attempts to present a psychoanalytic definition of love as it is intertwined with issues of narcissism, dependency, and loss.

Freud is reported to have said that the goal of life is "zu lieben und zu arbeiten" ("to love and to work"). Although love is implied as an active state in this statement, Freud (1914) did not focus on this aspect of love in his theory. He was concerned with the love object to which the libidinal energy was cathected. In clinical papers regarding problems in loving, he emphasized the lack of integration of tender and sensual feelings, and he states that their integration constitutes normal loving (Freud 1912). And, in fact, the failure to integrate these two feelings is still considered pathological (Schachtel, 1959; Khan 1974).

Reik (1944) took exception to Freud and clearly stated that love is not derived from the sexual but has its own origin. Reik indicates that the fact that love and sex often go together does not mean they must inherently do so and that sex can be performed without love. Love is an outgrowth of the stage of individuation. A person falls in love as a way to cope with feelings of "discontent," which is Reik's word for an awareness of one's insufficiency (1944). Thus love is a means for a person to cope with his individuality and his discontent or lack. This position, written shortly after Fromm's article "Selfishness and Self-Love" (1939) and later expanded in 1947, is in keeping with Fromm's position. Although there is no known influence of Fromm on Reik (that there was any influence is doubtful), Reik's position is similar to the existential approach of Fromm and of May (1969).

Fromm (1956) developed Freud's concept of "to love and to work" into "the productive orientation" in his book *The Art of Loving*. He describes four characteristics of love: care, responsibility, respect, and knowledge. Without the inclusion and integration of these characteristics, what looks like love is more likely to be infatuation or dependency masquerading as love. Thus Fromm (1956) clearly differentiated the subjective experience of love from the character of the person, emphasizing the character far more than the intensity of the subjective experience. Only the person who has individuated would have a character that is capable of loving.

In *Love and Will* (1969), May deals with the many facets of loving and the difficulties encountered in the contemporary cultural scene. He, too, separates the concept of loving from the romantic and views it as part of the personality. He also speaks of forms of love that are not part of sexuality. However, May stresses the existential aspects of loving as an authentic experience, which, when it is part of the personality, fills the existential void, or, in Reik's word, discontent.

Gediman and Bergmann are among the present-day Freudians writing of love. Gediman (1981) seems to equate loving with the passionate side of man. In her analysis of the *Tristan and Isolde* myth, she points out the dangers both of giving in to unrestrained passion and of connecting to the preoedipal mother as experienced in the image of the femme fatale. Since romantic love is derived from the blissful preoedipal symbiotic stage that preceded separateness, anxieties about engulfment and reestablishing the symbiotic tie may interfere with the ability to love. Bergmann (1980) has indicated that loving is sui generis and a means of refinding and improving upon the earliest love object; like Reik (1944), therefore, he does not consider love a sublimation of sex.

The object-relations and self psychologists seem to take a similar position. Winnicott (1965) maintains a distinction between loving as an expression of ego relatedness and passionate feelings as an expression of the id. Capacity for concern, for him, would be a precondition for a capacity to love. Klein (1964) and her followers (e.g., Segal 1974) stressed the resolution of the depressive position and the making of reparation as a precondition for loving. For the Kleinians the making of reparation is directly related to the experience of guilt over one's destructive capacities. Their view that the capacity for loving is related to the resolution of guilt is a distinctive one.

Kohut (1977) is similar to both the neo-Freudians and to Guntrip (1961) in his view of love as a result of the integration of personality, which includes the maintenance of values. Thus loving is the endpoint of the development of the self: a characteristic of an integrated self. For Kohut, (1964, 1977) the self is never separated from the self object. In his only direct reference to love in *The Restoration of the Self* (1977) Kohut states, in a footnote, that mature love includes an element of mutual admiration and a mutuality of self-esteem. Thus the other person is always present as the self object. Kohut (1964, 1977) does not use the concept of dependency. Perhaps it is subsumed under the concept of self object, or perhaps it is due to his emphasis on the narcissistic state, where, as will be shown later, dependency is denied.

For Guntrip (1961), love is part of the highest stage, called mature dependency. In this stage there is a recognition of the other as separate as well as the recognition of one's own need. There is no illusion of independence. For Guntrip (1961), a critical aspect of love is that there is no need to change the other person. The Jungians, one of the earliest schools to use the self as a concept, stress the self as the entity that engages in loving, and recognize that loving can only occur after projections and counterprojections are resolved (Edinger 1972). This definition of love is quite different from Kohut's where love includes mutual idealization, since in idealization there is projection.

One difference among the psychoanalytic schools on the concept of love is the role of idealization and unrealistic projections onto the other. Freud (1914) and Kohut (1977) indicate that love includes the overestimation of the love object. Fromm (1956), May (1969), and Jungians see this overestimation as part of an infatuation and view love as dependent upon the resolution of the projections and counterprojections, which allows the other person to be seen in his or her own right and not merely as a self object. The ability to see the other as he or she is requires giving up romantic notions, including the overestimation of the love object, and depends on the maturity and character of the person and his ability to pierce illusions. Perhaps the difference between these two orientations reflects the fact that Freud was connected to a drive theory and the others were committed to a self theory. Nevertheless, in his statement that the goal of life is "zu lieben und zu arbeiten," Freud implies a level of development that is in keeping with Fromm's (1956) productive personality, who is capable of loving, and with Guntrip's (1961) definition of love. Kohut (1977) comes close to this position as well, although he does not fully develop it, perhaps because his emphasis is on the narcissistic personality in whom idealization is an important defense. In such instances the failure to maintain idealization leads the person to feel criticized and potentially fragmented; his or her sense of self is lost.

The current psychoanalytic positions view loving as part of the character structure of the person, most specifically the self. It also implies that loving another requires the integration of tender and sensual feelings. A definition of love and loving derived from these writers would be as follows: A loving relationship is one in which the self of each partner, while connected in a shared identity, also flourishes and is enhanced individually. It includes sexual feelings and desires, but only when those are part of the total personality and not merely isolated sensual experiences. This definition of love does not imply an ideal state without anxiety. The enhancement of one partner may cause the other anxiety for several reasons. Their shared identity and its stability is threatened and it may be uncertain that a new shared identity will evolve. In addition, no person is so stable or mature as not to be threatened with the experience of envy in response to the other person's enhancement. In a loving relationship, however, these envious feelings and concomitant rage would be temporary reactions to the threat that one's enhancement may have for the other. The person would be able to transcend these feelings by expanding the self to include the other in a new shared identity.

If mature love can be considered to be the relatedness of two selves, which allows each to grow, then various difficulties in maintaining a self will inevitably interfere with the ability to love. A sense of self requires both the experience of oneself as separate and the mental image of oneself as separate. This state presupposes an ability to relate to an inner world and to an outer world. The self is not a reflection of others but the unique integration of the experiences that define oneself. It is this self that enters into a loving relationship with another self. Thus people who are fragmented may not be able to love. Being fragmented, they may relate with a part of themselves in every situation. Such people may have keener and more intense experiences than those not fragmented, since they are more in touch with earlier sensations. In their split they may be even more in touch with the intensities of sensual experiences than someone who has integrated tender and sensual feelings.

The narcissistic state, which is often equated with self as defined by Freud (1914), is not merely an instinctual drive but also the beginning of the self, or unity. The contribution of Kohut's self psychology may in fact be a redefinition of narcissism away from a drive theory to a concept of self based upon psychological principles (1964). Thus, for a subgroup of people, he emphasizes the importance of an integrated self and the difficulties in maintaining an integrated self. He clearly states, however, that at birth there ". . . is a *virtual* self" (1977, p. 101, italics his). Therefore he no longer relies on narcissism as a concept for the self, and he brings the self more directly into classical psychoanalysis in its own right. I have used the term *narcissism* both in relation to its self meaning and in its clinical sense as an overevaluation of the self, in other words a need to bolster a faltering self. An overevaluation of the self, albeit in a defensive stance, requires others to comply with this overevaluation, usually by being adoring and idealizing. Demanding that one be adored and idealized protects the person from feeling both a lack of confidence and of competence in the individual self. These lacks are the consequences themselves of an unstable and a split self.

Freud (1914) made the distinction between narcissistic and anaclitic love. This distinction states that a person loves someone according to the ego ideal (what one wishes to become), or according to one's dependency needs as in a love for a mother or parent. In both instances there is a recognition that the person who loves is in a state of need (or lack), which requires another person. Longing is an essential quality of loving and the experience of need. In the narcissistic form of loving, however, loving one's own image and not recognizing that this image is itself an introject that stemmed from some anaclitic relationship, is a way of negating dependency needs and longing.

The neo-Freudians, coming out of a social orientation, would see this need or lack as an inevitable aspect of the human condition, an existential reality, and loving as the normal way to fill the void. However, it is this very lack or need that the narcissist is trying to deny by an overestimation of himself and by an irrational self-aggrandizement that is aided and abetted by the current values of our culture. This defensive maneuver is the result of pain due to actual or fantasied disappointments in relationships. The pain is usually associated with themes of loss and dependency and the experience of separateness. In the anxiety about being alone and separate, the narcissist maintains an illusion of total self-sufficiency but also demands that others echo him and focus on him. Perhaps this pattern is an attempt to avoid the experience of total dependence upon someone else, which can also be maintained by splits of dependency upon more than one person.

The narcissist attempts to avoid the experience of separateness within his mind. His underlying grandiosity prevents him from experiencing others as separate from himself. The true narcissistic injury may be an event that has no relevance to oneself but that nevertheless affects one. The myth of Narcissus illustrates an irrational self-sufficiency and the avoidance both of separateness and of dependency. In the myth (D'Aulaire and D'Aulaire 1962; Graves 1968), Narcissus perishes after persistently gazing at his own reflection in the pond. He turns into the flower, Narcissus, as a result of his self-absorption, which is a punishment for not loving Echo. At his side was Echo, who because she betrayed a goddess was punished by being deprived of the capacity to hear any voice other than her own. Thus the relationship between Narcissus and Echo reflects two people who in their self-absorption can hear only their own voices or see only themselves and not the other person. Narcissus loses his status as a god in human form and becomes a plant. I believe that this is a significant image in that it represents a regression to an organic state that predates animal life. This image also reflects a regression to a symbiotic state, a return to mother earth, with a total loss of self and separateness. One is indeed rooted and connected to the nutrients in plant life, and one cannot survive without the attachment. In addition the capacity for ideation, thought, and reflection are lost.

The theme of punishment in the myth suggests guilt. Here the Kleinian concept of reparation for one's destructive fantasies is important. If love is the capacity to relate to another person with a "capacity for concern" then one needs to be able to feel guilt when it is appropriate to do so. The failure to be able to do so leaves the person in the manic state to cope with the depressive position. In the narcissist, guilt may be denied and the experience of shame and humiliation accentuated. I believe, however, that the narcissistic strivings may be an attempt to offset a sense of unlovability stemming from guilt, which manifests itself as self-hatred and shame. The guilt would be tied to the hurt one's own narcissistic goals may have for the other, and the shame stems from not being able to reach the ideal goal. A subjective sense of unworthiness may develop with a concomitant disbelief in one's ability to love. A stable sense of unworthiness interferes with loving because the person is not able to tolerate any good feelings and rejects closeness and tenderness when it is expressed. Instead the self is heavily weighted with darker feelings, such as anger, and is blocked from having good or even ambivalent feelings. Thus the self is threatened by good feelings and anger is provoked to maintain the status quo of unworthiness. This pattern is often seen in what is referred to as the negative therapeutic reaction, in which the patient's resistance is a reaction to good and tender feelings emerging in the treatment and not a response to negative countertransference.

The earliest experience of one's unlovability is the feeling of disappointment in not gaining or in losing the love and attention of one's mother, especially the narcissistic mother. Losing the position of being the apple of a mother's eye makes the child feel both rejected and unworthy. This loss of symbiotic oneness is experienced as embarrassing, and leads to feelings of self-hatred rather than of hatred of the mother. The narcissist's vulnerability to this loss which results in depression, and acting out, is described in O'Neill's *A Moon for the Misbegotten* (1952), and in Camus's *The Stranger* (1946). In both of these works, acting out of rage and sex results from the loss of the fantasied symbiotic tie brought about by the death of a mother. The acting out is an attempt to regain the narcissistic state of oneness with a mothering person or its symbolic representation as well as allowing for an expression of the rage that always accompanies a loss of symbiosis. It also protects the self from further fragmentation.

The biological tie with the mother ends with birth, and the psychological symbiosis begins. This psychological symbiosis lessens under the impact of development and differentiation, and with the beginning of group experience as expressed in oedipal problems. When the lessening of this tie causes too much anxiety, around separateness and aloneness, the child attempts to maintain this tie psychologically. It can be maintained in a symbolic form by striving for narcissistic goals, the achievement of which brings about a feeling of well-being in the sense of maintaining a good view in one's own and others' eyes. One's own eyes also includes one's introjects. Thus the attempt to reach ideal goals as a means of obtaining a sense of well-being and the consequent worthlessness when there is a failure to maintain such goals is a symbolic representation of the maintenance of self-esteem through contact with the mother in the earliest stages of development. Attempts to maintain well-being by such goals are connected to the attempt to maintain a state of being adored reminiscent of the earliest years. Adoration of the earliest years is substitutive of a loving relationship that recognizes differences and separateness.

The terms *symbiosis, fusion,* and *dependency* refer to different aspects of the mother-child interraction, and ultimately to any dyadic relationship. Unfortunately, these terms have been merged so that their respective meanings and nuances have been overlooked. The result is that any closeness and the difficulties it engenders between two people have been blurred. In the symbiotic state the two are united as one in a positive or negative manner. There is no individuation in symbiosis, and the loss of one means the death of the other, as in the *Romeo and Juliet* theme. Neither can outlive the other; there have been reports of spouses who have died shortly after a mate, as if one could not live without the other.

Fusion presupposes some separateness and differentiation which is then lost. In fusion there is a melting into one another and a loss of the boundary of the self. In symbiosis there is no boundary. On the positive side of fusion is the temporary melting into one another and the tactile sensations induced by the other. To experience this requires a freedom from restraints and the capacity to transcend the restrictions of one's personality. In addition, there is a psychological fusion whereby one becomes like the person one loves. The anxiety concerning fusion may be compared to the anxiety of a school phobic, who is afraid to go to school because he is afraid his mother (at home) won't be there when he returns. A person afraid of fusion is afraid of being stuck, often expressed in the image of a tunnel, which may be an expression of a sexual experience or of a malignant regression. To such a person to fuse is to be stuck in a malignant regression (Balint 1968) from which one does not expect to return and in which the self is lost. Kohut (1964) states that people with self disorders fear regression, for they may feel that their self will be permanently lost. This incapacity will affect their love capacity.

The ability to love requires the ability to tolerate momentary loses of self, to endure sensations that blur the distinction between self and other. A self that is split will not have the flexibility to allow for momentary fusions. Thus the experience of fused states in loving threatens the self and leads to experiences of confusion as the self faces alien experiences. Defensive maneuvers to offset these anxiety states, such as isolation and the maintenance of hostile interactions, develop in order to maintain a boundary between the two people and thus to avoid a state of fusion.

Dependency states recognize a distinction between the two parties involved. Paradoxically, separateness and dependency go together. Only after separateness can the issue of dependency be relevant, for before separateness there is no other upon whom to depend. A dependent state brings to the fore issues of control, dominance, submission, and other variations on the theme of a power struggle. This is particularly true in a society in which dependency needs are readily denied.

In the loving relationship, anxieties about need for the other and being dependent upon the other may lead to hostile, angry interactions, since the self of the dependent one is threatened with embarrassment because of open or implied expression of need. The vulnerability to rejection to which a person exposes himself as a result of expressing a need and the embarrassment that would be experienced if the need is not met often result in a denial of need or in the anxiety that the other will exploit one's need. Much of a person's demandingness is an indirect way of expressing need and of obtaining help without leaving him or herself open to rejection. Two young patients, each in their own way, expressed this pattern. Both needed some help from their parents and thought that their parents would reject them. In actuality the parents were reasonably supportive, but both patients felt that their need was so overwhelming that it would evoke a hostile reaction or even drive the other away. The intensity of their dependency needs were so interwoven with their love feeling that to love would be to overburden the other with dependency needs and destroy them. While it is true that dependency may itself be used in a hostile way to control others in a power struggle, the capacity to express need and to have it met in a realistic manner may be a prerequisite for moving from immature to mature dependency. It is for this reason, I suspect, that Guntrip (1961) refers to the movement from immature to mature dependency and not to independence.

Khan (1974) has written about the dread of surrendering to resourceless dependency, in which a person becomes completely passive without any inner resources. The wish for an ideal state is connected to this passivity and dependency in two ways. First, the ideal state usually means one in which one's dependency needs are fully met without any effort on one's part, as in the Garden of Eden. Second, seeking an ideal state may be a way to impose one's wishes onto another. What is ideal for me is to have you meet my desires and wishes without regard for yourself. In apparent weakness through passivity there is strength and in the name of idealization there is an attempt at domination.

In loving, there is always the concomitant risk of loss of the love object or of love itself. Loss implies the ruin and/or destruction of some one or thing that is valued. If one did not value the other there would be no loss. What is being lost may be the affective-cognitive bond that constitutes a loving relationship. To use Bowlby's (1969) phrase, it is an attachment by which the self of the loving person is connected to another and out of which it develops and maintains its self. Its loss threatens a person with depersonalization. The child's initial attachment is maintained through eye contact as the recent observational research of Stern (1976, 1977) has shown. The beginning of a response to a mirror image is the beginning of self, and this is connected to the mothering experience and to how one is viewed in the eye of others and subsequently in one's own eye. The loss of the mirror image, a precursor of self, may cause depersonalization, as illustrated in the opera *The*

Tales of Hoffman. The main character is enthralled by Guiletta, and at the moment of his enthrallment he loses his reflection, for he can no longer see himself in the mirror. With feelings of embarrassment, dread, and horror, he cries out, "I have lost my reflection." It is no accident that Guiletta's previous conquest was named Schlémil. As Laing (1959) has indicated, the loss of the ability to perceive and to be perceived is experienced as a loss of being. Thus at the moment of being captured by the other in passion, he is threatened with the loss of an inner image and, his capacity to reflect upon himself. This potential loss of self is also evoked by separation and ultimately death. It is interesting to note that the French refer to an orgasm as *la petite mort*.

The cognitive-affective bond that is essential to the development of the self and to the viability of the self is threatened by any loss or anxiety about separation. Yet it may paradoxically be true that the cognitive-affective bond from which we develop holds an allure for a return to it, but if acquiesced to, this allure threatens the developed self. This is particularly true where a strong self has not developed.

There are several other difficulties or distortions in loving. Where the self is split, there is likely to be a splitting in relationships in which a part of oneself is projected onto one person and another part on another person. The split self, then, maintains itself by having separate relationships and by projecting onto the other, with one part representing the good mother and the other part representing the bad mother. (This may vary for the female in that it would be the father, but it would be the mother image in the father rather than the father per se.) These two parts also represent the two types of loving, the narcissistic and the anaclitic, with the former representing the good and the latter the bad object. The self in these situations needs protection against the intrusion of ambivalence, which the split maintains. Intense fury is also kept in abeyance by the maintenance of the split. In addition, threats stemming both from loss and regression to resourceless dependency are also minimized.

The integration of tender feelings (love, compassion, affection, kindness) with sensual feelings, including sexual ones, still remains a critical aspect in difficulties in loving. Although times have changed since Freud, there is still emphasis on competition, which lessens the value of tender feelings. Since the tender feelings are often seen as a sign of weakness, they are dissociated and covered over by anger. I suspect that much of a patient's anger may be an indirect way of getting close without expressing tender feelings. An interesting twist has been noted by Carola Mann (at a conference), who in working with older people noted that men seem to be more tender as they were moving away from competition and that women were more competitive as they moved away from tender feelings. I would suspect that this may be true at an earlier age as well. Sullivan (1953) has most eloquently described one transformation, of tender feelings into hostility and anger, in his concept of the malevolent transformation. According to Sullivan, this transformation is exacerbated by a withdrawal pattern in which a person feels that he had only been happy before he had to interact with people. At some point, the cognitive-affective bond becomes so overwhelming or anxiety-producing that the pain becomes greater than the satisfaction. The person then retreats into a cocoon or an introversion, hoping to obtain satisfactions in fantasy. Such attempts are protective devices for a fragile self.

Bergmann (1980) has indicated another form of difficulty which stems from self-hatred. Earlier, I related self-hatred to guilt and hatred of others; but in some instances, self-hatred prevents mirroring, because if the other is like the hated self he or she is similarly rejected. Self-hatred may also cause difficulty in maintaining idealization or in the sharing of a common illusion. Denigration, belittling, and creating conflicts are part of the defensive aspects of the self.

Difficulty in allowing for expansion of the boundaries of the self is another issue. Boundaries shift in that the male may have feminine wishes and the female masculine ones. The psychological reality of bisexuality needs to be tolerated while the person is able to maintain the self-concept appropriate to him or her-self.

Psychoanalytic writers seem to agree that the capacity to love requires the person to be separate from the parental ties and be individuated. There are different meanings to this individuation. The Bible says that one must leave one's parents and cleave to another. This is more easily done physically than emotionally. Emotionally it means the recognition that much personal interaction is made up of projections and counterprojections in which the being of each is hidden or lost. Where there is a self that has been individuated, then there are two beings to glimpse and to relate to each other. Only such a relationship can be considered to be love. Thus the psychoanalytic process, through helping a person individuate, helps the person to love. By individuating, people are able to see others as they are and not as they wish them to be, and are able to relate to and nourish them while being nourished. Individuation means the loss of illusions that protect the self from feeling isolated and alone, and their replacement by realistic relationships to others. In the face of that great loss, death, it is our capacity for love that allows us to be, unlike Narcissus, connected to people and rooted in the human experience.

REFERENCES

Balint, M. 1968. *The basic fault.* London: Tavistock.
Bergmann, M. S. 1980. On the intrapsychic function of falling in love. *Psychoanalytic Quarterly* 49:56–77.
Bowlby, J. 1969. *Attachment and loss,* vols. 1–2. New York: Basic Books.
Camus, A. 1946. *The stranger.* New York: Knopf.
D'Aulaire, I., and E. P. D'Aulaire. 1962. *Book of Greek myths.* New York: Doubleday.
Edinger, E. F. 1972. *Ego and archetype.* New York: Putnam.
Freud, S. 1912. On the universal tendency to debasement in the sphere of love. *Standard edition* 11, p:179–90.
———. 1914. On narcissism: An introduction. *Standard edition* 14:73–102.
Fromm, E. 1939. Selfishness and self-love. *Psychiatry* 2:507–23.
———. 1947. Selfishness, self-love, and self-interest. In Fromm, *Man for himself,* pp. 119–41. New York: Rinehart.
———. 1956. *The art of loving.* New York: Harper.
Gediman, H. 1981. On love, dying together, and *Liebestod* fantasies. *Journal of the American Psychoanalytic Association* 29:607–30.
Graves, R. 1968. *New Larousse encyclopedia of mythology.* London: Hamlyn.
Guntrip, H. 1961. *Personality structure and human interaction.* New York: IUP.
Khan, M. M. R. 1974. *The privacy of the self.* New York: IUP.
Klein, M. 1964. *Love, hate, and reparation.* New York: Norton.
Kohut, H. 1964. *The analysis of the self.* New York: Norton.
———. 1977. *The restoration of the self.* New York: IUP.
Laing, R. S. 1959. *The divided self.* London: Pelican.
May, R. 1969. *Love and will.* New York: Norton.
O'Neill, E. 1952. *A moon for the misbegotten.* New York: Random House.
Reik, T. 1944. *A psychologist looks at love.* New York: Farrar and Rinehart.
Schachtel, E. 1959. *Metamorphosis.* New York: Basic Books.
Segal, H. 1974. *An introduction to the work of Melanie Klein.* London: Hogarth.
Stern, D. 1976. Mother and infant play: The dyadic intervention involving fa-

cial, focal, and gaze behaviors. In M. Lewis, and L. A. Rosenblum, eds., *The Effects of the infant on its caretaker*, pp. 87–254. New York: Wiley.

———. 1977. *The first relationship: infant and mother*. Cambridge: Harvard University Press.

Sullivan, H. S. 1953. *The interpersonal theory of psychiatry*. New York: Norton.

Winnicott, D. W. 1965. *The maturational process and the facilitating environment*. London: Hogarth.

13. Aspects of the Erotic Transference

Helen W. Silverman

Love can enter the treatment situation suddenly, with a good deal of noise and disturbance, or it can slip in shyly, stealthily, and slowly. In countless forms and in endless variety, it is an inevitable part of treatment. Patients enter treatment with the expectation that they are supposed to fall in love with their therapist. Laughing nervously in the first session, they ask, "Do I have to fall in love with you for treatment to work?" What happens phenomenologically to the patient, analyst, and the treatment when this intense emotion appears in the psychoanalytic situation? This chapter is an exploration of the phenomenon that Freud called transference love: specifically, how it is conceived, its manifestations in treatment on the part of the patient and analyst, and the gender differences in the experience.

Discovery of the erotic transference was simultaneous with, and in fact, the vehicle of the discovery of transference proper. It was in the treatment of Anna O. by Josef Breuer that transference was first noted, and seen then only as a disturbance and a disruption of treatment. It was the erotic transference of Anna O., eventuating in her hysterical pregnancy, which triggered the abrupt and dramatic termination of the treatment. Freud was struck by the power and force of the dynamic of love within the treatment. He concluded from these events that the arousal of love was not elicited by the analyst himself but by the very nature of the treatment situation. Only with that assurance did Breuer agree to collaborate in writing *Studies of Hysteria* with Freud. According to Jones (1953), Breuer was still, even ten years later, bothered by the failed treatment of Anna O., and particularly by the sexual aspects of the case. It was clear from contemporary accounts that Breuer was caught up emotionally with the treatment of Anna O., that he terminated the treatment in a panic, and that his wife, Freud, and even Freud's wife-to-be Martha were aware of the situation. Reflecting his theoretical interests at that time, Freud emphasized the importance of the patient's feelings and did not focus on the role of the analyst's contribution in the evolving erotic transference, nor did he explore the mutuality of the interaction. One could speculate that this view might have been influenced by Freud's realization of Breuer's discomfort and desire to protect him, arising out of his long-standing admiration and idealization of Breuer.

Transference love was described by Freud as the outbreak of a passionate demand for love, in which the patient, heretofore affectionate and intelligent, and working in treatment, is suddenly without insight and seems "swallowed up in her love." The patient declares her love for the analyst openly, deflects all her interest from the work of treatment, and puts the analyst in an "awkward position." He also described a more intransigent form of transference love in some patients where their elemental passions are such that it is accessible only to the "logic of soup with dumplings for arguments" and where gratification and not insight were desired (Freud 1915a, p. 167).

Freud tackled the important and still vital question of whether the love that is seen in treatment is the same as genuine love in his 1915 paper "Observations on Transference-Love." His eloquent and surprising answer is that "the state of being in love that makes its appearance in the course of treatment has the character of 'genuine love'" (p. 168). He goes on:

It is true that the [transference] love consists of new editions of old traits and that it repeats infantile reactions. But this is the essential character of every state of being in love. There is no such state which does not reproduce infantile prototypes. . . . Transference love has perhaps a degree less of freedom than the love which appears in ordinary life and is called normal; it displays its dependence on the infantile patterns more clearly and is less adaptable and capable of modification, but that is all, and not what is essential. (p. 168)

Transference love interested Freud "because it occurs so often and is so important in its real aspects, and partly because of its theoretical interest" (1915a, p. 159). After seeing it only as an interference with treatment, Freud came to view the transference as a powerful and central means for enriching and deepening analysis and as a path leading back to the retrieval of infantile history, memories, and loves. It was through the transference that earlier connections to love objects could be traced. Freud saw all love as a search for the original infantile objects and all later loves as an attempt to regain and integrate these infantile objects. It is noteworthy that Freud used the term *transference love,* and indeed he seems to be talking about love and falling in love, and not only about sexual feelings and erotic longings. In the subsequent psychoanalytic literature, however, this phenomenon is rarely described using the affectively connotative word *love,* but is usually referred to more narrowly as either erotic transference or erotized transference, without mention of love.

The phrase *erotic transference* has supplanted one of the aspects of transference that Freud termed transference love. The erotic transference includes feelings that may range from "strong affection to strong sexual attraction, from ubiquitous unconscious sexual transference wishes to conscious ego syntonic transference occupation" (Blum 1973, p. 69). The erotic transference is seen by many analysts as a relatively universal phase of analysis (Blum 1973; Frayn and Silberfeld 1986).

The other aspect of Freud's transference love, the more intransigent and stubborn "soup and dumpling" type, is referred to as the *erotized transference*. It is seen as a specialized form of the erotic transference, on the extreme end of the spectrum. Erotized transference was not a term used by Freud and seems to have been first introduced to the psychoanalytic literature by Blitzstein via quotations by Rappoport (1956) and Gitelson (1952). Blitzstein used the term *erotization* to indicate the desire of the patient to overplay the erotic component in the transference and to scream out that he wants his fantasy to be reality, a definition which emphasizes the conscious aspects. The implication that patients could control this reaction, if only they chose to, may reflect the analyst's annoyance, discomfort, and impatience. A definition differing in its emphasis is "an intense, vivid, irrational, erotic preoccupation with the analyst, characterized by overt, seemingly ego-syntonic demands for love and sexual fulfillment from the analyst" (Blum 1973, p. 63). Many varieties of erotic feelings and patient demands for gratification from the analyst are considered as erotized transference, including demands for physical contact, craving for sexual relations with the therapist, unlimited demands for approval and admiration, the need to please and comply, and dependent clinging with fear of object loss. In the erotized transference the patient no longer sees treatment as a therapeutic relationship but one in which demands for gratification must be fulfilled. It is in part for this reason, and in part because it makes both participants extremely anxious, that it may often lead to the inappropriate transfer or premature termination of patients.

The erotized transference has been considered by some analysts such as Greenson as unamenable to psychoanalytic treatment and one for which parameters of psychotherapy and support are more appropriate. The frustration of the analyst in dealing with patients in an erotized transference is vividly described by Greenson (1967):

> The patients were ready for action, they seemed to listen to interventions and interpretations but they were not influenced by ordinary analytic measures. If they agreed with an interpretation it was merely lip-service and as a means to get me to stop talking. They came to their hours eagerly but not for insight, only to enjoy the physical proximity. My interventions seemed irrelevant to them. (p. 339)

There is much discussion in the literature about the level of functioning of people exhibiting erotized transferences. Rappoport (1956) viewed it as a phenomenon of predominantly borderline patients who have difficulty with reality testing and who do not view the therapist *as if* he were the parent but who insist that *he is* the parent. Blum (1973) has stated that those people exhibiting an erotized transference were generally subjects of childhood seduction. Others theorize that the state of excitement manifested is related to earlier masturbatory excitement (Meltzer 1974). Sandler (1970) discussed erotized transference under special forms of transference and linked it with the psychotic transference in its loss of reality testing, therefore isolating it as a form of transference that is unusual and malignant.

Yet as Blum (1973) has aptly said, "Falling in love with the analyst is not a requirement for therapeutic success, nor is erotized transference always a harbinger of analytic failure" (p. 71). It is my impression that many patients have the potential for an erotized transference and that it is not necessarily an indication of manifestation of an ego defect. Support for this belief comes from Blum (1973), who states that the apparent loss of reality testing may only be an aspect of an unfolding transference neurosis and may be an ego regression that is partial and reversible. He does not regard psychoanalysis as an impossibility with an erotized transference but states that the analyzability of the transference depends upon the intact ego functions and the capacity for ego development. He holds that the erotized transference may occur and recede during the vicissitudes of the transference relationship.

There often seems to be some difficulty in deciding exactly where on the continuum of erotic or erotized transference a particular patient falls, although at the extreme ends there would probably be agreement. This may be related to what is perceived and experienced as disturbing by different analysts. One differentiating aspect of an erotic or an erotized transference appears to have to do with the intensity of sexualization and demand for gratification, and its accessibility to therapeutic intervention. The perception of the intensity of the erotic transference and the assessment of its amenability to the psychoanalytic method is, probably in large part, a function of the analyst's theoretical stance, personality, and countertransference to the particular patient. It is possible that an erotic transference in one patient might be more acceptable to a particular analyst than would an equally intense erotic transference on the part of another patient. It is also possible that an analyst's negative reaction to an erotic transference, such as anxiety, avoidance, rejection, may cause a normal erotic transference to become exacerbated or intensified.

In the rest of this chapter I will use the term *erotic transference* to describe the wide variety of behavior in which the patient expresses or in some form demonstrates sexual feelings and/or an idealized form of romantic or loving involvement with the analyst whether mild or extreme. Erotized transference will be used only when the author quoted uses that term. I believe that some form of erotic transference is universal and appears in all treatments, and that the more extreme erotized transference is on a continuum at one end. The absence of an erotic transference, therefore is in itself noteworthy, and an analyzable aspect of the treatment.

In reviewing the literature, I find no unique constellation of personality factors in which an erotic transference can be presumed to occur. It makes its appearance in almost all diagnostic categories and cannot be used as a tool of differential diagnosis, nor does it appear to be indicative of a particular personality dynamic.

The diversity of reasons given for the appearance and meaning of erotic transference suggest that it is, as Freud said, a "complicated process" (1915a) for which no one dynamic can account. The manifest content of the erotic transference is overdetermined, and its significance may not be completely understood until the later phases of the treatment. The erotized transference, according to Blum (1973), may be used as a defense against hostility, homosexuality, loss, or narcissistic injury or may represent the turning of childhood traumatic seduction into active repetition for mastery.

The use of erotized transference as a means of preserving the self and preventing fragmentation and as a means of preserving a sense of identity is discussed by Greenson (1967). He describes a female patient who used erotization as a last-ditch effort to keep from falling into an abyss of a homosexual regression. In another patient it served to enforce the massive denial that she was losing contact with people in general, and suffered from a loss of internal objects. He observed that what seemed like a sensual passion was more like an urgent, gnawing hunger.

Rappoport (1956) sees the underlying dynamic as a hunger for contact. It is not a yearning for love, in his view, because these regressed patients have never known adequate love, though they may have experienced sporadic contact. He suggests that even a verbal battle serves as a substitute form of contact. He links it with a preoedipal defect and views the stormy demands for genital contact as a disguise for an earlier type of contact. There is an overwhelming desire to make the analysis pleasurable and to make the analyst into a real parent. Nunberg (1951) regarded this effort not as a transference but as an attempt to transform the analyst into the actual parent. Rosenfeld (1969) has also noted that it is not uncommon to find in an erotized transference that is ostensibly oedipal one which proves to be preoedipal. He gives as an example patients who want to marry the analyst or make the analysis go on forever and thus remain married to the analysis, as in fact desiring to reestablish a mother-child relationship.

The erotic transference may be preoedipal and, simultaneously, be a restatement of the oedipal situation. In the earlier psychoanalytic writings it appeared as if the oedipal material is revealed and analyzed first, and then the preoedipal appears on cue. It is my impression, however, that these aspects are consistently intertwined and interwoven, and in fact part of the analytic task is to understand the various levels of emotional communication.

It is important to remember that the erotic transference contains, in addition to the residues of the preoedipal and the oedipal, later, adolescent and adult loves. The erotic transference should not be thought of reductionistically as representing only early parental figures. An example is a female patient in her thirties for whom the adolescent high school period is the focus of her erotic fantasy life. In her transference to the analyst she is constantly reenacting that period, testing her attractiveness, teasing, and checking out her popularity. The ultimate aim of the analysis of the transference is the integration of lost loves from all phases of development (Bergmann 1986).

Nevertheless, the early phases of development do exert an immensely powerful influence upon the development of love. Bergmann (1971) evocatively states that the symbiotic phase "leaves as a residue a longing which remains ungratified until love comes" (p. 39). He has expanded Freud's view of the aim of love as a refinding of the lost object (a person) and suggested that the aim of love may also be a refinding of a lost ego state (the blissful state of unity with the mother).

Patients manifesting an extreme erotic transference may be desperately and demandingly trying to force the fulfillment and refinding of the early symbiotic ego state with the analyst. The milder forms of the erotic transference may be expressing the same wish in a gentler and more reality oriented way. The erotic transference is intensified by the analytic situation itself, with the hopes attached to treatment for cure, reparation, and redemption. Analysis allows the sense of object loss to come to the fore through memory and free association. If, as Bak (1973) indicates, the state of being in love is triggered by object loss, separation, or lack of fulfillment of the ego-ideal and is an attempt at finding a substitute object, then it becomes clearer why patients are prone to fall in love with their analyst. Being in love is based on undoing the separation of mother and child. The imagery of love is drawn from the very early ego phases and often refers to the fusion of self and nonself. The person in love finds a substitute object: the loss is undone, and the original object replaced or resurrected. The use of the analyst as a substitute love object is also a way of keeping aggressive feeling out of the analysis and of protecting the analyst from the patient's hostility. If one is in love and desiring its return, how can one be expressing hate and hostility? In addition, it is likely that the analyst's presence as a reasonable, attentive, and responsive person may further stimulate the longing for closeness with the early object, and a return to a pleasurable state of connection. It is possible that the erotic transference can represent an early wished for object as well as the longing to reenact and reinstate an earlier ego state of symbiosis.

It was quite clear to Freud (1915a) that the emergence of a passionate love for the analyst was "largely the work of resistance" (p. 162). The patient may have been in love for a long time, but suddenly "the resistance makes use of her love in order to hinder the continuation of treatment" (p. 162). He noted that the appearance of transference love often occurs just at the point in time when the patient is on the verge of remembering some particularly disturbing or repressed part of her history. It seems that Freud was well aware of the fluctuating nature of the erotic transference phenomenon and of the movement from a friendly positive transference into an erotic one. Freud assumed that the presence of a love transference (in his women patients at least) was a normal and expectable part of treatment. He saw the erotic transference as a particular kind of resistance to the process of recollection and to the treatment itself. Implied also is the resistance to the aims of the analyst and an unconscious attempt to thwart his efforts.

The presence of aggression in the midst of love is part of the human condition, a paradox delineated in poetry and literature as well as psychoanalysis. Freud himself wrote that, "Every intimate emotional relation between two people which lasts for some time—marriage, friendship, the relations between parents and children—contains a sediment of feelings of aversion and hostility, which only escapes perception as a result of repression" (1921, p. 101).

Masquerading as love, the erotic transference is often a guise for intense feelings of hostility and aggression. Certainly the demands for love and for the breaking of the analytic rules are often not experienced as loving by the analyst, and at times, in order to protect himself from frightening and taboo erotic countertransference reactions, the analyst may label erotic transferences as hostile. Apart from this, however, the erotic transference itself can be seen both as having an underlying dynamic of hostility and as serving as a defense against hostility. Saul (1962) states that hostility based on early frustration arises once again in the analytic situation where the dependence, weakness, and libidinal frustration are aroused, and are embedded in the sexual desires toward the analyst.

Stoller (1979), one of the few analysts who has ventured to explore the subject of sexual excitement, has hypothesized that hostility is an essential ingredient of the erotic: "It is hostility—the desire, overt or hidden, to harm another person—that generates and enhances sexual excitement" (p. 6). He traces that hostility to repeated attempts to undo childhood traumas and frustrations that threatened the development of masculinity or femininity.

In discussing the nature of erotic excitement itself, Stoller (1985) has stated that it is experienced as if it were spontaneously and instantly produced, as if we play no part in its creation. When seen in the transference it is perhaps an unconscious attempt on the part of the patient to deconstruct the past, to make all erotic experience the insistent present. The phenomenological experience of suddenness and inevitability splits the present from the past, involves a denial of will and volition, and puts the experience outside of insight and understanding—it just is. Thus the erotic feelings become an enemy of insight and exploration— antithetical to the psychoanalytic endeavor. I think that Stoller provides an interesting perspective from which to view both the defensive function of an erotic transference and the analyst's subjective experience of the intransigence of the erotized transference.

It is most striking that the psychoanalytic literature on erotic transference was conceptualized and written almost exclusively about the male therapist and the female patient. Until recent years the only paper written by a woman analyst about a male patient with an erotic transference was Grete Bibring's (1936) insightful paper pointing to the importance of real as well as transference aspects of the therapist and the interplay between them. She suggests that in certain situations the sex of the therapist does have an effect on whether the patient can undergo or continue analysis. The controversy is still very much alive, with many analysts believing, in the traditionally held view, that maternal and paternal transferences can appear in analyses with an analyst of either sex, though in a different order and with variations in the ease with which it is elicited. Other analysts state that there is real question as to whether such transferences can be elicited and worked through by analysts of either sex. Concurrent with the growth of interest in the analyst's personality and its contribution to the analytic situation, attention has been increasingly paid to individual and particular aspects of the analyst. Specific interest in gender differences of the analyst in erotic transferences, perhaps a late fallout from the feminist movement, is reflected in an increasing number of papers published starting in the mid-eighties and continuing to the present.

The investigation of the transferences of the four possible patient-therapist dyads, male therapist–female patient, female therapist–male patients, male–male, and female–female, have suggested that differences do exist. Lester (1984) finds that in contrast to the commonly observed flamboyant erotic transference between male therapists and their female patients, the erotic transferences in the reverse situation (with a female therapist and a male patient) are generally muted, low-keyed, indirect, and relatively infrequent. She and her colleagues have reported nothing analogous to the erotized transference of the male-female combinations. Lester (1984) offers several reasons for the infrequency and low intensity of female-male erotic transferences. Most importantly, she views the inability of males to form paternal transferences to a female therapist as a result of the fear of seeing the analyst as a phallic woman, which makes one vulnerable to feelings of dependence and castration, and is a threat to gender identity. Similar findings have been reported by Karme (1979) and Person (1985). Person proposed that the erotic transference is used by women patients as resistance to the treatment, while men have resistance to the idea and awareness of an erotic transference. She suggests that the erotic transference varies as a function not only of the patient's personality structure but also as a function of the sex of the patient vis-à-vis the analyst. She also reports few or no cases of overt female-male erotic transference. Female-to-female transferences are somewhat more usual and can be intense. Totally absent are male-male transferences.

However, others (Goldberger and Evans 1985; Kulish 1986) have contended that these reports are incorrect in their assertions that erotic transferences do not occur with male patients–female therapists and that a significant paternal transference cannot be formed with a woman analyst. Goldberger and Evans (1985) raise some very important questions regarding these issues. They state that there indeed can be paternal transferences to a woman, as the classical psychoanalytic literature has held. They explain that if one is set to see oneself as a phallic woman, that is, as a woman with a penis, then one fails to see a paternal transference. They suggest that it may be easier for women to see themselves as phallic women than as having a variety of masculine attributes, and this may result in an inability to put oneself in the position of the father.

They seem to be talking about countertransference issues without using the word or elaborating on their suggestions. For instance, why would a woman prefer to see herself as a phallic woman than to imagine herself as a man, or in a man's role as father? One could hypothesize that it involves the potential threat to gender identity, which Stoller has indicated is basic to our sense of self. Kulish (1986) also questions the lack of erotic transference with female analysts, and while she tends to accept Lester's view that such transferences are infrequent, asks, if more common, why they are not being written about.

My own experience and that of female colleagues I have consulted do not seem congruent with the generalizations regarding an absence of erotic transference among male patients. On the contrary, many different types of transference were reported ranging from that more typical of an erotized transference in being direct, conscious, and demanding, to less direct transference manifestations in dreams, fantasies, and acting out. Also reported was the enacting of a direct communication outside the therapeutic hour, such as upon leaving or entering. For example, Mr. A., walking behind his analyst to the front door, commented with enthusiasm on her "impertinent ass." This was the first appearance of an erotic transference, which later unfolded in the treatment.

It is impossible to talk of transference without also attending to countertransference. Loewald (1986) points out that the word itself indicates that it is a transferential phenomenon. Blum (1986) has wondered why the interest in countertransference has risen so late in psychoanalysis. The reciprocal nature of transference and countertransference, how they entwine and are enmeshed with each other, so that a patient can have a transference to a therapist's countertransference, is a focus of current interest, and follows Racker's (1968) pioneering work. The image of the analyst as a blank screen, or a mirror, now has shifted to an image of two interacting mirrors producing an endless series of reflections that sparkle and bounce off one another. The erotic transference, however, has been discussed almost exclusively from the patient's side. Very little has been written in relation to the countertransferences evoked by a patient's transferences.

The area of erotic countertransference is especially taboo in psychoanalysis. Perhaps that is why, until very recently, there has been a notable silence in the literature regarding the countertransference response to the patient's erotic transference. Tower (1956) observes the strong condemnation of any sexual reactions by the analyst and assumes therefore that the temptations are great and ubiquitous, and to some extent trouble every analyst. Recently, several authors have attempted to deal with the sexualized countertransference (Gorkin 1985; Kumin 1985; Racker 1968). In the past, as Gorkin (1985) points out, more attention was paid to the aggressive countertransference and the usefulness of the sexualized countertransference was overlooked. He states that there is always a sexual countertransference to an erotic transference and that with careful self-analysis and investigation of the feeling aroused, it can prove extremely helpful in understanding the patient.

I think a major reason for the curtain over countertransference response to the erotic transference has to do with concerns about self-revelation to fellow professionals, fears of disapproval by peers, humiliation, discomfort, and embarrassment in talking about sex in public, professionally, and at all. It is not that analysts are not aware of their sexual countertransferences, they often talk about it privately among close colleagues; it is not yet acceptable to speak about it in public. Stoller (1976) has pointed out that sexual excitement is rarely spoken about as a subject in itself. In spite of the recent so-called sexual revolution, the puritanical current runs deep within American culture.

Freud (1915a) cautioned against imagining that it was the charm of the doctor that caused the patient to fall in love with him, suggesting that he was aware of the narcissistic pitfall of believing one is specially loved, deserving of it, and that one has special powers of cure. Apparently some therapists still need to be reminded of Freud's admonition, as sex with patients is not a thing of the past. A recent study (Gartrell et al., 1986) reported that seventy-six male psychiatrists and eight female psychiatrists out of a total of 1,423 who responded to a questionnaire admitted that they had had sex with a patient, though in most cases they claimed it had occurred out of the therapy setting. The majority of the psychiatrists gave love as the reason: 65% claimed to love the patient, and 92% believed the patient loved them. In spite of the fact that therapists may be conscious of the transference character of this love, doubt may enter their mind whether it is really "only transference" (Racker 1968). The loneliness of the analytic stance, including the daylong inhibition, anonymity, and the submerging of self, probably make one particularly vulnerable to this temptation.

It is significant that many studies have shown that far more male therapists have sex with their patients than women therapists. This may reflect the cultural patterns that women are not expected to take the initiative sexually, are reared to consider it ego-syntonic to reject a male's sexual advances, and that the incest taboo between mother and son is far more powerful than between father and daughter (Marmor 1972).

While more attention is being paid to gender differences in transference, particularly by women analysts, there too the restrictions on countertransference exploration exist. Although increasingly more references are made to countertransference, they tend to be asides, and extensive discussion of sexual countertransferences seems to be still taboo. It is likely that countertransference is one of the major issues in the understanding of erotic transference and in understanding the gender differences in the manifestation of the erotic transferences. Chasseguet-Smirgel (1984) believes there are probably no differences in the ability of patients to form transferences to analysts of either sex, "however, one can assume the analyst's countertransference differs between the two sexes" (p. 173). It is not clear why Chasseguet-Smirgel does not expect sex-dependent differences in the transferences as well.

Let us imagine what it may mean both consciously and unconsciously to a female analyst alone in the consulting room with a male patient who is professing love and sexual feelings toward her. The element of vulnerability and perhaps fear of male aggression and physicality would play a large part though perhaps on an unconscious level. A woman in authority may feel diminished when sexually addressed. She feels more comfortable when professional issues or competence are challenged than when sexuality is raised. She may fear being seen as provocative or seductive and may experience guilt, as women often do, for being unable to fulfill the demands of a man. Many of my women colleagues concurred and further elaborated upon how they can feel responsible for male arousal and then have to fight inner feelings of being obligated to do something for him, to take care of him, to slake his desire for which they were anyhow ultimately responsible. Guilt is felt about not giving something "real" when something real is asked, and an interpretation may seem a meager substitute. Talking about sexual feelings or love that cannot be responded to (encouraging something that cannot be gratified) may feel like putting salt on the wound. There may exist a wish to rescue and cure through love, and perhaps a temptation to fulfill the transference demand. There may also be sexual attraction and arousal, which give rise to embarrassment and confusion. If, ultimately, erotic transference represents a longing arising from symbiotic wishes, it may be more difficult for a female analyst to tolerate that with a male patient than with a female patient. The possibility of the male patient having an erection, quite visible from the couch, must bring into play many sexual fantasies and unconscious reactions. An erection is an actual physical event, removed from the realm of talk, interpretation, and fantasy. Perhaps it arouses conscious and unconscious fears of being physically overpowered and raped. These are reflections on what it is like to be a woman analyst in the presence of the erotic transference of a male patient. It should be clear that many of the issues are applicable to other therapist-patient dyads, and are not exclusive to the female-male dyad.

There may also be cultural reasons for the difficulty of the female-male erotic transference. It is culturally less acceptable for a love relationship between an older woman and a younger man than the reverse situation, perhaps because of the stronger taboo between mother-son incest than between father-daughter incest.

Gornick (1986) points out it is culturally permissible for men to talk sexually about women, but not in the woman's presence. When he does so in the transference it may be in the service of "turning the tables" and by sexualizing gain power, and reverse feelings of humiliation and shame, thus solving the dilemma of choosing between a dependent relationship with a maternal figure and the masculine role. Men can often perceive their sexual expression as hostile and hurtful, and experience a conflict of not wanting to hurt the one they love who is the source of basic needs. It is interesting that the dyad group in which there is the least information is male-male, suggesting that the difficulties in transference and countertransference feelings between two men are the most difficult in our culture.

Much of the failure to see the erotic transference with male patients is perhaps a result of avoidance which has its source in countertransference issues. Kulish (1986) has written that "gender carries inevitable blind-spots, biases, countertransference as well as special sensitivities, capacities, and understanding" (p. 402). These blind spots occur in subtle and not so subtle ways, consciously and unconsciously, verbally and nonverbally. Female therapists may overlook the erotic transference, especially when it is anxiety-provoking to them. For instance, a supervisee reported the statements a male patient regularly made at the beginning of each session about missing her, or comparing being with her to being with his wife, as distractions from the main business of the analysis and ignored these remarks in order to "get on with the analysis." The supervisee was a person of great intelligence and insight, quite able to handle transference with other patients, but her inability to pursue the material as she might have in another situation was a measure of her intense discomfort with the sexual aspect.

In another instance of avoidance and denial of sexual material, a male patient, an artist, produced, over the summer vacation, a series of drawings of a huge amazonian woman with whom he was entranced. The female analyst realized that he was expressing his feelings regarding her absence over the vacation but failed to see he was also talking of his continued love for her and related the material only to separation issues. This was a clear case of denial and avoidance on the analyst's part, using interpretation of the past to move away from the present, and avoiding themes indirectly expressed. The avoidance of the erotic transference/countertransference can occur in many ways, frequently out of the awareness of the analyst. Many writers, including Freud, speculated about unconscious-to-unconscious communication. More likely, this happens in tiny microsignals from one person to another, mostly nonverbal (Jacobs 1986). For example, the mere movement and averting of the eyes at a crucial sexual moment may communicate negation. Culturally, much of flirtation is through the eyes, and the meeting of eyes is often arousing and can be the vehicle for much erotic communication. The analogy of eyes and penetration was suggested by Gornick (1986).

The erotic transference often presents difficulties in management within the treatment. Freud (1915a) warned the analyst to be sure to maintain a neutral and wary stance in relation to the erotic transference, to be careful not to suppress or redirect its expression. He compared the handling of the erotic transference to a scientist who works with explosive substances and must use great caution. Blum (1973), however, states that a "loving resistance need not be more insuperable than belligerent attitudes or protracted negative transference" (p. 70). In handling the erotic transference it is necessary to be very tactful and empathic and not humiliate the patient nor minimize the need for love. A delicate balance exists between acknowledging the patient's legitimate right to be loved and analysis. An interpretation may be experienced as wounding when the analyst tries to redirect the love currently expressed to the past, especially when the patient is in the throes of the feeling. There is a need to understand one's own countertransference and to use that to understand what the patient is doing with the erotic transference. Several authors have described the unpleasantness of going through the experience of an intense erotic transference for both the patient and the analyst (Gorkin 1986; Kumin 1985).

The experience of a sexualized countertransference need not and in fact should not lead to acting out. On the contrary, awareness may facilitate treatment, elucidate hidden interactions between the patient and therapist, and help avoid subtle forms of acting out that frequently occur in sessions, such as bantering or avoiding sex as a topic.

Freud's emphasis on the general occurrence of love in the psychoanalytic situation without regard for the person of the analyst is related to the controversy about the seduction theory, as elucidated by Masson (1984). By making the seduction all the patient's fantasy Freud veers away from the possible real trauma and real actions by adults. Similarly, with the transference and countertransference aspects in relation to love, by emphasizing only the psychoanalytic situation one ignores the possible real contribution of the particular analyst, such as his or her response, gender, history, manners, or appearance.

The path of love in psychoanalysis is from distorted, unrequited, infantile fantasies of love to erotic transference and back to love again in real life. The ultimate aim of analysis is to help the patient find in his real life love, satisfaction, and fulfillment and to reduce the barriers to the quest of refinding the earlier desirable ego states in a mature love relationship. The difficulty, however, of translating the tendency toward idealization of the analyst as seen in treatment into love on the outside, has been noted (Bergmann 1971). This raises the question of whether the love the patient has for the analyst is ever really resolvable and whether in fact it should be. The termination of the analysis need not and perhaps should not terminate the core of love that the patient has had for the analyst. Perhaps the analyst becomes another lost object to be refound in real life, and the analytic state a lost ego state that contributes to the refinding of some similar level of intimacy in real life. What remains from a completed analysis is not the renunciation of the love of the analyst but a transmutation of those feelings into aim-inhibited and sublimated forms such as warmth and gratitude and the ability to continue on in life with hope.

REFERENCES

Altman, L. 1977. Some vicissitudes of love. *Journal of the American Psychoanalytic Association* 25:35–52.
Bak, R. 1973. Being in love and object loss. *International Journal of Psychoanalysis* 54:1–8.
Bergmann, M. 1971. Psychoanalytic observations on the capacity to love. In J. McDevitt and C. Settlage, eds., *Separation-individuation: Essays in honor of Margaret S. Mahler*, pp. 15–40. New York: IUP.
———. 1980. On the intrapsychic function of falling in love. *Psychoanalytic Quarterly* 49:56–77.
———. 1982. Platonic love, transference love, and love in real life. *Journal of the American Psychoanalytic Association* 30:87–111.
———. 1986. Panel on the nature and utilization of transference phenomena. Clinical controversies and interpersonal tradition: New York.
Bibring, G. 1936. A contribution to the subject of transference resistance. *International Journal of Psycho-analysis* 17:181–89.
Blum, H. P. 1973. The concept of erotized transference. *Journal of the American Psychoanalytic Association* 21:61–76.
———. 1986. Countertransference and the theory of technique: Discussion. *Journal of the American Psychoanalytic Association* 34:309–27.
Chasseguet-Smirgel, J. 1984. The femininity of the analyst in professional practice. *International Journal of Psycho-analysis* 65:169–78.
Frayn, D. H. and M. Silberfeld. 1986. Erotic transferences. *Canadian Journal of Psychiatry* 31: 323–27.
Freud, S. 1912. The dynamics of transference. *Standard edition* 12:97–108.
———. 1915a. Observations on transference-love. *Standard edition* 12:157–71.
———. 1915b. Thoughts on war and death. *Standard edition* 14: 275–300.
———. 1921. *Group psychology and the analysis of the ego*. *Standard edition* 18:67–143.
Gartrell, N., J. Herman, S. Olarte, M. Feldstein, R. Localio, 1986. Psychiatrist-patient sexual contact: Results of a national survey, I: Prevalence. *American Journal of Psychiatry*. 143:1126–31.
Gitelson, M. 1952. The emotional position of the analyst in the psychoanalytic situation. *International Journal of Psycho-analysis* 33:1–10.
Goldberger, M., and D. Evans. 1985. On transference manifestations in male patients with female analysts. *International Journal of Psycho-analysis* 66:295–309.
Gorkin, M. 1985. Varieties of sexualized countertransference. *Psychoanalytic Review* 72:421–40.

Gornick, L. 1986. Developing a new narrative: The woman therapist and the male patient. *Psychoanalytic Psychology* 3:299–325.
Greenson, R. 1967. *The technique and practice of psychoanalysis.* New York: IUP.
Jacobs, T. 1986. On countertransference enactments. *Journal of the American Psychoanalytic Association* 34:289–307.
Jones, E. 1953. *The life and work of Sigmund Freud.* New York: Basic Books.
Karme, L. 1979. The analysis of a male patient by a female analyst: The problem of the negative oedipal transference. *International Journal of Psycho-analysis* 60:253–61.
Kulish, N. 1984. The effect of the sex of the analyst on transference. *Bulletin of the Menninger Clinic* 48:95–110.
———. 1986. Gender and transference: The screen of the phallic mother. *International Review of Psychoanalysis* 13:393–404.
Kumin, I. 1985. Erotic horror: Desire and resistance in the psychoanalytic situation. *International Journal of Psychoanalytic Psychotherapy* 11:3–20.
Lester, E. 1984. The female analyst and the erotized transference. *International Journal of Psycho-analysis* 66:283–93.
Loewald, H. 1986. Transference-countertransference. *Journal of the American Psychoanalytic Association* 34:275–87.
Marmor, J. 1972. Sexual acting out in psychotherapy. *American Journal of Psychoanalysis* 32:3–8.
Masson, J. M. 1984. *The assault on truth: Freud's suppression of the seduction theory.* New York: Farrar, Straus and Giroux.
Meltzer, D. 1974. Narcissistic foundation of the erotic transference. *Contemporary Psychoanalysis* 10:311–16.
Nunberg, H. 1951. Transference and reality. *International Journal of Psycho-analysis* 32:1–19.
Person, E. 1985. The erotic transference in women and in men: Differences and consequences. *Journal of the American Academy of Psychoanalysis* 13:159–80.
Racker, H. 1968. *Transference and countertransference.* New York: IUP.
Rappoport, E. 1956. The management of an erotized transference. *Psychoanalytic Quarterly* 25:515–29.
Rosenfeld, H. 1969. The psychopathology of the erotic transference resistance in neurotic patients. *Bulletin of the Philadelphia Psychoanalytic Association* 19:102–07.
Sandler, J., C. Dare, and A. Holder. 1970. Basic psychoanalytic concepts: VIII. Special forms of transference. *British Journal of Psychiatry* 117:561–68.
Saul, L. 1962. The erotic transference. *Psychoanalytic Quarterly* 31:54–61.
Stoller, R. 1976. Sexual excitement. *Archives of General Psychiatry* 33:899–909.
———. 1979. *Sexual excitement: Dynamics of erotic life.* New York: Touchstone.
———. 1985. *Observing the erotic imagination.* New Haven: Yale University Press.

Swartz, J. 1967. The erotized transference and other transference problems. *Psychoanalytic Forum* 3:307–18.
Tower, L. E. 1956. Countertransference. *Journal of the American Psychoanalytic Association* 4:224–55.

14. Should Analysts Love Their Patients? The Resolution of Transference Resistance Through Countertransferential Explorations

Robert S. Weinstein

In 1926, on the occasion of Freud's seventieth birthday, Ferenczi wrote that psychoanalysis works through the deepening and enlargement of our knowledge, a task accomplished only through love. Thus, he believed, it is the analyst's love that ultimately heals the patient. This was, both then and now, a controversial position. What is surprising is how little has been written in the sixty years that have passed about the central and complex nature of love as its enters the analytic process. Far more has been written on the therapeutic uses of hate, about the analyst's rage, greed, grandiosity, competitiveness, despair, and hopelessness than about his love. Although we as analysts are supposed, by the public, to be experts on love, and although the subject certainly fascinates all of us, Tauber addresses the current dilemma well when he writes, "I have thought for a long time that what strongly blocks us is a profound unease in dealing with love, affection and tenderness in our work; we have acknowledged the need to deal with anxiety, hate, rage, etc. but are unclear about and evasive with love, affection and tenderness . . ." (1979), p. 66–67.

Therapists, of course, do have feelings and hearts, and none would disagree with the importance of the therapeutic alliance involving aspects of love such as positive regard, empathy, or the value of understanding. Freud did speak about love and recognized the power of love in the relation of physician to patient. He was more concerned, however, with freeing the analyst from the countertransference than in helping him use it therapeutically. Although in 1912 Freud wrote that the analyst "must turn his own unconscious like a receptive organ towards the transmitting unconscious of the patient" in order to reconstruct the patient's unconscious (p. 115), in a 1913 letter to Binswanger (1957) he stated, "One must always recognize one's countertransference and rise above it. Only then is one free oneself. To give someone too little because one loves him too much is being unjust to the patient and a technical error" (p. 50). Here we can see a loving and dedicated man concerned about how suppression of one's feelings can work against the interest of patients. Yet Freud recognized that analysts could be carried away by their feelings and apparently felt that it was often necessary to keep those feelings at bay. Marie Bonaparte quotes Freud as saying, "One must never love one's patients. Whenever I thought I did, the analysis suffered terribly from it. One ought to remain completely cool" (1985). This type of thinking led to the consequent conceptualization of the neutral, accepting, and relatively unresponsive analyst. Tauber and others have pointed out that the classical position is itself a countertransference phenomenon. "It is the therapist's fear of using himself and is directed against the therapeutic transaction; it indirectly discourages the patient's confidence and daring in respect of his own contribution" (Tauber 1979, p. 65).

The systematic study of one's countertransference reactions is now seen as a necessary condition for analytic success, and a number of theorists, including Winnicott (1947), Searles (1959, 1978), Weigert (1954), Epstein (1979), and Spotnitz (1985), have written about this, particularly in relation to the preoedipal disturbances, in which the patient's powerful emotions tend to evoke equally powerful emotions on the part of the therapist. Spotnitz (1985) tells us that to give too little of any kind of feeling because the analyst has too much is a technical error. He states, "The patient is entitled to whatever feelings—positive or negative—are needed to resolve his resistance to mature functioning. . . . these feelings should be a source, and tool, of communication" (p. 227). Winnicott (1947) calls this "the truly objective countertransference . . . the analyst's love and hate in reaction to the actual personality and behavior of the patient, based on objective observation"

(p. 195). By this he means that realistically induced emotions are to be distinguished from those reactions based on the analyst's idiosyncratic adjustment reactions.

In his moving paper "Oedipal Love in the Countertransference" (1959), Searles emphasizes that a successful analysis involves the analyst's deeply felt relinquishment of the patient both as a cherished infant and as a fellow adult who is responded to at the level of genital love. As he progressed in his work, Searles became convinced that there is a direct correlation between the affective intensity with which the analyst experiences awareness of loving and erotic feeling, as well as the unrealizability of such feelings, and the depth of maturation the patient achieves in analysis.

In my own experience the more powerful the feelings I have toward a particular patient, the greater his or her involvement is in the treatment process and the greater the likelihood of therapeutic success. I am speaking now about the inner awareness, not the overt expression, of such feelings. Inner awareness helps the therapist direct emotional communication toward the unconscious reciprocal emotional state in the patient, freeing the expression of repressed material. I hope to demonstrate here how the analyst's loving feelings can be used to resolve certain difficult transference resistances, thereby furthering progress in advanced stages of psychotherapy and psychoanalysis.

Three cases come to mind in which awareness of powerful stirrings within myself helped resolve a particular transference resistance and led to therapeutic progress. The first, a seemingly naive, passive, and moderately depressed young woman, was without a defined sense of self. It soon became apparent that primal scene memories and fantasies set the stage for certain behaviors that were destructive for her. She actually remembered sleeping in the same room as her parents as a very young child, turning as close to the wall as possible and covering her ears not to hear the sounds of sex coming from her parents' bed. This, along with certain subsequent events, led to the development of a profound fear both of self-assertion and of intruding upon others. Now, after a deep and lengthy analysis, which resulted in many professional and personal accomplishments, she can accept both her sexuality and her aggressive feelings and is no longer the timid, waiflike girl who first appeared in my office.

If asked, she might tell you that I deeply care about her and that feelings of mutual love and respect have been very much alive in the treatment. Recently, some interesting developments have emerged. Having received her long-awaited and well-deserved medical degree, she began actively to look for a life partner, basing her search on realistic goals. Time passed and there was not a satisfactory mate in sight, despite her devoting considerable energy to the search. All the men who became interested in her were found to be flawed—one too possessive and clinging, the other too childish, still another too self-abasing, and so on. The men she found compelling, special, and fascinating couldn't have cared less about her and were ultimately disappointing. The analysis seemed stuck. Perhaps because of this I found myself helping her choose the best wording for a personal ad. She was becoming annoyed at the status quo, and I, too, found myself irritated by what seemed at best a tenacious resistance, at worst very bad luck. Both of us wondered why I wasn't helping her to find a worthwhile person whom she could care about.

I am very fond of this woman. I have known her for a long time, watched her grow from a young girl to a developed and productive person as she shared intimate secrets and struggled hard to be honest with me and truthful to herself. Although she could be frustrating and irritating at times, the sessions were conducted in an atmosphere of warm regard. I began to question why I was not aware of sexual feeling toward her at this stage of treatment, and I realized we were colluding in a mutual suppression; neither one of us was speaking of the love relationship between us, thereby keeping erotic fantasies at bay. With this in mind I told her she was not finding the right man because she had already met him. Who? Me, of course! I was the ideal she was seeking; no one else could ever come close. After she laughed heartily at this suggestion, associations followed that validated the interpretation and opened up a new area for discussion and confrontation. If she couldn't have me, she secretly hoped for a clone in the guise of my best friend to whom I would introduce her. The patient was highly reluctant to give up our partially gratifying but hidden love relationship, which was, in part, a transference from father to me. This was what was keeping her from finding a full-time man in her real life. Once she began to see this and to deal openly with her feelings, new possibilties of relationships emerged. She no longer felt stuck in pursuing an unrealistic romantic ideal, began dating men seriously, and now has more than a few possibilities to choose from.

We are all familiar with transference love, but what I am illustrating here is how countertransference love and the acknowledgement of it to oneself with a particular patient can free the analyst to make what may seem to be an outlandish confrontation-interpretation in order to resolve a difficult transference resistance. As in all kinds of emotional reactions to patients, the analyst must contain the feeling until it is appropriate to communicate it to serve the emotional growth of the patient.

Certain patients seem incapable of love; the abuse of the analyst engenders hate. This may well be stressful for the analyst, but the feelings must be analyzed and contained until the patient is emotionally ready to be confronted. As Winnicott states,

> If the patient seeks objective or justified hate, he must be able to reach it, else he cannot feel he can reach objective love. . . . there is a vast difference between those patients who have had satisfactory early experiences which can be discovered in the transference, and those whose very early experiences have been so deficient or distorted that the analyst has to be the first in the patient's life to supply certain environmental essentials. (1975, p. 199)

One patient, who came into treatment overweight, angry, and self-destructive, became in the course of analysis a financial and social success but still could be easily wounded in his self-regard. When he felt attacked because I did not take his side, and instead told him he was being uncompromisingly selfish, he set out to hurt me. He threatened to quit therapy so as to show me what a rotten guy I was. He hoped that I would feel impotent, powerless, and humiliated as he did in my treatment of him. Since he was too sane to kill me, he saw his only option as leaving treatment precipitously knowing that I was both attached to him and interested in his emotional development. Of course, I hated him for this ploy, knowing that there was still analytic work to do, but he was not yet ready, nor did it seem therapeutically useful at the time for me to confront him with my negative feeling. Instead, I made a decision to use both my love and vulnerability in relation to this patient. I told him that, of course, I would be hurt if he left treatment this suddenly; we had been together a long time, and I did not yet have a sense of the completion of our work. It was not my intention to hurt him, and he was using what I had said to him to attack both himself and me. I understood, too, that leaving treatment to hurt me was something he felt compelled to do. I then brought the session to a close, and was aware that my hearty and loving greeting of my next patient may have been a way of discharging anger and hatred of him.

The next week he came to our scheduled appointment furious with me, letting me know what an uncaring son-of-a-bitch I was. No matter how he tried to hurt me, I would still go on, still live my life, still have other patients. He had heard me speak to my next patient as he had left the previous session. Now he would have to acknowledge his competitive fury and his own sense of worthlessness, work on himself rather than put me out of order.

Hate is a powerful, complex emotion. Some patients may seem to truly hate us, yet we feel no similar emotion. One session comes readily to mind, where a patient's explosive hatred paradoxically elicited warm and tender feelings. This countertransference reaction clued me into the patient's frustrated love and need for my understanding beneath the surface of her anger. This is the case of Miss T., a young woman just barely out of a suicidal depression after an unhappy love affair. I had been treating her nearly two years when, after a seemingly innocuously supportive comment of mine, she burst into a tirade of hopelessness and hate. Exploding, she stated,

I really feel I hate you. I don't want to be around you, just being around you makes me feel revolted—I really hate you. Don't take it personally. I don't know why but I don't like you either. I don't understand you. I hate you for my not being happier, why after all this time I have to be the only different person in this world. Your other patients get better but I have to keep proving to myself I am not happy.

Although hatred of me has often elicited vastly different feelings, the kind of hate Miss T. exploded with became more transparent when I understood why I still felt tenderness and compassion. It was her love and longing that she was speaking about, and what I really felt was that I should love her more than I did, guilty that my love went only so far. It was with this understanding that I told her if only I loved her more, there would be a chance for her happiness, but without it she was doomed to hopelessness and despair. With this she sighed and said,

You love J. [her sister-in-law who was previously in treatment with me] better anyway and M. [a patient of mine she knew] and people who make you feel more successful than I do. . . . . I have to keep an angry barrier even with you. With people I am afraid of losing I have to have an angry barrier. It's pathetic. I'm not functioning like a full human being, it's like starting from scratch. I don't want to make my mother happy by getting better. I don't want to make you happy either.

This session was a turning point in Miss T.'s treatment. With the revelation that she still wanted to be loved despite her feeling of losing out to her siblings and my other patients, Miss T. could begin to feel less despairing. She began to reach out toward others once again and toward a different kind of working alliance with me. She became less interested in having me fail out of vengeance and more concerned with her own self-regard.

In conclusion, the more feelings that can be experienced and integrated into the analysis both from analyst and patient, the deeper the experience will be and the greater the potential for constructive change to occur. For no human connection involving knowledge and love can occur without influencing all concerned. Erich Fromm writes that

> the essence of love is to "labor" for something and "to make something grow". . . . to love a person productively implies to care and to feel responsible for his life, not only for his physical existence but for the growth and development of all his human powers. Without respect for and knowledge of the beloved person, love deteriorates into domination and possessiveness. (1947, p. 99–100)

We as analysts function with respect and knowledge. This lets us use the intensity of our love and passion as emotional fuel to ignite the dormant powers of our patients, kindling their spiritual growth with our love and hope.

REFERENCES

Binswanger, L. 1957. *Sigmund Freud: Reminiscences of a friendship.* New York: Grune and Stratton.
Bonaparte, Princess M. In press. *Journals.* (Reported in the *New York Times,* Nov. 12, 1985, sec. C, p. 1 and 3.)
Epstein, L. 1979. The therapeutic function of hate in the countertransference. In L. Epstein and A. H. Feiner, eds., *Countertransference,* pp. 213–34. New York: Aronson.
Ferenczi, S. 1926. *Final contributions to the problems and methods of psychoanalysis,* New York: Brunner/Mazel, 1980.
Freud, S. 1912. Recommendations for physicians practising psychoanalysis. *Standard edition* 12:109–20.

Fromm, E. 1947. *Man for himself: An inquiry into the psychology of ethics.* New York: Rinehart.

Searles, H. 1959. Oedipal love in the countertransference. In Searles, *Collected papers on schizophrenia and related subjects*, pp. 284–303. New York: 1965. (Reprinted from *International Journal of Psycho-analysis* 40:180–90.)

———. 1978. Psychoanalytic therapy with the borderline adult. In J. Masterson, ed., *New perspectives on psychotherapy with the borderline adult*, New York: Brunner/Mazel. pp. 41–65

Spotnitz, H. 1985. *Modern psychoanalysis of the schizophrenic patient.* 2nd ed. New York: Human Sciences Press.

Tauber, E. S. 1979. Countertransference re-examined. In L. Epstein and A. H. Feiner, eds., *Countertransference*, pp. 59–69. New York: Aronson.

Weigert, E. 1954. Countertransference and self-analysis of the psychoanalyst. *International Journal of Psycho-analysis* 35:242–46.

Winnicott, D. W. 1947. Hate in the countertransference. In Winnicott, *Through pediatrics to psychoanalysis*, pp. 194–203. New York: Basic Books, 1975. (Reprinted from *International Journal of Psycho-analysis* 30:69–75.)

15. Mature Love in the Countertransference

Irwin Hirsch

There is little question that analysts frequently experience feelings of mature, adult love for their patients. Sometimes such feelings are transient, and at other times they endure over the course of analysis and for years beyond. This is not a rare occurrence with only special or unusual patients. The analytic situation lends itself to such feelings more than do types of psychotherapy, which are less intense and last for shorter periods of time. Analysts usually meet with people several times a week over the course of many years. During that time the analyst is frequently the object of the patient's loving feelings and certainly a central figure in the patient's life. The analyst watches important changes in the patient's life and comes to know, albeit secondhand, all the significant others in the patient's world. Over time, the patient exposes the worst and the best of him- or herself. Under those conditions of the patient's prolonged vulnerability, it is difficult not to experience either love accompanied by erotic feelings or love without sexual feelings.

Largely because of the way the classical psychoanalytic model evolved, the notion of countertransferential love has been fearfully regarded as akin to incest. The predominant fear is that loving feelings will be acted out in the relationship, in the form of excessive analytic gratification or, far worse, explicit sex. These fears have basis, for feelings of love could easily lead to either. Excessive gratification destroys the analysis, and sexual acting out is obviously a gross breach of ethics, responsibility, judgment, and goodwill. It is just as evident, however, that loving feelings should not lead to either of these serious pitfalls. Comparing love with other strong affects, every analyst acknowledges feelings of anger, for instance, without necessarily being frightened that he or she will act violently. Every therapist feels withdrawn or distant without expecting that they will fall asleep, or ask the patient to terminate treatment, or to leave the session. Feelings of love have been accorded special treatment, and such feelings are not nearly as frequently acknowledged by the analyst to him- or herself (I am not speaking of self-disclosure to the patient).

In addition to acting out through gratification or sex, it is feared that feelings of love will lead to a love cure rather than an analytic cure. This is a reasonable worry, since it is so difficult to discern what factors lead to analytic change and analysts do not want patients to get better only because they feel loved. The improvement is likely to be no more than a time-limited high. Being the object of loving feelings, however, is not inherently in conflict with the normal working-through process usually associated with analytic change. That such feelings exist does not necessarily mean that change is due to them. Some (e.g., Rogers 1961) have argued that unless strong positive regard exists as a base, the working-through process may not happen. Unconditional positive regard is a human impossibility, and Rogers may be speaking, euphemistically, about feelings of love. Many contemporary analysts believe that the more an analyst is aware of his or her feelings, the less likely that these feelings will dominate the treatment. Awareness allows the analyst to moderate his or her response, while supression of the normal feeling process is more likely to lead to acting out.

Historically, in the predominant classical school, countertransference has been associated with feelings that the analyst should not have, that may result in an interference with analytic neutrality and objectivity. Current thinking (e.g., Epstein and Feiner 1979), however, leans toward a less global approach. Distinctions are now more likely to be made among feelings that lead to acting out, feelings that do not, feelings that reflect the analyst's pathology, and feelings that are not problem-dominated. Further, analyst's feelings are seen as useful data about the patient and as an aid to bringing the patient's world to greater light. Though some analysts still define the term *countertransference* as referring only to the analyst's problems that interfere with treatment, the term has more and more come to refer to the totality of the analyst's feelings toward the patient. Similarly, there are still analysts who believe that any strong feeling the analyst has toward his or her patient reflects a problem and a departure from neutrality. This too, once a sentiment of a vast majority of analysts, is now not as widely held.

Some definitions of love in *Webster's New Collegiate Dictionary* (1960) and the *American College Dictionary* (1963) are a follows: "Ardent affection"; "A feeling of strong personal attachment induced by sympathetic understanding or kinship ties"; "A strong liking, fondness, goodwill"; "Tender and passionate affection"; "A strong or passionate affection for a person"; "Sexual passion or desire or its gratification"; "To take delight or pleasure in"; and "A feeling of warm personal attachment or deep affection." In discussing mature love, Fromm (1956) speaks of it as an openness to receiving and a wish to give. It is an active concern for the life of another and the growth of another. It is reflected in an ability to be responsive to the other and to let oneself see the other and fully know the other. Balint's (1968) discussion of mature love focuses on tenderness. One who is capable of mature loving is able to feel tender regard for long periods of time without necessarily demanding the same in return for that period of time. May (1969) emphasizes care as a precondition for love. He sees this as the ability fully to see or to recognize the other, to identify with pain and joy, to feel a tender concern and an ability to experience sadness in relation to the other. Kernberg (1976) also speaks of tenderness and the capacity to feel depressed by or to mourn the loss of the other. He emphasizes the combination of genital eroticism with the capacity to relate to the total person. His focus, however, is specifically on the patient's love of the analyst, while the other authors speak of love in general and so do not distinguish between the feelings of the analyst and those of the patient. This, of course, reflects different theoretical backgrounds.

Though many analysts do not write about or publicly discuss their experience of such feelings, it is difficult to imagine not having any of the above feelings over a prolonged analysis. A number of major questions remain, however, even when one acknowledges the mild, moderate, or strong presence of some or many of the sentiments defined. Of what relevance are these feelings to the analytic work? How are these feelings used or channeled, since they are not normally expressed directly or explicitly to the patient in the form of words? How are the analyst's feelings of love viewed and used differently in different schools of analytic thought or in differing theories of therapy? Much of this discussion will focus upon these questions.

The analyst's feelings of love, or any other feelings for that matter, take on significance in what Greenberg and Mitchell (1983) refer to as the relational models, in contrast with the drive-structure models. In the use of the blank screen within the drive-structure model, the analyst's feelings take on relevance only to the extent that they create an atmosphere. Interpretation is the mutative factor, but the setting needs an ambiance in which interpretation can be received (Greenson 1967; Stone 1961). Recently, Pine (1985) has referred to these atmospheric features as the silent or noninterpretive factors. He goes a bit further than the earlier classical writing in attributing some mutative properties to qualities such as empathy, confirmation, allowing for identifications, and being safer than the original family. Interpretation is still the primary contribution to analytic change but not the exclusive one.

The relational-model theorists, coming primarily from the interpersonal and object-relations schools of thought, tend to attribute more curative power to the analytic relationship than to interpretation per se. There are many different points of view regarding what kind of analytic participation is most mutative, but all agree that the formation of a new relationship is at least as important an element in eventual change as is interpretation.

What is broadly known as the object-relations school—Balint (1952, 1968), Winnicott (1958, 1965, 1974), Khan (1958, 1974), Guntrip (1969, 1971)—focuses on parent-child love configurations. Psychopathology is viewed as a deficiency disease, and patients are seen as adult children who were deprived of effective parenting. Part of the analytic aim is to provide an environment where the patient is allowed to abandon normal measures of protection and regress to the preverbal period when the troubles first began. Winnicott's concept of a "holding environment," with the analyst portrayed as a "good enough mother," captures the spirit of this group of analysts. They provide a noninterpretive, warm, maternal atmosphere. Words are insignificant, since, as Balint makes clear, preverbal problems cannot be significantly aided with words. Once the patient has regressed to a thoroughly dependent state, the analyst provides a parentinglike experience, which is intended to be better in quality than the original. The analyst is given more license to provide material gratification than in most analytic schools. Winnicott claims that the analyst does nothing more than what a good mother does with her child. Winnicott and Khan do not explicitly speak of the analyst's loving the patient, but Balint and Guntrip come very close to saying this. Balint specifically discusses a primary love that the patient lacks and is looking toward the analyst to provide. One does not get the impression that erotic love is of any moment here. The patient as defenseless, regressed child is in his or her most needy and vulnerable state, and the analyst's response can be viewed as, among other things, parent-to-child love.

Surprisingly, the object-relations school has met with little criticism by mainstream classical analysts. Essentially, they have referred to the type of analysis described above as geared toward "preoedipal" patients and not the classical, "oedipal level" patient. An examination of the literature clearly indicates that all the object-relations analyst's patients (neurotic and preoedipal) are worked with in the same manner and that this division is more political than substantive. It is ironic that Sandor Ferenczi, the precursor of object-relations theory, is one of the analysts most scorned and vilified by the Freudian mainstream. It was Ferenczi who, in his waning years, proffered the love cure: the naive assumption that since deficiency is what leads to psychological problems, replacement love is the only thing that will compensate. Unfortunately, Ferenczi died before he was able to integrate this into a more sophisticated and psychoanalytic approach. The object-relations theorists who followed him, Balint most directly and explicitly, took as their mission the integration of compensatory love and analytic technique. The experiments of Ferenczi lead, in orthodox circles, to almost a phobia about mentioning anything about the analyst's love, and this remains true today. Ferenczi's descendants manage to circumvent this by calling all of their patients preoedipal and allowing the orthodox analysts to believe that the two groups are working with different populations. In classical analytic thinking, sexuality is the primary expression of love and the focus of feelings of love, so that the more supportive parent-to-child love engaged in by the object-relations group is seen not as incestuous but as overzeaously nurturant.

The interpersonal model is an adult-to-adult one. Some have criticized it as adultomorphic. In a way, the interpersonal analysts are closer to the classical group in that they view words as central. Regardless of how immature a patient is or how far back the problems date, clarifications, observations, confrontations, and interpretations with words are still viewed as meaningful. The kind of words used to describe the analytic relationship reflect the view of the patient as peer adult: *intimacy, mutual influence, coparticipation, shared experience,* and *authenticity* are samples. The patient is seen not as an injured child, as he is by the object-relations group, but as an initiator, capable of making at least some choices about giving and receiving (e.g., Searles 1965, 1979; Singer 1965; Wolstein 1974, 1975a; Levenson 1983; Hirsch 1981, 1983; Mitchell 1984). The analytic ideal is a relationship in which each party is open to the observations of the other. The prototypical interpersonal analyst tries to create an atmosphere where the patient is as free to observe the analyst as the analyst is to observe the patient. The analyst does not necessarily confirm or disconfirm these observations or in any way openly self-disclose facts or personal matter. The analyst implicitly acknowledges that his or her unconscious is visible to the patient, as is the patient's to the analyst. The patient gains self-esteem, in part, by recognizing that his or her observations are potentially impactful and respected and that he or she is capable of giving as well as receiving. The relationship is conceptualized as a dialogue. Many interpersonalists (e.g., Fromm, May) have a strong existential strain and refer to Buber's (1958) notion of "I-Thou" relatedness. In speaking of love and relationships they sometimes sound cloying and ministerial. For this group openness of dialogue and clarification of experience can be ends in themselves. Explanations are less significant than descriptions; the "what" is more important than the "why." The analyst, in helping the patient to clarify experience, is implicitly telling the patient he or she knows firsthand about such experience (Singer 1977). Self-disclosure is usually not practiced, yet anonymity is viewed as unlikely. Similarly, Feiner (1977) describes the risk of taking too distant or too parental a stand when he talks of the importance of the analyst's being open to the patient's influence. He cautions against adherence to rigid technical procedures. The analytic experience, to some degree, is a mutual monitoring (Wolstein 1975b) of what is transpiring between analyst and patient, with less concern for issues of timing than in other orientations. It is assumed that the tenor of the analytic relationship has historical and current parallels and that these relational parallels are explored. The new relationship evolves out of an exploration of a reliving of the old relationship with the added feature that the process is mutually monitored. In addition to whatever love is felt explicitly by the analyst, feelings of love are channeled into the aim of establishing a coparticipant and an intimate, adult-to-adult relationship. Ehrenberg's (1974) notion of the intimate edge speaks to the principle of the analyst's staying with the most salient emotional features of the relationship at any given moment in the analysis. This ideal of the open attention to the immediate experience between two people with a minimization of interpersonal hierarchy approximates one ideal of mature adult love.

The study of both participants in the analytic field evolves out of Sullivan's (1953) concept of "participant-observation." The observer cannot be separated from the observed. Even prominent orthodox analysts (e.g., Spence 1982; Schafer 1983; Gill 1982), like McLaughlin (1981), Tower (1956), and Bird (1972) before them, have been writing about the degree to which the analyst influences and participates in the analytic process, both by dint of the analyst's theory and values as well as their actual behavior and feelings. Transference is viewed as a creation of both participants and not as emanating only from inside the patient's psyche. Countertransference as a given and not as an inherent problem, has now been the object of study for some thirty-five years.

The most interesting development to grow out of this merging of the interpersonal, liberal classical, and object-relational trends is delineated by Hoffman (1983). He refers to a group of analysts, whom he distinguishes as radical critics of the blank-screen paradigm, as analysts of the "social paradigm" or the new group of "participant-observers." I (Hirsch 1987) have used Fromm's (1964) term *observing-participant* to distinguish this orientation from other relational-model analysts. Hoffman refers to Levenson, Searles, Racker, Sandler, and Gill. This group, and others, view the analyst above all as a subjective participant who openly invites the patient to clarify and react to the nature of this participation.

Two features of this group of theorists make them most relevant to the study of analytic love. The first is that they view the analyst as engaged in a feeling process toward the patient or in response to the patient at all times. That is, the analyst is always feeling something. The second is that they see the analyst as unwittingly reliving with the patient a reasonable facsimile of the patient's early significant relationships. This is not done premeditatedly but is a natural outgrowth of the analyst's immersion in the patient's world.

Racker (1968) is most closely identified with the notion that the analyst is always experiencing strong feelings and is never neutral or objective. He speaks not of the analyst's personality but of the analyst as influenced by the patient. He refers to responsiveness and to the talionic principle; we tend to respond in kind to feelings addressed to us. Thus, anger breeds counteranger, schizoid withdrawal and rejection evoke withdrawal in return, and love promotes delight and a return of love. According to Racker's point of view, love is a common, everyday feeling on the part of the analyst. It is not necessarily enduring but is frequently present. It comes from the blissful feeling of being loved and valued, and the glow is felt and returned to those who generate it. Love is always part of the interchange, just as are anger, hate, abandonment, and so on. It does not have a special place in contrast to other feelings, and certainly no taboos are associated with it. It is not verbally disclosed by the analyst any more than hate, lust, boredom, or other responses are normally disclosed. The patient undoubtedly sees it and responds to it, and the analyst does not deny it any more than he or she denies the patient's other observations. In fact, Racker sees lack of awareness of any feeling as the greatest analytic danger. To be unaware is to be "drowned" in the countertransference, and acting out at such points is much more likely. Awareness of love and other feelings assist the analyst in understanding the meaning of the interchange and always provides useful data.

Searles (1965, 1979) speaks of his love for his patients in a somewhat different way. He doesn't view it as necessarily a talionic response to the patient's love but as stemming more from the person of the analyst and his or her particular feelings for particular patients. It is a more personal view of countertransference than countertransference as primarily evoked by the patient. Searles is more revealing about his feelings in his writing than any other analyst of whom I am aware. He unabashedly speaks of love, lust, hatred, and violent feelings in his writing and perhaps directly to some of his patients. Reading him, many analysts wish that they too had the courage to acknowledge such sentiments. Analysts who, even to themselves, tend to deny their feelings about patients are made uncomfortable by his work. People who work intensively with patients, however, know that the feelings Searles talks about are universally experienced and admitted only to oneself or perhaps to one's personal analyst. Searles sees the analyst as fully a person in the analytic dyad, one who cannot help but bring his or her uniqueness into the exchange. The analyst is not simply the responder but is often the initiator, for better or worse. When Searles talks of oedipal love, he is one of the few who states that the parent's sexual love for the child precedes the child's sexual interest in the parent. He is different from Racker in that he sees the analyst as also likely to initiate feelings of love or lust. Nothing inherent in either role makes one party likely to have feelings that the other could not.

Gill (1983, 1984) also speaks of the analyst as initiator. He notes that the analyst is often quite unaware of what he or she is conveying and that these responses have strong impact on the patient. Gill, (as well as Searles, Hoffman, Levenson, and Wolstein) relies on the patient to convey to him what he, the analyst, is yet unaware of. Again, the analyst does not use self-disclosure to confirm or disconfirm but respects the perceptions as likely or plausible. Gill has not yet written specifically about analytic love, but from all indications he would include this as a very plausible experience for the analyst to be having at any given moment.

Levenson (1972; transformation), Sandler (1976; role responsiveness), and Searles (1965; therapeutic symbiosis) all speak of the inevitability of the analyst's repeating with the patient clear parallels to the patient's past and current relationships. Gill and Hoffman are in accord with this viewpoint and see it as a central or the central part of every analysis. Some of the ways an analyst engages with a patient reflect the unique personal properties of that analyst; others reflect patterns strongly pulled for by the patient. In repeating the core interactional patterns (and making these patterns verbally explicit as they occur), the analyst experiences the feelings felt by the key early figures in the patient's life. In most instances patients have felt some love in their early life. Patients whose functioning is highest and who do the best in life have probably felt more love. Indeed, many patients have been fortunate enough to receive considerable love. The more love a patient has felt, the more the loving patterns will be repeated in the patient's current life and in the analytic dyad. Much-loved people are easier to love. Deprived people are often so angry that love usually comes harder. They tend to fight love or drive it away. If one believes that early patterns are relived in the analytic dyad, it is impossible not to acknowledge that early patterns of love are among the prominent repetitions. It makes little sense that only problem areas will be repeated. Though Racker (1968) has spoken of talionic love and Levenson (1975) of intimacy, Searles (1965) has written the most poignantly about the repetition of what has earlier been defined as love. It is the logical extension of this so-called radical, observing-participant group to begin to focus on the unwitting replay of good early relational patterns as well as bad ones.

One final way in which analytic love will be addressed is through examination of the analytic virtues of empathy, understanding, and "thereness." Boyer and Giovacchini (1980), in criticizing analytic approaches that stress gratification, state that knowing and understanding are the primary ways in which analytic love is conveyed. From their perspective, gratification is infantilizing and disrespectful to the patient, whereas understanding and being fully present and forthright are more genuinely loving. Bergmann (1985) comes close to acknowledging that analysts inevitably feel love for their patients and recommends that this love be sublimated into the analytic work. Singer (1965) speaks of the analysts' confrontations as a way of conveying that they care enough to say frankly what they see. It is a way of being there in the present, of being fully with the patient. Kohut (1984) used himself differently than Boyer and Giovacchini or Singer did, but he considered his efforts toward emphatic relatedness as close to love. It is difficult to maintain prolonged empathic involvement without strong positive attachment to the patient. To know is to love. Kohut's empathy is often displayed by silence or knowing when not to intervene. As is true of the majority of analysts, understanding is conveyed with few words. For Boyer and Giovacchini in a more quiet way, and for Singer, who may be somewhat more active and may feel less protective toward the patient, love is conveyed by observing painful things at the risk of provoking rage or hurt or scorn. Whether knowing or understanding is conveyed conservatively and quietly or by a more confronting approach, the patient's experience of being deeply known can be a form of love given by the analyst.

Although the love of analyst toward patient is rarely explicitly expressed, each analytic school has an implicit view of love in the analytic situation. The classical Freudians have always emphasized the sexual aspects of love. Patients have been viewed as inevitably having strong sexual feelings in the transference, since the term *transference* has been associated with the oedipal situation. They have seen countertransference love as tantamount to incestuous wishes and, therefore, it has always been cast in a rather negative light. According to many authors associated with the British object-relations school, this love has been of a mother-child configuration. The atmosphere is maternal and warm, and the analyst's compensatory actions and mannerisms have a large role in healing the deficient child. Countertransference love is not usually directly addressed (with the exception of Balint who speaks of "primary love") but is conveyed in the form of nurturant supplies. The interpersonal group comes closest to speaking explicitly of countertransference love but unfortunately sometimes sound as if they are preaching. They stress the equality of the analytic relationship and focus considerably on analytic intimacy, mutuality, shared experiences, and coparticipation. The relational model is clearly adult to adult, not father to child or mother to child. This way of viewing the analytic relationship lends itself most to the likelihood of open writing about mature countertransference love. Countertransference love per se is not usually discussed in the literature, nor at professional conferences, but is probably inevitable in, and possibly essential for, fruitful, long-term analytic experience.

REFERENCES

American college dictionary. 1963. New York: Random House.
Balint, M. 1952. *Primary love and psychoanalytic technique.* London: Tavistock.
———. 1968. *The basic fault.* London: Tavistock.
Bergmann, M. 1985. Transference love and love in real life. *International Journal of Psychoanalytic Psychotherapy* 11:27–45.
Bird, B. 1972. Notes on transference: Universal phenomenon and hardest part of analysis. *Journal of the American Psychoanalytic Association* 20:267–301.
Boyer, B., and P. Giovacchini. 1980. *Psychoanalytic treatment of schizophrenic, borderline and characterological disorders.* New York: Aronson.
Buber, M. 1958. *I-thou.* New York: Scribner's.
Ehrenberg, D. 1974. The intimate edge in therapeutic relatedness. *Contemporary Psychoanalysis* 10:423–37.
Epstein, L., and A. Feiner, eds. 1979. *Countertransference.* New York: Aronson.
Feiner, A. 1977. Countertransference and the anxiety of influence. *Contemporary Psychoanalysis* 13:1–15.
Fromm, E. 1956. *The art of loving.* New York: Harper and Row.
———. 1964. *The heart of man.* New York: Harper and Row.
Gill, M. 1982. *The analysis of transference,* vol. 1. New York: IUP.
———. 1983. The interpersonal paradigm and the degree of the therapist's involvement. *Contemporary Psychoanalysis* 19:200–37.

———. 1984. Psychoanalysts and psychotherapy: A revision. *International Review of Psycho-analysis* 11:161–79.
Greenberg, J., and S. Mitchell. 1983. *Object relations in psychoanalytic theory.* Cambridge: Harvard University Press.
Greenson, R. 1967. *The technique and practice of psychoanalysis.* New York: IUP.
Guntrip, H. 1969. *Schizoid phenomena, object relations and the self.* New York: IUP.
———. 1971. *Psychoanalytic theory, therapy and the self.* New York: Basic Books.
Hirsch, I. 1981. Authoritarian aspects of the psychoanalytic relationship. *Review of Existential Psychology and Psychiatry* 17:105–33.
———. 1983. Analytic intimacy and the restoration of nurturance. *American Journal of Psychoanalysis* 10:359–71.
———. 1987. Varying modes of analytic participation. *Journal of the American Academy of Psychoanalysis* 15(2): in press.
Hoffman, I. 1983. The patient as interpreter of the analyst's experience. *Contemporary Psychoanalysis* 19:389–422.
Kernberg, O. 1976. *Object relations theory and clinical psychoanalysis.* New York: Aronson.
Khan, M. M. R. 1958. Introduction to D. W. Winnicott, *Through pediatrics to psychoanalysis.* London: Hogarth.
———. 1974. *The privacy of the self.* New York: IUP.
Kohut, H. 1984. *How does analysis cure?* Chicago: University of Chicago Press.
Levenson, E. 1972. *The fallacy of understanding.* New York: Basic Books.
———. 1975. Changing concepts of intimacy in psychoanalytic practice. *Contemporary Psychoanalysis* 10:359–69.
———. 1983. *The ambiguity of change.* New York: Basic Books.
May, R. 1969. *Love and will.* New York: Norton.
McLaughlin, J. 1981. Transference, psychic reality and countertransference. *Psychoanalytic Quarterly* 50:639–64.
Mitchell, S. 1984. Object relations theories and the developmental tilt. *Contemporary Psychoanalysis* 20:473–99.
Pine, F. 1985. *Developmental theory and clinical process.* New Haven: Yale University Press.
Racker, H. 1968. *Transference and countertransference.* New York: IUP.
Rogers, C. 1961. *On becoming a person.* Boston: Houghton Mifflin.
Sandler, J. 1976. Countertransference and role responsiveness. *International Review of Psycho-analysis* 3:43–47.
Schafer, R. 1983. *The analytic attitude.* New York: Basic Books.
Searles, H. 1965. *Collected papers on schizophrenia and related subjects.* New York: IUP.
———. 1979. *Countertransference and related subjects.* New York: IUP.
Singer, E. 1965. *Key concepts in psychotherapy.* New York: Basic Books.
———. 1977. The myth of analytic anonymity. In K. Frank, ed., *The human*

dimension in psychoanalytic practice. pp. 181–92. New York: Grune and Stratton.
Spence, D. 1982. *Narrative truth and historical truth*. New York: Norton.
Stone, L. 1961. *The psychoanalytic situation*. New York: IUP.
Sullivan, H. S. 1953. *The interpersonal theory of psychiatry*. New York: Norton.
Tower, L. 1956. Countertransference. *Journal of the American Psychoanalytic Association* 4:224–55.
Webster's new collegiate dictionary. 1960. Springfield, Mass.: Merriam.
Winnicott, D. W. 1958. *Through pediatrics to psychoanalysis*. London: Hogarth.
———. 1965. *The maturational process and the facilitating environment*. New York: IUP.
———. 1974. *Playing and reality*. New York: Penguin.
Wolstein, B. 1974. Individuality and identity. *Contemporary Psychoanalysis* 10:1–14.
———. 1975a. Toward a conception of unique individuality. *Contemporary Psychoanalysis* 11:146–60.
———. 1975b. Countertransference: The psychoanalyst's shared experience and inquiry with his patient. *Journal of the American Academy of Psychoanalysis* 3:77–89.

16. The Classical Psychoanalytic Stance: What's Love Got to Do With It?

Andrew B. Druck

I

To speak of "love" in the classical psychoanalytic stance is to navigate between the Scylla of those who believe that the analyst's personality has no place in the psychoanalytic process and the Charybdis of those who see a "corrective emotional experience" as the primary mutative factor in analysis. There is reason to believe, however, that the former position is a reaction to the latter (Lipton 1977) and that a middle view is possible, one that acknowledges the analyst's love without abandoning major tenets of psychoanalytic theory of technique. It is this view that we will explore here.

When we speak of love in the analytic stance, we should be clear, first of all, that we are not discussing the transference. We are also not discussing countertransference since, by definition, countertransference refers to something unusual, out of the ordinary, a disturbance in the analytic stance either due to personal difficulties in the analyst or difficulties in the analyst due to feelings projected into him by the patient (Kernberg 1975; Ogden 1982). The issue here is not love resulting from disturbance in the stance but, rather, love by the analyst toward the patient that is *inherent* in the nondisturbed analyst working in a classical manner.

What then do we mean by the analyst's love? The term *love* does not refer to direct expression of sexual or anaclitic urges by the analyst toward the patient, either in action or verbally. It does not mean being "better" parents, lovers, or friends to patients than they have previously experienced, even though the therapeutic relationship might be better in some ways than the patient's relationships outside of therapy. It does not refer to active manipulations designed to facilitate a corrective emotional experience. All of these conceptions are nonpsychoanalytic in that they ignore unconscious intrapsychic conflict, the repetition compulsion, transference, symbolic and verbal expression, change through insight, and a host of other tenets fundamental to psychoanalysis.

What is meant by analyst love is aim-inhibited love, an interest and caring, which forms the background to the interpretive work in the foreground. Perhaps it has been defined best by Modell, in his discussion of the "holding environment." Modell writes:

> The gratifications that result from the analyst's functioning as a "holding environment" . . . are not the consequence of the analyst's special activity, that is, actively giving reassurance, love, or support, but are an intrinsic part of "classical" technique. Here, gratification appears to contradict the rule of abstinence, but the nature of the gratification is quite different from that associated with libidinal or aggressive discharge. *It moves silently, it is not orgastic.* (1976, p. 293, my emphasis)

Stone (1961) also believes that there is an aim-inhibited variation of parental love inherent in the psychoanalytic situation. He emphasizes the implicit and background aspects of the analyst's love and cautions that if it moves to the foreground of the psychoanalytic stance, in a manner that goes "beyond what may be inherent in the attitude of a friendly physician" (p. 58), then it becomes a threat, rather than an aid, to the analysis.

From the standpoint of self psychology, this background love may be understood as an aspect of the self-object transference and assumed to exist even in the analysis of neurotic patients although it may never be addressed (see, e.g., Adler 1980). Yet it need not be understood only within a self-psychological theoretical framework. Schafer (1983) considers the analyst's love in his discussion of the analyst's "second self," which he defines as a form of one's personality

> that integrates one's own personality into the constraints required to develop an analytic situation. It is within this form that one expresses his or her humanity analytically. On this basis a special kind of empathic intimacy, strength, appreciation and love can develop in relation to an analysand which it would be a mistake to identify with disruptive countertransference. (p. 291)

Stone (1961) has written of the analyst's love as forming the backdrop for "legitimate 'transference gratification'" (p. 49). The implicit gratification makes possible development and analysis of transference and it helps to sustain the working alliance. He states:

In gratifying this "mature" wish of childhood, there is also in the analytic situation, as in childhood, an acceptable form of love which, in an economic sense, may well contribute importantly to the incentive for mastery of unneutralized and unelaborated erotic and destructive drives. This may be one of the primary conditions of psychotherapy in general. . . . (p. 50)

Grunes has also discussed a form of therapist love in work with disturbed patients. He writes that the "therapeutic object relationship," provides a certain sustenance for the patient and is an object relationship necessary for the development of certain ego functions in the context of a treatment geared towards insight (1984, pp. 139–40). For the disturbed patient, Grunes states, the therapeutic object relationship is ". . . the matrix of change in treatment" (p. 139). One would assume that the more disturbed patient requires more sustenance than the neurotic patient in analysis. However, while its expression might need to be more explicit with the disturbed patient, we have seen that Stone (1961) and others argue that the sustenance of aim-inhibited love is present and crucial even with the neurotic patient, where its expression is more implicit.

These analysts see the analyst's love as present and inherent in the classical psychoanalytic stance. They might disagree on the role and importance of the love, ranging from those who would view it as more central and mutative with the more disturbed patient (Adler 1980; Grunes 1984; Modell 1976, 1978) to those who see it as nonspecific accompaniment of analysis with the neurotic patient, perhaps facilitating general internalization (Kernberg 1980), facilitating insight, and providing some of the nonspecific nurturance that sustains the working alliance and provides real, nonspecific relationship gratification along with the more illusional, symbolic, transference relationship (see Grunes 1984). Generally, the more disturbed the patient, the greater is the importance given to the love inherent in the analyst's stance.

2

The question of love and its place in the classical psychoanalytic stance has been somewhat controversial, primarily because to speak of loving feelings by the analyst, even of an aim-inhibited nature, has seemed to open the door to emphasis on cure through suggestion and internalization and has appeared to threaten the principles of analytic abstinence and neutrality. Since insight through interpretation, in a climate of abstinence, is so fundamental to classical psychoanalytic theory of technique, many classical analysts have been wary of anything that might open a Pandora's box.

Classical analysts have always regarded insight as the primary mutative factor in psychoanalysis. In fact, the central role of insight has been made part of the very definition of psychoanalysis. Gill, in a widely accepted definition of the "essence of psychoanalytic technique," once defined psychoanalysis as follows: "Psychoanalysis is that technique which, employed by a neutral analyst, results in the development of a regressive transference neurosis and the ultimate resolution of this neurosis by techniques of interpretation alone" (1954, p. 775). Technical concepts such as neutrality and abstinence are meant to facilitate analysis of the transference neurosis and to minimize change through factors other than insight, particularly change through forms of identification with the analyst. The latter is understood to be more central and mutative in psychotherapy than in psychoanalysis.

The traditional focus on insight has been accompanied by a suspicion of other mutative factors, such as internalization. The suspicion takes the form of denying or minimizing the existence or importance of nonspecific processes of support or internalization which seem to exist in any analysis (Pine [1976] is one of many who discuss such factors), and consequently denying or minimizing the specific role of the therapist other than as interpreter of transference. For example, Gray (1973, 1982), in a series of classic papers on analytic listening, empasizes an analytic focus on insight into the patient's ego defenses as they are expressed within the hour, and sees an authoritative role (even a benign one) on the analyst's part as an attempt to cure by authority rather than by insight. For Gray, such a cure may be important to psychotherapy with more disturbed patients; however, it is inferior to cure through insight, a cure that is within the reach of the neurotic patient in psychoanalysis.

Kernberg has echoed the emphasis on insight as mutative, even for the more disturbed patient. For Kernberg, it is not only the therapist's empathic activity, analogous to the mother's empathy for her child, which is important. Kernberg gives greater primacy to the way in which the therapist-patient relationship *differs* from the mother-child relationship, in the ". . . totally rational, cognitive, almost ascetic aspect to the therapist's work with the patient . . ." (1977, p. 303), a dimension Kernberg sees as ultimately mutative in work with the borderline patient.

Friedman (1969) and Lipton (1977) have discussed the controversies and differences in opinion in Freud's work and in the work of later analysts over the role of the *patient's* attachment and "love" for the analyst in facilitating the therapeutic alliance. Most modern classical analysts are suspicious of the patient's attachment, viewing it as fundamentally transferential and as leading to cure based on identification, which is, at best, a form of "transference cure" inferior to insight and, at worst, a defense against insight. Friedman (1978) described analyst suspicions of the mutative role of attachment to the analyst at the Edinburgh Symposium on Curative Factors in Psychoanalysis, which took place in 1961. At this symposium, when Gitelson suggested that patients' motives are structured to some extent by the analytic relationship, a relationship activating primary needs for a maternal supportive and integrative matrix, and that the patient internalizes these nonspecific aspects of the relationship, the structure of the relationship as well as the content of particular interpretations, he was criticized by other participants, who, Friedman writes, ". . . did not want to hear about any curative factors except understanding as conveyed by interpretation" (1978, p. 535). In the same way that the mutative role of the patient's love and attachment to the analyst is controversial, one can assume that the mutative aspects of the analyst's love would be equally controversial.

Friedman (1978) and Lipton (1977) have shown how views of the proper psychoanalytic stance, of the very definition of "classical" technique, have shifted in response to controversies with psychoanalysis. In our times, "classical" technique has been identified most with those who strongly deemphasize noninterpretive factors in the analytic process and who tend to view the role of the analyst almost exclusively as "interpreter" of transference within what has sometimes been characterized as the "blank-screen" model (Hoffman 1983). Other attributes of the analyst are minimized. This view is most cogently articulated by Brenner (1976, 1979), who consistently deemphasizes the effect of the analyst's actions on the transference and who recommends responding to *any* event, including patient reactions to the analyst's behavior, by analyzing the transferential aspects of such behavior. Brenner states that,

"Provided his analyst is competent . . . it is a patient's own illness that determines whether he experiences the analytic situation in and of itself as a source of pain, as essentially neutral, as a welcome anodyne, or as a positive source of pleasure" (1979, pp. 152–53).

It should be emphasized that these points of view are fundamental to classical psychoanalytic technique because they express and safeguard a commitment to insight and autonomy for the patient, goals that are quickly given up by many therapists who emphasize change based on internalization, ego building, and transmuting internalizations, that is, change based more on a variation of a new relationship between patient and analyst than on change through insight. While this emphasis on insight as mutative is important, the manner in which the caution (or suspicion) of factors other than insight has been emphasized has led to a conception of psychoanalysis that has appeared to be theoretically restricted and unidimensional. Those who believe that the analyst has a function that involves more than only analysis of the patient's transference distortions, and that factors in the psychoanalytic process other than insight also play a mutative role and need to be taken into consideration, may feel that they must leave the classical analytic position in order to find a theory of treatment that takes these factors into account. Further, analysts who feel that they need to be gratifying to patients, particularly more disturbed patients, may feel they cannot be more "giving" within the classical model. Thus, instead of considering whether there are inherent aspects of the analyst's love within the classical model, and whether they can attempt to amplify on such inherent love in work with more disturbed patients, they may be led to throw the baby out with the bathwater, so to speak, and abandon the richness of the classical model. These analysts are not necessarily against insight as the primary mutative agent in analysis. Rather, it is the manner in which some analysts attempt to insure the primacy of insight that they find questionable. What has been designed to protect the core of analysis—insight through interpretation of transference—may create more difficulties than it prevents.

All this is unfortunate because Brenner expresses only one direction in classical technique. There are others, such as Loewald (1960) and Stone (1961), who have criticized the prevailing emphasis on the analyst's ascetic and frustrating aspects. Stone (1981) has questioned whether it is in fact "classical," and suggests that it is better termed "neoclassical" technique. Loewald, Stone, and others have given more emphasis to the human function of the analyst in a way that does not sacrifice commitment to insight and analysis of transference. These analysts examine the other side of Brenner's position, the side that gives credence to the analyst's actual role. They do not seek to eradicate all evidence of the analyst's presence, and they raise questions such as the following: What are the effects of the analyst's actual behavior? Is there inherent love in the analytic stance? How does this facilitate or retard insight? If we ask these questions, then our appreciation of psychoanalysis with the neurotic patient is increased, and, further, the therapist working with the more disturbed patient has theoretical room within the classical position to attempt to modify the analytic stance in a manner that is sensitive to the difficulties of the patient but that retains, as much as possible, emphases and elements of the classical stance; thus the therapist would attempt to express and enhance inherent elements of the stance, rather than see himself as violating it. He is then able to practice what Pine (1976) has termed "psychoanalytically oriented supportive psychotherapy," a therapy that draws from the insights of classical psychoanalysis rather than a therapy understood to be in opposition to these insights.

3

The most common theoretical understanding of the analyst's love has been through the analogy of the parent-child model. The analyst-patient relationship is compared with the parent-child relationship and similarities drawn from one situation to the other. The model has been criticized on several grounds. There are those who feel that too much focus on the similarities between parenting and analysis leads to too great a focus on factors such as relationship and empathy and a deemphasis on what is different about parenting and analyzing (see Kernberg 1980). Some feel that the analogy invites the therapist to play a role and attempt to provide new and better parenting and a corrective emotional experience for the patient. Finally, some feel this model infantilizes the patient; the patient is an adult and ought not to be considered a child.

The first two criticisms have a certain validity, but only as useful cautions in analysis and not as serious problems. The third criticism involves a misunderstanding both of the model and of psychoanalysis.

Freudian analysts understand that they are dealing with an adult. This understanding is embodied in conceptions of the patient-analyst relationship, where, as Stone writes, "There is, throughout the process, the presence of the patient as an integrated adult personality, larger than the sum of his psychic parts or functional systems" (1961, p. 55). Stone emphasizes the patient as adult throughout his work. It is the patient as adult who voluntarily enters into a technical arrangement with his analyst within which he adopts, in certain respects, a formally childlike role with a therapeutic goal and purpose he rationally understands. Aspects of the classical stance include expectations of the patient such as the working alliance, where it is understood that the patient as adult is responsible for understanding his associations and the transference. It also includes expectations of the analyst toward the patient, such as the courtesy and humanness described by Stone (1961, 1981; Langs and Stone 1980). However, the Freudian analyst then focuses on the child in the man: childhood wishes, childhood fantasies, and, of course, the transference neurosis. The analyst encourages a therapeutic regression (transference neurosis) and looks at the irrational aspects of the patient. This is not turning the patient into a child or infantilizing him; it is recognizing, analyzing, and, finally, accepting the child in the man.

The parent-child model has been elaborated by Winnicott (1954), Stone (1961), Blanck and Blanck (1974, 1979), Modell (1976), Pine (1976), Myerson (1981), Buie and Adler (1982), Grunes (1984), and others. All of these authors have approached the model from somewhat different theoretical contexts and attempted to use it to deepen understanding both of the analyst's functioning within classical psychoanalysis and of ways in which the analyst can work analytically in psychotherapy with patients who have severe disturbances in ego functioning. Pine, for example, writes of the parent as helping the child name feelings, or anticipate frustration, and makes suggestions for how the therapist may help his patients in an analogous manner (1976).

Loewald (1960), in his influential paper dealing with the neurotic patient in analysis, has used the parent-child model to help clarify and expand our ideas regarding the mutative factors in psychoanalysis. In contrast to Brenner, Loewald allows for the mutative effect of factors operating in conjunction with insight and gives the analyst a major role as object of internalization, all in the context of a classical stance. Loewald does not see the patient as a closed system and the analyst solely as a recipient of transference. He thinks the nondistorted aspects of the analyst affect the analysis and he understands this effect using the parent-child model. Loewald writes that the analyst, like the parent, has an image of the patient/child as he is now and as he could be in the future. The patient/child sees the gleam of what he might be, or what Loewald calls a "vision" of the child's future, in the analyst's eye and internalizes it.

> This vision, informed by the parent's own experience and knowledge of growth and future, is, ideally, a more articulated and more integrated version of the core of being that the child presents to the parents. This "more" that the parent sees and knows, he mediates to the child so that the child in identification with it can grow. (1960, p. 229)

Ideally the image of the patient/child in the future reflects the patient/child's capacities more than it does the analyst/parent's narcissistic wishes. Loewald states: "I only want to indicate . . . the positive nature of the neutrality required, which includes the capacity for mature object relations as manifested in the parent by his or her ability to follow and at the same time be ahead of the child's development" (1960, p. 230). Thus in the parent-child model we see both a recognition of the analyst's love and an acknowledgment that processes of internalization are mutative in analysis, all within the classical psychoanalytic stance and with a continued recognition of insight as the central mutative factor in analysis.

The parent-child model is also relevant in our understanding the limits in analysis. These limits are manifested in administrative details such as beginning and ending sessions on time, without regard for the patient's state of mind at the end of the hour (within limits), and in aspects of the analytic attitude such as neutrality and abstinence. There is always a tension, seen sometimes as between love and hate, other times as between experience and insight, and still other times as between merger and separation. This tension is reflected in the analyst's stance, both in the analytic attitude (which combines great empathic intimacy within a professional role) and in the analytic arrangements. Winnicott has stated, "The analyst expressed love by the positive interest taken, and hate in the strict start and finish and in the matter of fees. Love and hate were honestly expressed, that is to say not denied by the analyst" (1954, p. 285). Generally, as we see from Winnicott's remark, the limits of the analytic stance are discussed in terms of hate. If we think of the limits of analysis in this way, would this not argue for the idea that, in addition to love, the analyst's hate is also an intrinsic element of the analytic stance?

One could easily make this argument. However, this may be a matter of theoretical preference. Since so many actions reflect the balance of love and hate, one might just as easily understand limits from the love end of the spectrum (sublimation) as from the hate end (neutralization). For example, returning to the parent-child model, the parent actively loves his child and demonstrates his love in a multitude of ways that are giving. But how do we understand the action of a parent who, when asked to carry a child who is old enough to walk, tells the child that he must walk himself? or do the homework by himself? If a parent interferes with a child's emerging attempts at separation and individuation, by, for example, feeding the child instead of letting it feed itself, is this an expression of love? If a father hugs his adolescent daughter less intensely than he did when she was younger, is this neutralization of hate?

I would suggest that, even though one could make a good case for understanding these examples and the limits in analysis as derivatives of hate, one may just as fruitfully speak of parental and therapist restraint motivated by love, a love that recognizes the patient's or child's need for autonomy and space. Stone (1961, 1981) has spoken of the patient's wishes for union with his analyst, and Tarachow (1962) and Langs and Stone (1980) have written of a corresponding pull in the analyst toward union with the patient. For the analyst not to act on these wishes and to maintain a self-abstinent position may require not sadism but, rather, self-discipline. In many cases, it is easier to answer questions and joke with a patient than it is to restrain these wishes for contact. We might even term gratifications and love by the therapist that go beyond either the inherent love in the stance or the needs of a disturbed patient (for the therapist as a holding introject, for example) as incestuous, using Loewald's analogy of incest as occurring when the object of identification, an object in relation to which the child's sexual needs are developed, itself becomes the object of these developed sexual needs (Loewald 1978). Psychoanalysts never attempt to understand behavior from its manifest content alone, and it is necessary to understand why a therapist sets limits and whether he does so sadistically; however, it is just as possible that the therapist exhibits derivatives of love as well as of hate in his restraint.

4

We can understand the concept of analytic neutrality from the perspective of restraint. According to Laplanche and Pontalis (1973), neutrality can be understood from three points of view. First, there is an overall attitude of neutrality, or respect, for the patient's values, religious beliefs, goals in life, and overall decisions. Second, on a level closer to the clinical material, the analyst must be neutral with regard to manifestations of transference. He must not encourage certain transference and discourage other transference. Finally, on the level of analytic listening, the analyst must listen to all of what the patient says and attempt to understand it without attempting to fit it into his own predispositions. Anna Freud refers to this aspect of neutrality when she states that the analyst should listen "from a point equidistant from the id, the ego, and the superego" (1946, p. 30). All these levels require some restraint by the analyst, some degree of distance, so that he can listen with "evenly-hovering attention" (S. Freud 1912) and respond with respect rather than with the countertransference of his own values and unresolved conflicts.

There have been other discussions of the function of neutrality within the psychoanalytic process. Some focus on its role in eliciting and facilitating that which is unique in analysis, the analysis of transference (Shapiro 1984). Schafer (1983) sees it as helping to create an atmosphere of safety in analysis, which helps prepare the patient for interpretation. Poland sees it as a way through which the analyst acknowledges the power position he has in the patient-analyst relationship. Since the analyst is given so much power, he must be certain to guard the patient's autonomy and allow the patient to express his true self without analytic impingement. Poland sees neutrality and empathy as representing different poles in the analyst-patient relationship. He writes:

> Empathy has a special link to neutrality, both having roots in the conflicting pressure toward merger and toward differentiation. Empathic perception arises in the context of felt separateness, an effort to open into the feelings of the other. Neutrality is the technical manifestation of respect for the essential otherness of the patient. (1984, p. 299)

Despite these rationales, the concept of neutrality is often used to support the caricature of the stiff, cold, overintellectualized Freudian analyst. When we look at discussions of neutrality, however, we see that it is always discussed from the point of view of concern for the patient, and coldness is specifically condemned. Poland states, for example, that

Classical psychoanalysis is not a spectator sport. . . . analysis is practiced for the sake of the analysand. Neutrality is required for the sake of the patient's analytic work; it is not an unconcerned indifference. (1984, p. 286)

Schafer writes:

There does exist a stereotype of the Freudian analyst as one who maintains an acid, stiff, utterly impersonal atmosphere in the analytic session. But in fact there is always room in analytic work for courtesy, cordiality, gentleness, sincere empathic participation and comment, and other such personal, though not socially intimate, modes of relationship. (1983, p. 9)

Gill states:

Neutrality does not mean that the analyst is a stick of wood without spontaneity. It does not mean that he may not laugh at a joke, or make one, or show irritation, or find tears in his eyes when a patient relates a moving incident. This neutrality is not contradicted by the analyst's feeling a general benevolent friendliness toward his patient. Indeed without such an attitude on the analyst's part, an analysis is bound to fail. Such friendliness is not countertransference but the realistically desirable attitude of the therapist to the suffering patient. (1954, p. 776)

We can see that, from a theoretical point of view, neutrality is understood as facilitating the analytic process (analysis of the transference) and as a form of respect for the patient. Coldness is seen not as an essential attribute of neutrality but as a manifestation of countertransference or ignorance. (Shapiro [1984] cites the woodenness of first-year psychiatric residents, attempting to emulate what they don't understand, in this context.) Thus there is much evidence to support the view that neutrality may be understood as a form of love for the patient, manifested in restraint and respect.

From a practical point of view, the principle of neutrality is applied differently by different analysts who emphasize different aspects of the analytic stance. Brenner (1976, 1979), for example, emphasizes the function of the analyst as the analyzer of transference. For Brenner, nothing said by the patient is taken at face value. It is as if everything said or done by the patient is the manifest content of a dream that needs analysis. Brenner deemphasizes the precipitants of the patient's reactions (what we might call the equivalent of the dream's day residue) and does not consider internalization to have mutative significance. Yet Loewald (1960), while also emphasizing insight and analysis of transference, has a very different view of the analyst's role and of the importance of internalization. Schafer (1983) has also discussed his conception of the basic elements of the "analytic attitude."

These and many other classical analysts differ in the way they apply neutrality and other technical and theoretical concepts of psychoanalysis. We would expect this, since all of us understand and apply these concepts through our own personalities; once they are learned and internalized, they become ours, and any analyst's analytic work is ultimately the result of his own character and the manner in which he has internalized what he has learned through the filter of his character. Some may choose to emphasize the inherent love, others may feel more comfortable with restraint. (In this regard, the differences in emphasis between Brenner [1976, 1979] and Stone [1961, 1981] are illuminating.) We have seen, however, that there is ample evidence to assume that love in the analyst is an inherent part of the conceptualization of the analytic stance, and that the analyst is free to emphasize derivatives of this aspect of the stance as he finds it clinically useful.

In summary, we have seen that, while some classical analysts prefer to emphasize the more ascetic "blank-screen" aspects of the analyst, a significant number of analysts view the analyst's primary interpretive role in the context of a background of aim-inhibited love. Finally, we have attempted to show that neutrality refers to respect for, rather than indifference to, the patient.

REFERENCES

Adler, G. 1980. Transference, real relationship and alliance. *International Journal of Psycho-analysis* 61:547–58.
Blanck, G., and R. Blanck. *Ego psychology: Theory and practice.* New York: Columbia University Press.
———, and ———. 1979. *Ego psychology II.* New York: Columbia University Press.
Brenner, C. 1976. *Psychoanalytic technique and psychic conflict.* New York: IUP.
———. 1979. Working alliance, therapeutic alliance, and transference. *Journal of American Psychoanalysis* 27 (Supp.): 137–57.
Buie, D., and G. Adler. 1982. Definitive treatment of the borderline personality. *International Journal of Psychoanalytic Psychotherapy* 9:51–87.

Freud, A. 1946. *The Ego and the mechanisms of defense.* New York: IUP.
Freud, S. 1912. The dynamics of transference. *Standard edition* 12:97–108.
Friedman, L. 1969. The therapeutic alliance. *International Journal of Psychoanalysis* 50:139–53.
———. 1978. Trends in the psychoanalytic theory of treatment. *Psychoanalytic Quarterly* 47:524–67.
Gill, M. M. 1954. Psychoanalysis and exploratory psychotherapy. *Journal of the American Psychoanalytic Association* 2:771–97.
Gray, P. 1973. Psychoanalytic techniques and the ego's capacity for viewing intrapsychic conflict. *Journal of the American Psychoanalytic Association* 21:474–94.
———. 1982. "Developmental lag" in the evolution of technique for psychoanalysis of neurotic conflict. *Journal of the American Psychoanalytic Association* 30:621–56.
Grunes, M. 1984. The therapeutic object relationship. *Psychoanalytic Review* 71:123–43.
Hoffman, I. Z. 1983. The patient as interpreter of the analyst's experience. *Contemporary Psychoanalysis* 19:389–422.
Kernberg, O. F. 1975. *Borderline conditions and pathological narcissism.* New York: Aronson.
———. 1977. Structural change and its impediments. In P. Hartocollis, ed., *Borderline personality disorders,* pp. 275–306. New York: IUP.
———. 1980. *Internal world and external reality.* New York: Aronson.
Langs, R., and L. Stone. 1980. *The therapeutic experience and its setting.* New York: IUP.
Laplanche, J., and J.-B. Pontalis. 1973. *The language of psychoanalysis.* Trans. D. Nicholson-Smith. New York: Norton.
Lipton, S. 1977. The advantages of Freud's technique as shown in his analysis of the rat-man. *International Journal of Psycho-analysis* 58: 255–73.
Loewald, H. 1960. On the therapeutic action of psychoanalysis. In Loewald, *Papers on psychoanalysis,* pp. 221–56. New Haven: Yale University Press, 1980.
———. 1978. The waning of the oedipus complex. In Loewald, *Papers on psychoanalysis,* pp. 384–404. New Haven: Yale University Press, 1980.
Modell, A. H. 1976. "The holding environment" and the therapeutic action of psychoanalysis. *Journal of the American Psychoanalytic Association* 24:285–307.
———. 1978. The conceptualization of the therapeutic action of psychoanalysis. *Bulletin of the Menninger Clinic* 42:493–504.
Myerson, P. 1981. The nature of the transactions that occur in other than classical analysis. *International Review of Psychoanalysis* 8:173–89.
Ogden, T. H. 1982. *Projective identification and psychotherapeutic technique.* New York: Aronson.

Pine, F. 1976. On therapeutic change: Perspectives from a parent-child model. In *Psychoanalysis and contemporary science* 5:537–69. New York: IUP.
Poland, W. S. 1984. On the analyst's neutrality. *Journal of the American Psychoanalytic Association* 32:269–99.
Schafer, R. 1983. *The analytic attitude*. New York: Basic Books.
Shapiro, T. 1984. On neutrality. *Journal of the American Psychoanalytic Association* 32:269–82.
Stone, L. 1961. *The Psychoanalytic situation*. New York: IUP.
———. 1981. Notes on the noninterpretive elements in the psychoanalytic situation and process. In Stone, *Transference and its context*, pp. 153–175. New York: Aronson, 1984.
Tarachow, S. 1962. Interpretation and reality in psychotherapy. *International Journal of Psycho-analysis* 43:377–87.
Winnicott, D. W. 1954. Metapsychological and clinical aspects of regression within the psycho-analytical set-up. In Winnicott, *Through Pediatrics to Psychoanalysis*, pp. 278–294. New York: Basic Books, 1975.
Wolf, E. S. 1983. Aspects of neutrality. *Psychoanalytic Inquiry* 3:675–89.

Index

Abend, S., 84, 85
Adams, H., 15, 21
Adler, G., 214, 215, 220
Adolescence, 12, 111-13
   acting-out behavior in, 116-17
   love in, 12
   role of music in, 52
Agape, 15-16, 17
Altman, L., 2, 26, 27, 28
Ambivalence, 8, 156
Analyst's love
   as curative factor, 157, 194
   in Freudian theory, 213-25
   in interpersonal theory, 205-9
   parent-child relationship and, 219-22
Andreas-Salomé, L., 90-91
Anyi, Ivory Coast, 37-39
Apaches, Mescalero, 35-37

Bach, S., 25
Bak, R. C., 2, 15, 179
Balint, M., 2, 27-28, 122, 149, 167, 202, 203-4, 210
Bank, S., 83, 85
Bellak, L., 156
Benedek, T., 134
Bergman, A., 125
Bergmann, M. S., 1-2, 17, 25, 28, 93, 96, 101, 160-61, 170, 179, 188, 209
Bernays, A., 82
Bessel, H., 15
Bettelheim, B., 42
Bibring, G., 181
Binswanger, L., 193
Bird, B., 206
Blanck, G., 220
Blanck, R., 220
Blos, P., 106, 111, 112, 116
Blum, H. P., 175, 176-77, 178, 183, 187
Bonaparte, M., 193
Bonding, 147-49
Bowlby, J., 113, 149, 168

Boyer, B., 209
Boyer, L., 35, 37, 38, 48n3
Boyer, R. M., 35, 38, 48n3
Brenner, C., 64, 66, 217-19, 220, 224-25
Breuer, J., 173-74
Brown, P., 20
Buber, M., 205
Buie, D., 220

Campbell, J., 16, 19, 21, 22, 23
Camus, Albert, 165-66
Capellanus, Andreas, 22
Carey, J. T., 57
Chasseguet-Smirgel, J., 97-98, 101, 185
Childhood
   attachment insufficiency in, 150-51
   overexposure to single parent in, 153
   overinvestment in parenting figure in, 152-53
   psychic abandonment in, 151-52
   sibling relationships in
      Freud on, 81-82
      mature love relationships and, 81-91
Christianity
   concept of love in, 18-21
   courtly love and, 23
   cult of Virgin Mary in, 20-21
   marriage and, 20
   sex attitudes in, 19-20
Clark-Stuart, K. A., 113-14
Colonna, A., 81
Countertransference, 99, 150, 196-98, 200-202, 213
   erotic countertransference, 183-87
   gender differences in, 185-87
   hatred and, 197-98
   love in, 200-210
   reactions to, 193-94
   transference resistance and, 192-98

D'Arcy, M. D., 15
D'Aulaire, E. P., 164

D'Aulaire, I., 164
Davis, H. B., 8
de Reincourt, A., 15, 17, 18, 20, 21, 22, 23
De Rougemont, D., 4, 15, 23, 32
Demosthenes, 18
Dependency, 167-68
 fear of, 168
Developmental approach, 2, 111-13, 125-28, 147-49, 165-67
Devereux, G., 33-35, 47
Domash, L., 5, 6, 9, 11
Dover, A. J., 18
Druck, A. B., 10

Edinger, E. F., 161
Ehrenberg, D., 206
Empathy, 94, 96, 116, 154, 155, 209
 blocks in, 156-57, 209
Endleman, R., 3, 8, 32, 42, 49n6
Epstein, L., 193, 201
Erikson, E. H., 66, 113, 134
Eros, 15-16, 17
Erotic countertransference, 183-87
Erotic transference, 173-89
 erotized transference, 175-77
 female therapists and, 186-87
 Freud on, 173-75
 gender differences in therapist and, 181-83
 hostility and, 180-81
 management of treatment and, 187-88
Evans, D., 182-83
Existential psychoanalysis, 160

Fairbairn, W. R. D., 59, 127, 128, 129
Fantasies, 111-20
Father
 brother as oedipal substitute for, 90
 need for, in adolescence, 113-17
Feiner, A., 201, 205
Fenichel, O., 64, 94
Ferenczi, S., 192, 204
Fleiss, R., 138
Frayn, D. H., 175
Free association, 96-97
Freeman, D. M. A., 48n3
Freud, A., 125, 223

Freud, S.
 on aggression, 180
 on analytic neutrality, 223
 on distinction between narcissistic and anaclitic love, 2, 163
 on ego, 136
 on idealization in love, 8, 106, 162
 on love, 24-27, 58, 64, 81-82, 104, 113, 123, 159, 174
 on love of patients, 193
 on love relationships, 134
 on repetition compulsion, 135
 on transference, 64-66, 135, 184, 187
 on transference love, 173, 174, 175, 177
 on transference resistance, 180
 on use of unconscious, 193
Freudian theory, 2, 24-28, 58, 64-65, 81-82, 90-91, 104, 111-13, 134-36, 140-41, 163, 173-79, 213-25
Friedman, L., 217
Fromm, E., 27, 47, 159, 160, 162, 198, 202, 205, 206
Fusion, 166-67

Gadlin, W., 5
Gartrell, N., 184
Gassner, S., 136
Gaylin, W., 14
Gediman, H., 160-61
Gender differences
 according to Plato, 17-18
 in love, 54, 56-58, 60
 in therapist, 181-83
Gill, M. M., 79n2, 144n2, 206, 208, 216, 224
Gilligan, C., 59
Giovacchini, P., 209
Gitelson, M., 175, 217
Goldberger, M., 182-83
Gorkin, M., 95, 184, 188
Gornick, L., 186, 187
Graves, R., 164
Gray, P., 216
Greece
 conventions of love in, 16-18
 homosexuality in, 18
Greenacre, P., 64
Greenberg, J. A., 129, 131, 135, 203
Greenson, R., 176, 178, 203

Grunes, M., 215, 220
Guilt, 46, 165
Guntrip, H., 59, 126, 127, 129, 161, 162, 168, 203-4

Hatred
  countertransference and, 197-98
  of self, 170
  See also Hostility
Hawthorne, Nathaniel, 19
Hazo, R., 26
Herdt, G., 42-43
Hippler, A., 49n6
Hirsch, I., 10, 11, 205, 206
Hofer, W., 64
Hoffman, I. Z., 79n2, 206, 208, 217
Holmes, J., 83
Homosexuality
  in Greece, 18
  in New Guinea, 42-43
Horner, A., 101-2
Hostility
  erotic transference and, 180-81
  love and, 8, 26
  sexual excitement and, 100-101
  See also Hatred
Huizinga, J., 22, 23, 24
Hunt, M. M., 15, 18, 20, 22

Idealization
  of love object, 3, 18, 24, 47, 105-6, 110, 162
  in pathological love relationships, 106
  role of, 8, 114
  of self-representation, 106
  theoretical views of, 8, 162
  of women, 22-24
Ideals of love, 15-18, 21
Individuation, 170-71
Inner world, 128-32
Interpersonal analysis, 160-62, 204-6
Ireland, W., 3, 8
Isolation, 27

Jacobs, T., 187
Jacobson, E., 116
Jaeger, C. S., 23
Jones, E., 82, 173
Jung, C. G., 52
Jungian analysis, 162

Kahn, M., 83, 85
Kaplan, D. M., 19
Karme, L., 182
Kernberg, O. F., 25, 28, 59, 106, 116, 125-26, 202, 213, 215, 216-17, 219
Khan, M. M. R., 160, 168, 203-4
Kiell, N., 84
Kierkegaard, S., 19
Klein, M., 59, 138, 161
Kohut, H., 96, 99, 122, 159, 161, 162, 163, 167, 209
Kosseff, J., 126, 127, 128
Kris, M., 84, 85
Kulish, N., 182, 183, 186
Kumin, I., 184, 188

Laing, R. D., 169
Lane, P. R., 11
Langs, R., 220, 222
Laplanche, J., 64, 65, 223
Lasky, J. F., 5-6
Lawner, P., 7, 9, 134, 137, 138, 144n2
Lerner, L., 15
Lesser, R., 83
Lester, E., 182, 183
Levenson, E., 137, 205, 206, 208
Libido, 15-16, 24-26
Lipton, S., 213, 217
Little, M., 130
Loewald, H. W., 25, 65, 136, 138, 183, 218-19, 220-21, 222, 225
Loewenstein, R. M., 141
Lomas, P., 130
Lomax, A., 53
Lorenz, K., 148
Love
  abstract, 15, 28
  adolescent, 12, 42, 111-13
  aim-inhibited, 10, 24, 213-25
  ambivalence in, 8, 14, 56
  anaclitic, 24-25, 104-5
  analyst's, 157, 194, 205-9, 213-25, 219-22
  as basic human need, 1
  being in, 32, 122-32
  capacity to, 25, 122, 123, 167, 170, 171
  in Christianity, 19-20
  courtly, 21-24
  cultural, 2

Index

Love (*Continued*)
  as a cure, 201
  as defense against separation, 2, 179
  definition of, 1, 102, 202
  dependency in, 167-68
  deprivation of, 11
  developmental approach to, 1-2, 111-13, 125-28, 147-49, 165-67
  ego and, 26-27
  eros, 15-16, 17
  falling in, 6, 122-32
  fear of, 15
  gender differences in, 18, 28, 54, 56-58, 60
  genital, 26
  guilt in, 165
  idealization in, 25, 47, 105-6
  idealization of, 4, 14
  ladder of, 17
  learning to, 1
  loss of, 15, 167-69, 179
  mature, 102-3, 163, 200, 202, 210
  music and, 4, 28, 52-62
  narcissistic love, 24-25, 104-6, 163-64
  object choice in, 32, 33, 81, 84, 93, 104-5
  oedipal, 25, 111, 194, 208
  parental, 1, 9, 152-53
  passionate, 9, 11, 26, 94, 101
  pathological, 104
  preoedipal, 25
  primary, 27
  problems in, 5, 169-70
  romantic, 3, 8, 32, 44, 161
  self and, 12, 162-63
  sexual, 24-28
  sibling, 5, 81-92
  sublimated, 28, 209
  tender, 102, 169, 202
  testing, 11, 133
  transcultural, 31-32
  as unfulfilled desire, 21
  women and, 18, 20, 24, 52
Lumsden, D. P., 48*n*3
Lusaka tribe, 39-41

Macalpine, I., 64
McLaughlin, J., 206
Mahler, M. S., 2, 25, 48*n*1, 101, 125, 148

Malcolm, J., 53
Mann, C., 170
Marital therapy, 69-70
Marmor, J., 185
Marriage
  in Christianity, 20
  maternal transference in, 73
  reciprocal transference in, 63-78
  sibling relationships in childhood and, 86-87
Marshall, D. S., 43
Martines, L., 18
Masson, J. M., 188
Masterson, J., 116
Matthew, St., 19
Maurois, André, 15
May, H. G., 19, 20
May, R., 159, 160, 162, 202, 205
Mead, M., 43
Meissner, W., 123
Meltzer, D., 176
Menninger, K., 64
Mescalero Apaches, 35-37
Metzger, B. M., 19, 20
Miller, A., 112
Mitchell, S. A., 129, 131, 135, 203, 205
Modell, A. H., 214, 220
Mohave Indians, Arizona, 33-35
Money, J., 52
Mooney, H. F., 55, 56
Morgenthaler, F., 37
Mother
  bonding, 147-49
  as earliest love object, 2, 25, 112, 113
  loss of tie with, 164-65
Mt. Zion Psychotherapy Research Group, 136-37, 140, 141
Mulliken, S. F., 5-6
Murdoch, Iris, 101
Music, conceptions of love in, 52-61
Muslin, H. L., 144*n*2
Myerson, P., 220

Narcissism
  pathological love relationships and, 105-6
  self and, 163-65
Narcissistic impairment, 93-94
Narcissistic injury, 164

Narcissistic love, 24-25, 104, 163-64
Narcissistic object choice, 104
Narcissistic transference, 96
Narcissus, myth of, 164
Newman, L., 81
Nielsen, G., 115, 116
Nunberg, H., 178

Object
  abusive, 94-95
  choice of, 32, 33, 81, 84, 93, 104-6
  consistency, 36, 48
  constancy, 48
  loss of, 15, 110, 168-69
  usage, 102
Object-relations theory, 122-32, 179, 203-4
  inner world in, 128-32
  love and, 161
  schizoid symptomatology in, 127-28
  splitting of self in, 126-27, 169
O'Faolain, J., 18
Ogden, T. H., 137, 213
O'Neill, Eugene, 165-66

Palmer, Robert, 60
Parent-child relationship, 4-5
  deficiency in, 105
  as model for analyst-patient relationship, 219-22
  as model for love relations, 93, 104, 147
  sibling relationships in childhood and, 85
Parents
  ambivalent wishes in, 156
  overexposure to single parent, 153
  overinvestment in parent, 152-53
  unconscious identification with, 106
Parin, P., 37, 39, 48n3
Parin-Matthèy, G., 37
Participant-observers, 206
Pathological love relationships
  frequency of, in Western culture, 45-46
  idealization in, 106
  narcissism and, 104-10
  as reason for therapy, 5
Paul, St., 19, 20
Pauletich, A., 54, 56
Person, E., 182
Perversions, 93-103
  dynamics of, 94-95
  treatment of, 96-98
Pessen, E., 55
Pine, F., 112, 125, 203, 216, 219, 220
Pisan, Christine de, 23
Plato, 3, 16-18, 25
Pleasure, 25-26
Poland, W. S., 223-24
Pontalis, J. B., 64, 65, 223
Promiscuity, in tribal-transitional societies, 44-45
Provence, S., 83-84

Racker, H., 79n3, 106, 183, 184, 206-7, 208
Rappoport, E., 175, 176, 178
Reich, A., 95, 97, 106
Reik, T., 26-27, 159, 160, 161
Resistance
  countertransference and, 192-98
  testing of love and, 140-41
  transference and, 2, 65, 95
Richards, A., 79n2
Ritvo, S., 84, 85
Rogers, C., 201
Róheim, G., 42
Rosenfeld, H., 178
Rossner, S., 83-84
Rycroft, C., 123

Sadomasochism, testing of love and, 138
Sambia, New Guinea, 42-43
Sampson, H., 136
Sandler, J. C., 65-66, 137, 176, 206, 208
Saul, L., 180
Schachtel, E., 160
Schafer, R., 134, 140, 206, 214, 223, 224, 225
Schizoid symptomatology, 127-28
Schlachet, B. C., 4
Schneider, H. K., 43-44
Schuster, I. G., 39-40, 48n5
Searles, H., 138, 193, 194, 205, 206, 207-9
Segal, H., 161
Self, 159-71
  erotized transference and, 178
  hatred of, 170
  loss of love and, 168-69

Self (*Continued*)
  narcissism and, 163-65
  splitting of, 169
Self psychology, 8, 161-62
Setzman, E. J., 6-7, 8
Sexual attitudes, in Christianity, 19-20
Sexual drive, 27-28, 31
Sexual excitement, 94
Sexual feelings, integrated with tender feelings, 45, 102, 169
Sexual hostility, 100
Sexual love, 24-28
Sexual passion, 59
Shakespeare, William, 53, 56
Shapiro, T., 223, 224
Sibling relationships in childhood
  brother as oedipal substitute for father, 90
  Freud on, 81-82
  marital relationships and, 86-87
  mature love relationships and, 81-91
  parent-child relationship and, 85
Silberfeld, M., 175
Silverman, H. W., 9, 10, 11
Singer, E., 205, 209
Singer, I., 14, 15
Solnit, A., 83-84
Soulé, H., 82
Spence, D., 206
Spinoza, Benedictus de, 26
Spitz, R., 148
Splitting of, 126-27, 169
Spotnitz, H., 193
Stein, H. F., 48n3
Stern, D., 148, 168
Stoller, R., 9, 93, 94, 100, 101-2, 180-81, 184
Stone, L., 64, 203, 214-15, 218-19, 220, 222, 225
Strachey, J., 137, 139
Sublimation, 15, 26, 97-98
Sullivan, H. S., 52-53, 170, 206
Symbiosis, 25, 166

Tarachow, S., 222
Tauber, E. S., 192, 193
Tender feelings, 169-70

Testing of love, 133-45
  sadomasochism and, 138
  in therapeutic relationship, 138-44
  transference and, 138-39, 140-41
Therapeutic relationship
  empathic blocks in, 156
  erotic transference
    female therapists and, 186-87
    management of treatment and, 187-88
  testing of love in, 138-44
Thomas, K., 24
Tower, L. E., 183-84
Transcultural approach, 31-32
Transference
  concepts of, 64-66
  erotic, 173-89
  erotized, 175-77
  gender differences in, 181, 183
  love, 2
  maternal, 67, 68, 73, 181
  neurosis, 63
  outside therapy, 64-66
  paternal, 67, 181
  to female therapist, 132
  reciprocal in marriage, 63-78
  resistance to, 95
  reverse, 106, 108-9
  testing of love and, 138-39
Tribal-transitional societies
  compared to Western society, 45-48
  promiscuity in, 44-45
Trust, 137-38

Varga, M. P., 6, 8, 9
Virgin Mary cult, in Christianity, 20-21
Volkan, W., 106

Waelder, R., 64
Wachtel, P., 135
Waxenberg, B., 4
Weigert, E., 193
Weinstein, R. S., 10
Weiss, J., 136, 141
Western society, tribal-transitional societies compared to, 45-48
Winnicott, D. W., 102, 116, 123, 125, 129,

131, 138, 147, 161, 193-94, 196, 203-4, 220, 221
Wolstein, B., 205, 208
Women
  absence of, 17
  expectations of love in, 52
  fear of, 24
  idealization of, 22

Zetzel, E. R., 138
Zuckberg, J. O., 7, 11, 148, 149